HUMOUR, HISTORY AND POLITICS IN LATE ANTIQUITY AND THE EARLY MIDDLE AGES

Although the topic of humour has been dealt with for other eras, early medieval humour remains largely neglected. The essays collected here go some way towards filling the gap, examining how the writers of early medieval sources deliberately employed humour to make their case.

The essays range from the late Roman Empire through to the tenth century, and from Byzantium to Anglo-Saxon England. The subject matter is diverse, but a number of themes link them together, notably the use of irony, ridicule and satire as political tools. Two chapters serve as an extended introduction to the topic, while the following six chapters offer varied treatments of the themes of humour and politics, looking at different times and places, but at the Carolingian world in particular. Together, they raise important and original issues about the ways in which humour was employed to articulate concepts of political power, perceptions of kingship, social relations and the role of particular texts.

GUY HALSALL is Senior Lecturer in History, Birkbeck College, University of London. His publications include *Settlement and Social Organization: The Merovingian Region of Metz* (Cambridge, 1995).

HUMOUR, HISTORY AND POLITICS IN LATE ANTIQUITY AND THE EARLY MIDDLE AGES

EDITED BY

GUY HALSALL

CAMBRIDGE
UNIVERSITY PRESS

PUBLISHED BY THE PRESS SYNDICATE OF THE UNIVERSITY OF CAMBRIDGE
The Pitt Building, Trumpington Street, Cambridge, United Kingdom

CAMBRIDGE UNIVERSITY PRESS
The Edinburgh Building, Cambridge CB2 2RU, UK
40 West 20th Street, New York, NY 10011-4211, USA
477 Williamstown Road, Port Melbourne, VIC 3207, Australia
Ruiz de Alarcón 13, 28014 Madrid, Spain
Dock House, The Waterfront, Cape Town 8001, South Africa

http://www.cambridge.org

First published 2002

Printed in the United Kingdom at the University Press, Cambridge

Typeface Baskerville Monotype 11 / 12.5 pt.   *System* LATEX 2ε   [TB]

A catalogue record for this book is available from the British Library

Library of Congress Cataloguing in Publication data

Humour, history and politics in late antiquity and the early
Middle Ages / edited by Guy Halsall.
p.   cm.
Most of the papers were first presented in a series of sessions at the fifth International
Medieval Congress at the University of Leeds, 1998.
Includes bibliographical references and index.
Contents: 'Don't worry, I've got the key' / Guy Halsall – Laughter and humour in
the early medieval Latin west / Danuta Shanzer – Humour and the everyday in
Byzantium / John Haldon – The lexicon of abuse, drunkenness and political illegitimacy
in the late Roman world / Mark Humphries – Funny foreigners: laughing with the
barbarians in late antiquity / Guy Halsall – Liutprand of Cremona's sense of humour / Ross
Balzaretti – 'He never even allowed his white teeth to be bared in laughter': the politics
of humour in the Carolingian renaissance / Matthew Innes – Alcuin's *Disputatio Pippini* and
the early medieval riddle tradition / Martha Bayless – Laughter after Babel's fall:
misunderstanding and miscommunication in the ninth-century west / Paul Kershaw.
ISBN 0 521 81116 3
1. Civilization, Medieval – Humor.   2. Classical wit and humor.   3. Laughter in
literature.   4. Europe – History – 476–1492.   5. Europe – Social conditions – To 1492.
6. Aliens in literature.   I. Halsall, Guy.   II. International Medieval Congress
(5th: 1998: University of Leeds)
D80 .H86 2002   306.4'81 – dc21   2001052873

ISBN 0 521 81116 3 hardback

For Ken Taylor (20.viii.1944–8.viii.1998),
who would have laughed

Contents

Notes on contributors

ROSS BALZARETTI has lectured in History at the University of Nottingham since 1990. His main early medieval research interests are in north Italian social and cultural history, especially that of Milan. Recent publications include articles on 'Men and sex in tenth-century Italy', 'Theodelinda, "most glorious queen": gender and power in Lombard Italy', 'The politics of property in ninth-century Milan: familial motives and monastic strategies in the village of Inzago' and 'Sexual cultures in the early medieval west'. He has been on the editorial collective of *Gender & History* since 1993.

MARTHA BAYLESS is associate professor of English at the University of Oregon, specialising in humour and medieval cultural history. She has a B.A. from Bryn Mawr College and a Ph.D. in medieval Latin literature from the University of Cambridge. Her books include *Parody in the Middle Ages: The Latin Tradition* and *Collectanea Pseudo-Bedae* (edited with Michael Lapidge).

JOHN HALDON is professor of Byzantine History in the Centre for Byzantine, Ottoman and Modern Greek Studies, and head of the School of Historical Studies at the University of Birmingham. He studied at Birmingham, Athens, Oxford and Munich, and has written numerous books and articles on many aspects of late Roman and Byzantine social and institutional history. He is also interested in the comparative history of pre-modern states. He is editor of the journal *Byzantine & Modern Greek Studies*. His most recent books include *Warfare, State and Society in Byzantium 565–1204* (1999), *Byzantium: A History* (2000), *The Byzantine Wars* (2001) and (with Leslie Brubaker) *Byzantium in the Iconoclast Era (ca. 680–850): The Sources* (2001). With Leslie Brubaker he is currently completing a major reassessment of the iconoclast period (*Byzantium in the Iconoclast Era (ca. 680–850):*

A Historical Survey (forthcoming, Cambridge University Press)), and is planning a major new project on medieval logistics.

GUY HALSALL teaches in the School of History, Classics and Archaeology at Birkbeck College, London. His current research focusses upon the role of the barbarian migrations in the transformation of western Europe from Roman Empire to post-Roman kingdoms. Besides numerous articles on early medieval social history and archaeology, he is author of *Settlement and Social Organization: The Merovingian Region of Metz* (1995), *Early Medieval Cemeteries: An Introduction to Cemetery Archaeology in the Post-Roman West* (1995), *Warfare and Society in the Barbarian West, 450–900* (2002) and editor of *Violence and Society in the Early Medieval West* (1997).

MARK HUMPHRIES is a lecturer in the Department of Ancient Classics at the National University of Ireland, Maynooth. His research interests include the social history of ancient religions (especially early Christianity), urbanism in late antiquity, and late Roman political ideologies. He is author of *Communities of the Blessed: Social Environment and Religious Change in Northern Italy AD 200–400* (1999), and a contributor to *The Cambridge Ancient History*, vol. XIV and *The Cambridge History of Greek and Roman Warfare* (forthcoming).

MATTHEW INNES lectures in the School of History, Classics and Archaeology at Birkbeck College, London. His research focusses on the role of historical tradition in early medieval culture, and on the relationship between freedom, property and power. In addition to numerous articles, his publications include *State and Society in the Early Middle Ages: The Middle Rhine Valley, 400–1000* (2000); (as coeditor) *The Uses of the Past in the Early Middle Ages* (2000); and *The Plough, the Sword and the Book: Community and Authority in Western Europe, 300–900* (forthcoming).

PAUL KERSHAW was educated at Jesus College, Cambridge, and King's College, London, and is currently assistant professor in the Corcoran Department of History, University of Virginia. His publications include articles on 'Power, prayer and illness in Asser's Life of Alfred'; 'The Alfred–Guthrum treaty: scripting accommodation and interaction in Viking-Age England'; and 'Time's abuse and the negligence of men: changing attitudes to the inscriptions of early medieval Brittany'. He was a contributing author to W. Davies et al., *The Early Medieval Inscriptions of Brittany/Les Inscriptions de la Bretagne du Haut Moyen Âge*

(2000), and M. Handley et al., *CISP Database of all Non-runic Inscriptions from Ireland, Scotland, Isle of Man, Wales, South-Western England and Brittany, 400–1100 AD* (http://www.ucl.ac.uk/archaeology/cisp/database/), and is currently preparing a book on royal peacemaking and the image of the peacemaking king in early medieval Europe.

DANUTA SHANZER was educated at Bryn Mawr College and Oxford University. After serving as director of the Medieval Studies Program at Cornell from 1992–2000, she is currently professor of Classics and director of graduate studies in Classics. She specialises in Latin of the later Roman Empire, both prose and poetry, and in medieval Latin. She is the author of *A Philosophical and Literary Commentary on Martianus Capella's De Nuptiis Philologiae et Mercurii Liber 1* (1986) and *Letters and Selected Prose of Avitus of Vienne* (coauthored with Ian Wood) (2002), and is coeditor (with Ralph Mathisen) of *Culture and Society in Later Roman Gaul: Revisiting the Sources* (2001). Current projects include work on the early medieval judicial ordeal, marriage, inheritance and the church, humour, hagiography and obscenity. She is currently the North American editor for *Early Medieval Europe*.

Preface

Most of the papers in this volume were first presented in a series of sessions at the fifth International Medieval Congress at the University of Leeds in 1998. John Haldon's chapter, however, was first given as his inaugural lecture at the University of Birmingham and I am very grateful indeed to Professor Haldon for allowing it to be included in this volume. The success of those sessions prompted their conversion into this book of essays. I should like to thank the authors for providing a set of such stimulating and original essays and also for their patience during the long and frustrating time spent finding a suitable and responsible publisher for the volume. In that connection I am also most grateful to William Davies and the Syndics of Cambridge University Press for rescuing the project with such enthusiasm and efficiency just when it seemed to be floundering.

Three other papers were delivered during the original conference sessions, but for various reasons do not appear here:

Hugh Magennis, 'A funny thing happened on the way to heaven: comic incongruity in Old English saints' lives.'
Ivan Herbison, 'Comic subversion in *Judith*.'
Stuart Airlie, '"With scoffing and derision": the power of ridicule and irony in Carolingian political narrative.'

I am grateful to all three speakers for excellent, entertaining papers, which sparked interesting and equally enthusiastic debate. By putting forward ideas taken on board by the contributors to this volume, they have contributed significantly to the final version. Similarly, I would like to thank all those who attended the sessions at Leeds for their interest in, and contributions to, the debate, most notably Professor Pauline Stafford for instigating a general debate on the topic at the end of the final session. I am also grateful to Professors David Ganz and Barbara Rosenwein for their support for this project. I must also thank Paul Kershaw for suggesting the cover illustration.

The production of the book has, however, been tinged with some sadness. Probably the person who did most to shape my own sense of humour, and instil in me a willingness to look for and – gently – to find a funny side to otherwise serious things, was my godfather, Ken Taylor, who died of a heart attack, much too soon, just a few weeks after the conference where these papers were delivered. It is to his memory that I dedicate my work on this project, in the sure knowledge that he would have found it all (especially the dry academic exegesis) very funny.

GUY HALSALL

Abbreviations

Amm. Marc.	Ammianus Marcellinus, *Res Gestae*: *Ammianus Marcellinus*, ed. and trans. J. C. Rolfe (3 vols., London 1935–9)
ANRW	*Aufstieg und Niedergang der römischen Welt* (Berlin)
CCSL	*Corpus Christianorum, Series Latina* (Turnhout, 1953–)
CSEL	*Corpus Scriptorum Ecclesiasticorum Latinorum* (Vienna, 1865–)
EME	*Early Medieval Europe*
Ep(p).	*Epistula(e)*
JRS	*Journal of Roman Studies*
LPER	*Liber Pontificalis Ecclesiae Ravennatis*
MGH	*Monumenta Germaniae Historica*
PC	*'Paris Conversations'*
PG	*Patrologiae cursus completus. Series Graeca*, ed. J.-P. Migne (167 vols., Paris, 1857–76)
PL	*Patrologiae Cursus Completus. Series Latina*, ed. J.-P. Migne (221 vols., Paris 1844–63)
PLAC	*Poetae Latini Aevi Carolini*
SRG	*Scriptores Rerum Germanicarum*
SRM	*Scriptores Rerum Merovingicarum*

'Don't worry, I've got the key'

Guy Halsall

A man is walking down the street when a neighbour runs up to him and says, 'Hey, your house is on fire!' 'Don't worry,' replies the man, 'I've got the key.'

This joke, possibly the best in this collection of essays (certainly that which got the biggest laugh at the conference where these papers were originally presented[1]), is to be found in John Haldon's treatment of 'Humour and the everyday in Byzantium',[2] and makes a useful focus for this introduction. Identifying the humorous in late antique and early medieval writing is very often a question of locating the key.

That, however, presupposes the willingness to look for the key in the first place, and this seems to have been conspicuously absent in previous generations of scholarship. At several points in the following chapters, we shall encounter footnotes pointing out how previous researchers have either not noticed that a work was intended to be funny, or have rejected interpretations of late antique or early medieval works which see them as anything other than entirely earnest.[3] Even a genre as overtly intended to amuse as riddle collections has, in its continental manifestations, been neglected.[4] Recently, historians have looked increasingly at humour and its uses;[5] the ancient world[6] and Anglo-Saxon England,

---

[1] With the possible exception of the occasion when Matt Innes tripped over the overhead projector's extension lead.

[2] Below, p. 64.   [3] For example, below, p. 86, n. 60; p. 102, n. 55

[4] Bayless, below, p. 157.

[5] See, for example, *Humour and History*, ed. K. Cameron (Oxford, 1993); *A Cultural History of Humour*, ed. J. Bremmer and H. Roodenberg (London, 1997), with bibliography at pp. 242–52.

[6] In addition to works on Roman humour found in the footnotes of the essays in this collection, see: D. Arnould, *Le Rire et les larmes dans la littérature grecque d'Homère à Platon* (Paris, 1990); *Le Rire des anciens: actes du Colloque Internationale, Université de Rouen, Ecole Normale Supérieure, 11–13 janvier 1995*, ed. M. Trédé, P. Hoffmann and C. Auvray-Assayas (Paris, 1998); *Laughter Down the Centuries*, vol. III, ed. S. Jäkel, A. Timonen and V.-M. Rissanen (Turku, 1997).

with its distinctive corpus of literature,[7] have been well served. The late antique and early medieval periods in Europe, however, have not yet received their share of this attention.

There are a number of possible reasons for this neglect. One might simply be that, as is often said, history is made in the present; in many ways it is also made in the image of the present. Humour, it would seem, has appeared too flippant a subject for a self-consciously serious discipline such as history. Over the past 150 years, much early medieval historiography has been about reconstructing political history, and the history of institutions, lay and ecclesiastical. Humour has seemed irrelevant to this sort of project. As Matthew Innes says,[8] the study of the Carolingian period reveals this attitude particularly well. A clever writer like Notker of St-Gall – Notker the Stammerer – who used humour to make very serious points, suffered the fate of prolonged exclusion from the canon of 'respectable' sources. Though the great academic scholars of past generations may seem easy targets as humourless tweed-clad 'old fogies' (perhaps unfairly; for all I know, Georg-Heinrich Pertz and Georg Waitz may have had a great laugh in their spare time in the offices of the *Monumenta Germaniae Historica*, though it does seem slightly unlikely[9]), it must be stressed that attitudes have been slow to change. More recent historical projects, the history of gender most notably, have been equally if not more self-consciously humourless; the recovery of the role of women and of gender relations in the past were, and are, not in themselves laughing matters, and that also appears to have informed the nature of historical writing. Thus Ross Balzaretti[10] points out that, even with recent attention to past laughter, humour and gender has remained a neglected topic – oddly, as humour is in many ways a particularly gendered aspect of social practice.[11]

There may therefore be something in the idea that for humour in late antique and early medieval Europe to become a topic, it had to wait for the emergence of a generation of historians who not only saw that history has its funny side but also, conversely, that humour and its past uses are, themselves, serious subjects. Maybe early medieval humour

---

[7] See, recently, *Humour in Anglo-Saxon Literature*, ed. J. Wilcox (Cambridge, 2000) and references therein.

[8] Below, p. 131.

[9] D. Knowles, *Great Historical Enterprises: Problems in Monastic History* (London, 1963), pp. 65–97, for a brief but very useful history of the *Monumenta*.

[10] Balzaretti, below, p. 114.

[11] Thus, note that it is a *man* who is warned of his house burning down, just as that tiresome trio, forever going into a pub, are an English*man*, a Scots*man* and an Irish*man*.

had to wait for a generation of historians with a *sense* of humour. This generation also sees that very serious points can be made through satire, irony and ridicule. To say that a passage in the sources is satirical or ironic is not to denude it of serious content. To study late antique and medieval texts to find instances of humour is not to belittle them or to miss the point by looking at peripheral ephemera. It is also possible that the search for humour in past texts, which, as we shall see, are rarely obvious places to look for jokes, mirrors broader changes in the nature of comedy over recent decades, which have often, in the world of post-modernism, focussed on conscious, self-referential irony.

Be that as it may, a more obvious reason for the neglect of late antique and early medieval humour lies in the unpromising nature of the source material. Danuta Shanzer outlines the fate of classical humour in her paper.[12] The obvious comedic genres of the ancient world, and their rich traditions, seem to have withered in late antiquity. This presents something of a contrast with humour in the eastern half of the old Roman Empire, that which became 'Byzantine'. John Haldon demonstrates a much clearer continuation of overtly humorous genres there.[13] At first sight it seems as though we can contribute to the ongoing debate on the Pirenne thesis[14] by adding to Pirenne's list – of gold, spices, silk and papyrus – another commodity which the Arab conquests prevented from reaching the west: jokes.[15] But, as with so much of the Pirenne debate, there is more to it than that. The great comic genres of antiquity appear to have atrophied long before the Fall of the West. Even the last western satirical play of the classical tradition, the fifth-century *Querolus*, can be condemned as not particularly amusing[16] (although that, of course, may just be because we don't get the joke any more[17]) and the genre of satire seems to have disappeared earlier still. There was continuity, too, though continuity from the specifically late Roman situation. Shanzer points out the continuation of late antique humorous techniques such as the use of bons mots and grim irony in narrative histories. The fate of this strategy in the works of fifth- and sixth-century writers, and the way in which it

[12] Below, pp. 25–37.   [13] Below, pp. 48–71.

[14] See, recently, *The Sixth Century: Production, Distribution and Demand*, ed. R. Hodges and W. Bowden (Leiden, 1998); *The Long Eighth Century*, ed. I. L. Hansen and C. J. Wickham (Leiden, 2000).

[15] Honesty demands that I credit Paul Kershaw as originator of this joke, though he may yet not thank me for this acknowledgement!

[16] Shanzer, below, p. 25.

[17] For some discussion of what the joke may actually have been about, see R. Van Dam, *Leadership and Community in Late Antique Gaul* (Berkeley, 1985), pp. 25–56, and J. F. Drinkwater, 'The Bacaudae of fifth-century Gaul', in *Fifth-century Gaul: A Crisis of Identity?* ed. J. F. Drinkwater and H. Elton (Cambridge, 1992), pp. 208–17.

was employed to respond to the changing world of those centuries, are further explored in my own chapter.[18] Riddles, a particularly common early medieval form of learned humorous expression, also derive their inspiration from a late Latin writer, Symphosius.[19]

That apart, we are usually forced to seek humour in non-humorous types of writing, and this can be problematic, as shall become clear. Nevertheless, some early medieval historical writers have long been suspected of deliberate humour. Gregory of Tours is one such.[20] In the introduction to his Penguin translation of Gregory's *Histories*, Lewis Thorpe included a section entitled 'Humour and irony'.[21] Thorpe, as often in his translation, seems to have correctly identified an aspect of Gregory's style,[22] though his insight did not spawn much further discussion of the bishop's sense of humour until, in a seminal chapter of his *Narrators of Barbarian History*, Walter Goffart argued that Gregory was a satirist.[23] This has not convinced everyone, and Shanzer criticises the thesis below, pointing out that Goffart's model of how Gregory would have acquired models for satirical history is 'too conjectural'.[24] The *satura* or mishmash of the *Histories*' organisation may result in them *appearing* to have the characteristics of satire – disjointed elements resembling a modern comedy sketch-show – but this structure seems to result from quite other demands. Gregory's view of causation, rather than, as in many modern views, being 'horizontal', with history unfolding as the cumulative result of previous human interactions, was typological and 'vertical'. That is to say, if people committed particular acts in particular ways or circumstances then a particular consequence, of divine provenance, would descend upon them. This, obviously, is the reasoning behind the narrative structuring of miracle collections and many saints' lives, especially Gregory's, into small self-contained incidents with actions and divinely ordained reward or punishment. The *Histories* fall into disjointed

[18] Below, pp. 89–113.   [19] Bayless, below, p. 157.

[20] The absence of a chapter on Gregory's humour is perhaps a glaring lacuna in this volume. However, Gregory's humour has already been discussed. Simon Loseby is apparently working on a study of Gregory's jokes, and I shall make a number of comments about Gregory in this introduction. The forthcoming collaborative work, *The World of Gregory of Tours*, ed. K. Mitchell and I. N. Wood (Leiden, 2002) will doubtless also address the Goffart thesis and related aspects of Gregory's style.

[21] *Gregory of Tours: The History of the Franks*, trans. L. Thorpe (Harmondsworth, 1974), pp. 46–9.

[22] Thorpe's translation often captures the sense of Gregory's Latin, although often at the expense of mangling its technical meaning.

[23] W. Goffart, *The Narrators of Barbarian History, AD 550–800: Jordanes, Gregory of Tours, Bede. Paul the Deacon* (Princeton, 1988), pp. 197–203.

[24] Below, p. 32; see also, for example, the riposte by R. Van Dam, *Saints and their Miracles in Late Antique Gaul* (Princeton, 1993), p. 148, which makes a similar point.

independent episodes not as a result of Gregory's desire to write satire but because they are written to the same pattern as his hagiography. Recent analyses, notably Goffart's, have accustomed us to the injunction to read all of Gregory's works, *Historiae* and *Miracula*, as part of a unified and coherent project. Thus the self-contained stories of secular goings-on are in many ways best understood as a sort of anti-hagiography. Instead of immediate miraculous healing or cure, or chastisement of enemies, demonstrating the eternal power or merit of the godly, to strive after worldly rewards in these episodes produces at best only transient benefit, but more often no good at all – usually quite the reverse.

Nevertheless, to say that the *Histories* were not written as satire does not imply that they were written without deliberate humour, or even without *elements* of satire or parody. Laughter is very commonly the response of modern audiences to Gregory's tales, and it is often hard to see that this humour is not deliberate. By juxtaposing the eternal merit and everlasting rewards of the saintly with the pointless doings of the worldly, Gregory seems clearly to have intended to ridicule the latter, especially when the deaths and other punishments of wrongdoers often contain elements of farce.[25] This sort of humour could be and was used effectively in didactic and homily in east and west. John Haldon draws our attention to Anastasius of Sinai, who used humour to ridicule his parishioners and alert them to the folly of their ways.[26] It is possible, if perhaps not probable, that ridicule is also used to similar effect in Salvian's *On the Governance of God*;[27] Saint Jerome was an adept at this technique. It may seem odd to look for humour in hagiography but, as Shanzer points out and as we shall see below, it is to be found there in plenty.

Laughter, as Ross Balzaretti says, is also the common modern response to the stories of Liutprand of Cremona, whose English translator likewise appreciated the sense of the original.[28] Liutprand's humour is less controversial than Gregory's in that he very often cues it with a comment which makes clear that he regards the succeeding tale as funny.[29] Nevertheless, his humour has long awaited a sophisticated discussion, especially in regard to the ways in which it is used to reinforce ideas about gender. A third author whose overt use of humour has been noted is Notker. As mentioned, Notker's jokes long earned him a form of scholarly damnation, but they have also, in the end, meant that he is one of

---

[25] Gregory seemingly never tired of informing his readers of the heresiarch Arius' death on the toilet; see also Shanzer, below, p. 28, n. 17. For other episodes with clear farcical elements see *Histories* 3.7–8, *MGH SRM* 1.1, ed. B. Krusch and W. Levison (Hanover, 1951).

[26] Haldon, below, pp. 62–3.   [27] Halsall, below, p. 98.

[28] Balzaretti, below, p. 115 and n. 6.   [29] Balzaretti, below, pp. 116–17.

the few early medieval historical writers to have had serious attention devoted to his use of humour.[30] The influence of David Ganz's seminal 1989 study of Notker is evident in several chapters of this book. Matthew Innes and Paul Kershaw develop, in slightly different ways, our under-standing of Notker's humour from the base provided by Ganz. Building on Ganz's analysis, Kershaw in particular makes Notker a rounded and sympathetic character by pointing out how this writer, who himself cre-ated an identity based upon his stammer, found amusement in the failure to communicate clearly.

Beyond these writers, the search for humour becomes more difficult. Most humour retreated into genres which did, and do, not proclaim themselves to be deliberately funny. Jacques Le Goff has seen most of the period with which this volume is concerned as one of repressed monastic laughter.[31] This may not entirely be the case, even if the sources of humour are largely ecclesiastical, and sometimes monastic, in origin. Shanzer draws attention, as mentioned, to hagiography, and there is probably more humour that has yet to be discovered in this possibly unexpected source.[32] In addition to the grim humour of persecutors and – sometimes – martyrs, and the humour of the everyday props which Shanzer points out, there is also slapstick and the ridiculing of sinners. As one example, drawn from Gregory of Tours' *Glory of the Confessors*,[33] take the story of Maurus, a man whose ill-treated slave ran away and took sanctuary in the church of Saint Lupus at Troyes. Maurus pursued the slave and, dragging him from the altar, mocked the saint who could not prevent him from recovering his property. Whereupon, his tongue 'was bound by divine power. The man was transformed and began to dance about the entire church, lowing like an animal and not speaking like a man.' Thus the sinner is ridiculed, before receiving the ultimate divine sanction: death. This would appear to be deliberately humorous, perhaps because, just as it invites the audience to laugh at Maurus' misfortune, and at his (seemingly) jester-like antics,[34] this is immediately followed

---

[30] D. Ganz, 'Humour as history in Notker's *Gesta Karoli magni*', in *Monks, Nuns and Friars in Medieval Society* (Sewanee Medieval Studies 4), ed. E. B. King, J. T. Schaefer and W. B. Wadley (Sewanee, TN, 1989), pp. 171–83.

[31] J. Le Goff, 'Laughter in the Middle Ages', in *A Cultural History of Humour*, ed. Bremmer and Roodenberg, pp. 40–53. See also, Balzaretti, below, p. 127.

[32] See also H. Magennis, 'A funny thing happened on the way to heaven: humorous incongruity in Old English saints' lives', in *Humour in Anglo-Saxon Literature*, ed. Wilcox, pp. 137–40.

[33] Gregory, *Glory of the Confessors* 66, *MGH SRM* 1.2, ed. B. Krusch and W. Levison (Hanover 1969); *Gregory of Tours: Glory of the Confessors*, trans. R. Van Dam (Liverpool, 1988).

[34] Note, in particular, that part of the punishment concerns Maurus' ability to speak 'like a man'. On the humour of communication breakdown, see Kershaw, below, pp. 179–202. For the similarity

by the punch line of the extreme vengeance of the saint, bringing the reader – or listener, since it seems clear that Gregory intended these stories to be read aloud, and appears to have used them himself as sermons[35] – back down to earth with a bump.

Humour in the past is endlessly fleeting. As Shanzer says, humour comes only in passing moments in comedic genres.[36] Furthermore, it is not unusual to find that a joke is not as funny when heard a second or third time, especially when the humour works on the principle of a sudden evaporation of expectations. On the other hand, a joke can *gain* in humorous value; we might not get, or see, the joke the first time. So humour is a passing moment in terms of both stimulus *and* response. Even then, not everyone in an audience finds a particular joke or comedy funny. One of the problems of writing the history of humour, as in my own paper in this volume, is that it is often difficult to persuade an audience that a story was meant to be funny when not all (or perhaps none) of that audience finds it in any way funny any more. How much more difficult does this become when one has to admit that probably not everyone in the original audience found it funny either? Historical humour is an incredibly slippery topic. The phrase 'you had to be there', often employed when a joke falls flat, is never more appropriate than in the study of humour in history. We can locate instances which seem funny to us in ostensibly non-humorous writings, but were they intended to be funny?

In trying to answer this question, this book makes a direct contribution to the ongoing debate on the history of emotions. The question of what is funny and why makes a particularly good case-study. Because we find something amusing, can we inscribe our response on to past audiences? Balzaretti reports that people still laugh at the things that Liutprand of Cremona thought were funny. If the genre of writing, or, as in Liutprand's case, a cue within a source, lets us know that a tale was thought to be funny,[37] can we analyse *why* it was humorous? The Byzantine joke with which we began makes a useful example. The laughter that it provoked when told at the conference[38] was largely based upon its almost surreal value to a modern audience, or its value as a piece of nonsense: what use is the key if your house has burnt down? When originally told in the

---

with a jester, see the discussion of Attila's court, below, pp. 17–18, which makes clear that the spectacle of a man dancing around and talking nonsense was precisely the sort of thing which early medieval people *did* find funny.

35 Van Dam, *Saints and their Miracles*, p. 144.   36 Below, p. 25.   37 Balzaretti, below, pp. 116–17.

38 And, I can report, on the many subsequent occasions when I have retold it.

Byzantine Empire, however, the humour was based upon a quite different factor. Haldon explains the joke's punch line[39] as meaning 'mind your own business'. If explained to a modern audience this robs the joke of its humour: 'Hey, your house is on fire'; 'Mind your own business'... A Byzantine audience would doubtless have been equally askance at an explanation for the modern British response to the joke. Of course, the explanation of jokes tends to dissipate their humour in any case.[40]

There are, furthermore, instances in early medieval writing where we can be fairly sure that a joke is being told but have no idea why it was funny, or whom the joke is on. Another example can be drawn from the work of Gregory of Tours. Domnolus, Abbot of St-Lawrence, Paris, feared that King Chlothar I was about to offer him the see of Avignon, so he let the king know that he did not want the job: 'he looked upon being sent to Avignon as a humiliation rather than an honour and he begged the king not to submit him, a simple man, to the boredom of having to listen to sophisticated arguments by old senatorial families, or to counts who spent all their time discussing philosophic problems'.[41] This seems to have been a joke, but exactly why is unclear. Is Gregory poking fun at southern, classically educated aristocrats, or (since he came himself from an 'old senatorial family') at uncouth northerners (Domnolus has a Frankish name, fairly rare in the sixth-century Gallic church)? Or at something so culturally specific that no trace of it at all emerges from the text?[42] We shall never know. Looking for the key here is as fruitless as it is in understanding the joke cracked by Louis the Pious' court jester during the Easter celebrations. That joke,[43] at the expense of Hatto, an otherwise unknown aristocrat, is now utterly incomprehensible. As Haldon says,[44] to understand jokes like this we need to know the details, and here the necessary details are quite beyond our purview. On the other hand, whether or not we still find the joke funny, study of a historical culture can at least let us know that something *was* funny and why. Thick description, to borrow Clifford Geertz's phrase,[45] can provide a key.

---

[39] Below, p. 64.

[40] Herein lies perhaps the biggest joke of the entire project: putting together a book with the enticing word 'humour' in the title and yet filling it with (mostly) dry discussion of largely serious medieval texts. That joke, dear reader, is on you!

[41] Gregory, *Histories* 6.9.

[42] Similarly I have often wondered why, at *Histories* 7.27, Gregory makes a brief aside in a story about the mutually fatal duel between Eberulf and Claudius to tell us that Claudius' wife was from Meaux, information which has no bearing on any part of the story. What was it about women from Meaux...?

[43] For which see Innes, below, p. 149.   [44] Below, p. 50.

[45] C. Geertz, *The Interpretation of Cultures* (New York, 1973).

It can also help with the difficulties of trying to reconstruct past humour from sources that are not obviously comic, and which do not introduce funny stories as such. This is a problem that my own chapter faces and may, understandably, not convince everyone as a result. If, however, we can 'find the key' by reconstructing norms and codes from the texts of a past society we should be able to find cases of clear incongruity and inversion. Where we can locate such instances, even if a story no longer strikes us as amusing today, a strong possibility, at least, is presented that that story was thought funny in the past.

Much of the debate on the history of emotions has focussed upon whether or not, or the extent to which, emotions are socially constructed. As outlined, for example, in Barbara Rosenwein's recent interesting edited volume, *Anger's Past*,[46] the sides in the debate may be characterised as primordialists, who believe in a certain timeless physiological and psychological 'human nature' in the expression of emotions, and social constructionists, who believe that emotions are only constructed within specific social circumstances. As will have become clear, neither view seems entirely satisfactory. Humour is a mix of psychological and physiological constants and cultural specifics. The physiological manifestation of the 'laughter reflex' has, it would seem, always been the same, but nevertheless there is apparently no clear biological, functional reason for laughter; whatever the physiological constancy of the response, the stimulus is socially contingent.[47]

Laughter itself can be a controversial topic within societies. As will be seen, the church could hold a very negative view of laughter,[48] well expressed in a reported speech of Saint Nicetius of Trier:

My beloved, you must avoid all jokes and all idle words; for, just as we have to present to God our body entirely pure, so we ought not to open our mouths unless it is to praise God. There are three ways by which a man is ruined: when he thinks, when he speaks or when he acts. Therefore, my beloved, avoid levity, malice and every other evil.[49]

Yet, even if this was a view that came to predominate in this period, there was nevertheless more than one possible Christian opinion on the

---

[46] *Anger's Past: The Social Construction of an Emotion in the Middle Ages*, ed. B. H. Rosenwein (Ithaca, NY, 1997), with references. See also the 'debate' on the subject in *Early Medieval Europe* 10(2), pp. 225–56, and my review of Rosenwein's volume, *Early Medieval Europe* 10(2), break pp. 301–3.

[47] See Haldon, below, p. 48.

[48] Explored in this volume by Innes, below, pp. 143–7; Kershaw, below, pp. 181–2; and Haldon, below, pp. 60–2.

[49] Gregory of Tours, *Life of the Fathers* 17.1, *MGH SRM* 1.2, ed. Krusch and Levison; *Gregory of Tours: Life of the Fathers*, trans. E. James (2nd edn, Liverpool, 1991).

subject.[50] In this volume, Paul Kershaw and Martha Bayless draw attention to other Christian readings of the subject. Nevertheless, the clear prominence of a view akin to Nicetius', especially in monastic writings, would hardly justify us in concluding that no one, or even that no monks, ever laughed. Similarly, at the time of writing this introduction, a heated debate is taking place in Britain about the screening of an edition of a satirical programme, 'Brass Eye', dealing with the media's coverage of paedophilia. Was it funny or not? Should we have laughed or should we not? The very fact that groups within a society feel the need to try to define what is and what is not funny is a graphic indicator of the fact that humour is *not* ultimately entirely governed by social norms. The differences in ideas of humour within a society, and the communications breakdowns which that can engender, can themselves be a location of humour. Kershaw[51] discusses Notker's tale of a bishop who thought that something Charlemagne said was a joke when it was nothing of the sort, and suffered the consequences. Emotions and their expression are not even constants *within* societies; this is as true of laughter as it is of fear or rage. It has consistently proved impossible to control laughter and humour, and as a result humour can be a valuable tool in social politics. The mocking, joking chants hurled at Byzantine emperors might be a case in point.[52]

Yet it is not true even to say that laughter might depend upon the group *within a society* in which one situates oneself. If it were, there would be no need to repress laughter. Many if not most of us will admit to an occasion where we have had to stifle a laugh, or where we have suffered from an 'attack of the giggles' at what social convention would lead us to believe was an entirely inappropriate moment or occasion. If we are honest, many of us will also admit to laughing at a 'sick' joke, or a joke about a subject in which we 'know' (according to learnt values) that really we ought not to find humour.

Much humour *is* entirely culturally specific: for example, the precise nature of the norms whose inversion makes people laugh, or the precise characteristics given to particular social groups.[53] Much humour depends on incongruity,[54] but what is or is not held to be incongruous is highly socially contingent. The precise situations wherein laughter is

---

[50] See, e.g., J. Le Goff, 'Le Rire dans les règles monastiques du haut moyen âge', in *Haut Moyen Age: culture, education et société. Etudes offerts à P. Riché*, ed. M. Sot (Nantes, 1990), pp. 93–103.

[51] Below, pp. 191–2.   [52] Haldon, below, pp. 64–5.

[53] Such as men and women – see Balzaretti, below, pp. 119–28; or foreigners – see Haldon, below, pp. 58–60, Halsall, below, pp. 89–113 and Kershaw, below, pp. 194–5.

[54] Halsall, below, pp. 89–90.

held to be appropriate are something else that can vary enormously from one society to another. On the other hand, if dominant ideas about what is or is not funny are widely accepted they can genuinely rob a situation or a joke of its humour. All this makes humour, when we can locate it, very important in looking at past societies.

It is still possible for us to share the same response to a story, and understand why it was, and still is, funny. Humour does seem to have its analytical constants. We can study puns and riddles, such as those discussed by Bayless,[55] and see that they can be explained by modern theories of humour such as Freud's.[56] When we know that a passage was intended to be humorous, it seems to be possible to discuss why it was so, in accordance with modern theories, particularly those about humour and incongruity.

The drawback of the social constructionist view, as with all ultimately structuralist modes of interpretation, is that it is static, and thus unable to deal with change. As, like all relativist interpretations, a rather safe and cosy view of the past, it obviates the need to discuss conflict, and humour is often a matter of conflict: conflict between expectations and outcome; conflict between social groups manifested by ridicule; conflict between ideas of what is or is not funny. If it were true that our understanding of what was and what was not funny, and our knowledge of what was or was not an appropriate moment to employ humour, were entirely socially contingent, dependent upon knowledge received as children, then it is difficult to see how change through time could occur, except through interaction with other cultures. If this was the case, twenty-first-century Europeans ought still to be laughing, not merely at the mother-in-law jokes so beloved of the stand-up comedians of the 1970s, but also at fifth-century western-European ethnic stereotypes and at hunchbacks wearing armour (for which see below). The irony, therefore, is that if pursued to its logical conclusion the social constructionist model produces a timeless, eternal view of emotions.

Humour can play an important role in social change. The nexus of the complex interaction between the socially specific and the more general psychological aspects of humour is the individual social actor and his or her practice. Humour is a particularly individual phenomenon, after all, and so brings this out especially clearly. Social structures are mental

---

[55] Below, pp. 157–78.
[56] E.g. S. Freud, *The Standard Edition of the Complete Works of Sigmund Freud*, vol. VIII, *Jokes and their Relation to the Unconscious*, ed. J. Strachey, with A. Freud, A. Strachey, A. Tyson and A. Richards (London, 1960).

templates made up of the sum total of previous interactions, those considered 'correct' and those that are not. Thus they are constituted by action, and are generative rather than simply constricting. Each interaction between individuals has the capacity, by adding to a society's cumulative 'memory bank', to alter that structure. As we shall see, humour presents very useful ways of attempting to modify the structure by such interaction. The knowledgeable social actor makes use of his or her awareness of the structure to play with, as well as within, the rules. Humour is a particularly effective strategy to employ in such practice. Such informed social practice is an interaction between socially contingent learnt structures and norms, more general psychological and physiological aspects and the characteristics, aims and objectives of the individual.[57] This allows change and innovation to take place, and it restores some freedom of action to the inhabitants of the past. For example, in the field of literary composition, Gregory of Tours, in his *Histories*, Alcuin, in his *Disputatio regalis et nobilissimi iuvenis Pippini cum Albino scholastico*,[58] and Liutprand of Cremona, in his *Antapodosis*,[59] though very well aware of the rules of genre, were not confined by them. They played with them to create something new. The solution might be to adapt and paraphrase Marx's classic formulation of the relationship between structure and agency: man makes jokes but not in circumstances of his own choosing.[60]

Most of the essays in this volume explore humour's political uses, whether the politics in question be 'high politics' – those of the Roman or post-Roman court – or more general social politics. This, again, is why humour is important historically. There can surely be few better indices of the dominant views of a society than occasions when their inversion was regarded as so ludicrous as to be funny. As this volume demonstrates, the most common form taken by this humour is ridicule. Mark Humphries shows how the comic denigration of an emperor's personal morality, specifically his sobriety, undermined his standing with an audience. Cicero had recommended this as a technique. The humour involved went beyond simply laughing at a drunkard, however. The ability to control one's own passions and desires was central to the claim

---

[57] This paragraph, as will be very clear, is heavily influenced by the work of Pierre Bourdieu, notably *Outline of a Theory of Practice*, trans. R. Nice, (Cambridge, 1977), and A. Giddens, *The Constitution of Society: Outline of the Theory of Structuration* (London, 1984). For further discussion of the problem, see Haldon, below, pp. 53–5, and Innes, below, pp. 153–6.

[58] *Dialogue of the Royal and Noble Youth Pippin with Albinus the Scholar*; see Bayless, below, pp. 157–78. Bayless provides the text, with translation and commentary, of the final, riddling section. The whole text can be found translated in *Carolingian Civilization: A Reader*, ed. and trans. P. E. Dutton (Peterborough, Ontario, 1993), pp. 123–8.

[59] See Balzaretti, below, pp. 114–28.   [60] For the real quote, see Haldon, below, p. 53, n. 8.

to be able to rule legitimately. This idea had a long life in east[61] and west, and Matthew Innes, in his chapter, explores its fate in the Carolingian period, when an emperor might equally claim the moral high ground by refusing to display emotion overtly. Innes traces a possible Roman imperial model for this behaviour but, as Humphries demonstrates, there was more than one model of imperial behaviour even in the late Roman period; the smile could be as important in the display of imperial qualities in the fourth century as it was in the ninth, and, as a symbol, it could be contested.[62] Furthermore, it is clear from fourth-century sources that the mode of impassive imperial deportment in which Innes traces the model for Louis the Pious' behaviour as emperor, at least as described by Thegan, was appropriate only in certain circumstances.[63] At the very end of the Roman Empire in the west, Remigius of Rheims could see nothing wrong in the idea of a model king having a joke, as long as it was with the right (young) people.[64] It is possible that Louis may have smiled but just refused to laugh – which, indeed, is how he behaves in Notker's story of his interruption by a fool during the Easter procession.[65]

The Christian model discussed by Innes is perhaps more relevant; Saint Martin never *laughed*, we are told, but his face nevertheless shone with joy (*laetitia*). Yet the meaning of Saint Martin's smiling refusal to display overt emotion could also be contested, and indeed ridiculed. Gregory of Tours tells how Martin's successor as bishop of Tours, Brictius, was asked by a sick man where he could find Martin: '"If you are seeking that crazy fellow", answered Brictius, "just cast your eyes in that direction. In his usual half-witted way, he is staring at the sky." '[66] Brictius' response to Saint Martin's deportment is reminiscent of that of some modern university students: impassive meditation of the joy of heaven mistaken for a form of catatonia. However, at precisely the time that Thegan wrote his account of Louis' behaviour, Rudolf of Fulda, who was himself closely involved in politics, wrote his *Life of Leoba*, which drew heavily upon the Martinian model in his description of Leoba's behaviour: 'But though she was always cheerful, she never burst out into laughter through excessive hilarity.'[67] This seems to clinch Innes' argument about the importance of this Christian model in defining

[61] Haldon, below, p. 64, shows that accusations of drunkenness as a way of demeaning an emperor's legitimacy continued into the Byzantine east.
[62] Humphries, below, p. 83.
[63] See, e.g., J. Matthews, *The Roman Empire of Ammianus* (London, 1988), pp. 231–8.
[64] See, below, n. 106.   [65] Below, pp. 149–50. This is the occasion of the 'Hatto joke'.
[66] *Histories* 2.1. The translation is Thorpe's (above, n. 21).
[67] Rudolf, *Life of Leoba*. The translation is C. H. Talbot's, from *Carolingian Civilization*, ed. and trans. Dutton, p. 318.

correct behaviour and thus appropriating the moral/political high ground in the 830s.

We must therefore seek a very contingent explanation for Louis the Pious' appropriation of Martinian behaviour and his refusal to 'bare his teeth in laughter'. Louis' reign was beset by problems; Thegan's description of the unlaughing emperor was written in the aftermath of one crisis. Some historians have plausibly sought the troubles of Louis' reign in the end of the vigorous military expansion which characterised the reign of his father, Charlemagne.[68] Charlemagne's court presents comparisons with Louis'. Innes contrasts descriptions of Charlemagne's court and its performance of secular songs with Louis' disdain of such entertainments, and shows clearly how this, too, stemmed from the emperor's adoption of monastically influenced modes of thought and behaviour. Bayless points out that Charlemagne's was also a court at which at least some elements, apparently including the ruler himself, enjoyed witty verbal games and exchanges.[69] As she also says, this wordplay could find Christian justification, too.[70] This was a confident court, one wherein the emperor had sufficient security in his position to embrace rituals of community. Louis' was quite different. Whatever Louis' own abilities,[71] it cannot be denied that Charlemagne was not an easy act for anyone to follow. When combined with the other problems faced by Louis' régime, it is perhaps not surprising that this emperor chose to eschew (or to present himself as eschewing), and thus raise himself above, the horizontal bonds that unified the rest of the court. The response to humour can be a valuable tool in social politics. The 'Brass Eye' debate mentioned above has seen politicians and the editors of various newspapers (not all of whom even watched the programme) stake a claim for moral superiority by portraying themselves as not having laughed. Even then, as Kershaw shows, it is possible through subtle reading of the different sources to show a certain common ground between depictions of Charlemagne and his son.[72] Both, in different ways, portrayed themselves as the 'fixed points of order'.[73]

Closely related to the concept that an ability to control emotions manifested the capacity to rule legitimately were ideas of what distinguished

---

[68] See, e.g., T. Reuter, 'The end of Carolingian military expansion', in *Charlemagne's Heir: New Perspectives on the Reign of Louis the Pious (814–40)*, ed. P. Godman and R. Collins (Oxford, 1990), pp. 391–405; also his 'Plunder and tribute in the Carolingian empire', *Transactions of the Royal Historical Society*, 5th series, 35 (1985), pp. 75–94.

[69] Below, pp. 162–4.   [70] Below, p. 160.

[71] For reappraisal of which, see *Charlemagne's Heir*, ed. Godman and Collins (Oxford, 1990); Innes, below, p. 134.

[72] Below, p. 193.   [73] Below, p. 193.

the civilised man from the barbarian. Barbarians were distinguished by their lack of reason; their inability to master their passions.[74] Thus, as Humphries says, the failure of a Roman emperor to control his feelings not only impugned his right to rule, it brought him close to not being a Roman at all.[75] With the early medieval transformation of the Roman–barbarian dichotomy into the Christian–pagan opposition, one can see how these ideas had come to be translated by Louis the Pious' day. The distinction between Romans and barbarians was one of the most important structuring principles of classical writing and, though it was a rather shifting, rhetorical opposition, it was largely based upon these ideas of the mastery of emotions. That the barbarians could not achieve this meant they were unfree. In turn their political systems did not count as true governments,[76] and thus barbarians lived in a perpetual state of unfreedom. Humour could be used to mock this state of affairs and reinforce Roman ideas of superiority. As with Louis' response to the circumstances of his rule, the harping on these ideas of superiority by some writers may have become more strident during late antiquity because of the insecurity of their position. The dry aphorism of Theoderic the Ostrogoth, that 'The poor Roman imitates the Goth, the rich Goth imitates the Roman', on the other hand, may have issued from Theoderic's position of power, as may the bon mot of Athaulf, king of the Visigoths, about barbarians' inability to live according to the law.[77] The humour directed against barbarians worked not only simply by mocking the supposed nature of the Other; it also worked by ridiculing instances when the barbarian tried to play the Roman. The language barrier that created the concept of the barbarian in the first place could also be used to create comic difference, and underline a sense of superiority; this was as true in the ninth century, as Kershaw shows, as it had been in classical antiquity, and as it remained in Byzantium.[78]

Another key structuring principle in late antique and early medieval views of the correct order of the world, was, of course, the division between man and woman. In one of the stories I discuss below, dealing with inversion of the norms of barbarian behaviour, it is interesting that gender stereotypes are also transgressed, perhaps underlining the topsy-turvy nature of the situations presented. Whether this was itself

[74] Halsall, below, pp. 91–93.   [75] Humphries, below, pp. 77–8.
[76] See below, pp. 91–2.
[77] For Theoderic's comment, see Anonymous Valesianus 12.61; *Ammianus Marcellinus*, vol. III, ed. and trans. J. C. Rolfe (London, 1939). Also Shanzer, below, p. 34, n. 56. For Athaulf, see Halsall, below, pp. 99–102.
[78] Kershaw, below, pp. 194–5; Haldon, below, pp. 58–60 for the Byzantine view.

humorous is in this instance doubtful, but it helps to set up a situation where the normal structures of society are abandoned. Everything is all over the place. This creates a scene where a ludicrous outcome might be expected. When Amalasuntha rules the Goths and tries to bring up her son as a Roman, something which infuriates the Goths, she behaves like a man; on the other hand, the Goths who object to this education and wish to replace it with a proper barbarian education (the upshot of which is rapidly revealed) claim that the pursuit of letters was 'far removed from manliness' (only an irrational barbarian could think that).[79] Similarly, gender is involved in Agnellus' depiction of Bishop Gratiosus of Ravenna, referred to as mother by his *familia* (upon whom the joke is, in the end), instead of as father, as would be usual.[80] Ideas of rationality and the control of emotions also played a significant part in early medieval ideas of what distinguished man from woman. This becomes clear in the story told by Liutprand of Cremona and analysed by Balzaretti about the Greek woman who intercedes with Tedbald for the safe return of her husband.[81] As Balzaretti says, the woman behaves in many ways like the early medieval stereotype of a woman, for example in displaying extreme emotion, weeping and tearing her face in grief. Yet other parts of the story presumably, as Balzaretti also says, display inversion and incongruity. She claims lordship (over the marriage bed) and has left her stereotypical domain, the castle, to move into the very male world of the army to make her demands. Balzaretti suggests very plausibly that, for contemporaries, these may well have been the story's funniest elements.

Thus all of these aspects of ideas of society, the control of desire and emotion at the highest levels of society, the difference between the civilised man and the barbarian, and the opposition between man and woman, are related. Fun can be poked at an Other simply by making use of the stereotype, but using inversion and incongruity can also often create humour. As is pointed out repeatedly in this volume, to identify and understand the incongruity requires reconstruction of the thought-world of the past. These ideas of the proper way of things are almost invariably those of the dominant élite.[82] As has been well known since the work of Mikhail Bakhtin, such inversions do not undermine the norms, but

---

[79] Amalasuntha: Halsall, below, pp. 106–7.   [80] Kershaw, below, p. 186.

[81] Below, pp. 115–20. Note, again, the combination of the (at least partial) inversion of one structural norm of society, that based upon gender, with the use of another set of stereotypes. In this case the woman is a Greek. That she was a foreigner may have added another dimension to the story's amusement value.

[82] Haldon, below, p. 64.

serve to reinforce them. Notker's story of the Vikings' apparent subversion of the Franks' political use of baptism rituals[83] in fact serves only to underline their own barbarism. By the same token, drawing attention to humorous usage of stereotypes does not imply that those stereotypes were not taken very seriously. The humour, after all, comes from the very 'reality' of the stereotype and the strength of belief in the 'right' order of things; otherwise the inversion would not be funny.

This humour, as is seen repeatedly in the succeeding essays, is almost entirely élite.[84] Though it can often take a fairly base form, the humour discussed here is nearly always that of the learned classes, lay and ecclesiastical: mostly puns, heavy irony and witty conceits, doubtless evoking wry smiles rather than belly laughs. Early medieval demons may be made to speak like rustics but the joke is still told by the pope.[85] Only occasionally do we catch a glimpse of commoner varieties of humour and, truth to tell, when we do it rarely makes for edifying reading. Once again, the humour focusses on ridicule: on laughing *at*. A story in Priscus of Pannium's account of his embassy to the court of Attila the Hun possibly brings us closer to hearing the raucous laughter of early medieval crowds at fairs, feasts or parties, than any of the learned puns, inversions and riddles discussed here; it is not a welcoming sound. 'After the songs a certain crazed Scythian came forward, who forced everyone to burst out laughing by uttering monstrous and unintelligible words and nothing at all sane.'[86] Then in came Zercon the Moor: 'On account of the deformity of his body, the lisp of his voice and his appearance he was an object of laughter.' Attila's brother Bleda had thought him hilarious because of the way he walked and spoke, and used to dress him up in armour, to make him even funnier; eventually he even had him married off to a noblewoman, which Bleda appears to have thought an hilarious prank.[87] Attila, to his credit, did not find either amusing, although that may have been, as Innes points out,[88] because he was trying to act like a Roman emperor. Certainly it did not make him treat Zercon more humanely. The 'crazed Scythian' brought on and encouraged to speak provoked laughter according to what have been termed 'mastery theories' – in other words, laughing at mistakes which the audience has learnt

---

[83] Kershaw, below, pp. 195–7.   [84] Haldon, below, p. 64.

[85] Shanzer, below, p. 46.

[86] Priscus, fragment 13.1, in *The Fragmentary Classicizing Historians of the Later Roman Empire*, ed. and trans. R. C. Blockley (Liverpool, 1981). The translation is from *The Age of Attila*, ed. and trans. C. G. Gordon (New York, 1960).

[87] Priscus, frag. 13.2, in *Fragmentary Classicizing Historians*, ed. and trans. Blockley.

[88] Below, p. 141.

not to make.[89] The Huns 'burst out laughing' because they knew that the unfortunate man was speaking nonsense and he did not. As with some of the more learned humour discussed in this volume, Zercon was funny because of incongruity: a man with a speech impediment forced to speak in public like an orator; a man with a physical deformity made to don armour and play the soldier. All the established expectations of a public speaker or a warrior are dashed.

Another glimpse of this type of humour comes in Gregory of Tours' *Histories*.[90] Having discovered a plot against his life, Childebert II of Austrasia had the conspirators rounded up. 'Some had their hands amputated and were afterwards released, some had their ears and noses cut off, and were released to be ridiculed' (*ad ridiculum laxeverunt*). Haldon discusses Byzantine analogies for this tale of mutilation, and ridicule was a common feature of early medieval western rituals of punishment.[91] This was an extension of the idea that a political opponent might be reduced in the eyes of an audience, and his (or her) capacity for power thereby diminished, by the use of ridicule. In Cicero's works this was accomplished by verbal assault;[92] late antique and early medieval rulers and legislators simply made the violence more corporeal. It may be that, in a society that bound masculinity and secular power more closely to martial ability than Roman society had done, it is not surprising that the humorous belittling of an enemy in the form of physical disfigurement began to take a more prominent place alongside the ridicule of his or her personal habits and morality.[93] Disputes seem more often to have been resolved via the threat, at least, of violence in the post-Roman period than in Cicero's day.[94] Carolingian court intellectuals may have done a great deal of their jousting with words,[95] but even Theodulf of Orléans and Alcuin – the same Alcuin whose intricate, joking wordplay is analysed by Bayless below[96] – were far from being above using armed force to settle their differences.[97] Is it possible that humour itself became more violent?

---

[89] C. P. Wilson, *Jokes: Form, Content, Use and Function* (London, 1979), p. 17.

[90] *Histories* 10.18.

[91] Byzantine analogies: Haldon, below, pp. 65–6. For the west, see, e.g., Shanzer, below, p. 28; Innes, below, p. 132

[92] See Humphries, below, pp. 76–79.

[93] Though there is doubtless a contrast between early medieval and Roman ideas of masculinity as expressed in the capacity for physical violence and warfare, it should not be overstated.

[94] G. Halsall, 'Violence and society in the early medieval west: an introductory survey', in *Violence and Society in the Early Medieval West*, ed. G. Halsall (Woodbridge, 1998), pp. 1–45.

[95] Innes, below, p. 131.   [96] Below, ch. 7.

[97] See J. L. Nelson, 'Violence in the Carolingian world and the ritualization of ninth-century warfare', in *Violence and Society*, ed. Halsall, pp. 90–107, at p. 93; P. Fouracre, 'Carolingian justice: the rhetoric of improvement and contexts of abuse', *La giustizia nell'alto medioevo, secoli V–VIII* (Settimane di Studi 42) (Spoleto, 1995), pp. 771–803.

The glimpses we have of non-élite humour reveal some linkages with the things which the dominant classes found humorous. After all, Constantine IX and his learned biographer, Michael Psellos, both thought it would be uproariously amusing to dig pits in a garden before a party, so that the guests would fall into them.[98] King Alboin of the Lombards had a cup made from the skull of his enemy, Cunimund, and offered it to his wife to drink from – his wife being Cunimund's daughter. [99] One might wonder if the skull-cup itself was a sort of pun – a play on the fact that 'head' and 'pot' could be the same in Vulgar Latin: *testa*.[100] In much the same vein, one can today buy a mug (large cup) in the shape of a mug (face). Generally, though, non-élite humour lies beyond us. We know that there were public performances of plays, and mimes, and that jesters were to be found in royal and aristocratic households.[101] They were the sorts of thing, as Innes describes, of which the church disapproved and sought to keep clerics away from, perhaps because of the fact that many such performances took place on holy feast days.[102] Exactly what these plays comprised of, or the nature of the jokes told by jesters, can only be guessed at; if the jokes were all as funny as the one about Hatto told by Louis the Pious' court fool, one might imagine that theirs was a precarious living . . .

Much of the humour of the fool, though, could serve not to question but to underline the political order. After all, what better way of making public a claim for moral authority than having a jester who, by making jokes about the powers that be, served to underline that questioning such structures, funny though it might be, was itself the prerogative and the behaviour of a fool, something outside correct order? How

[98] Haldon, below, p. 65. Then again, people falling over unintentionally (or at least apparently unintentionally) seems to be one of the constants of humour, which a significant portion of all societies sees as funny. How else can one explain the staggering popularity of the British comedian Norman Wisdom in Communist Albania? Another such constant might be people wearing odd things on their head; see Kershaw, below, p. 182, n. 12.

[99] Shanzer, below, p. 37.   [100] Shanzer, below, p. 32, and n. 39.

[101] M. Richter, *The Formation of the Medieval West: Studies in the Oral Culture of the Barbarians* (Dublin, 1994), usefully discusses the semantic field of *scurrus*: it encompasses the overlapping and closely linked roles of the jester, and the professional performer of oral tradition and (often humorous) secular lays. Whether such figures were necessarily descendants of allegedly archaic Germanic traditions of rulers having *skalds* at their courts seems at best a moot point given the state of the evidence. There are parallels for such entertainers in late antiquity. None the less, some of the sophisticated literary discussion of the role of such figures in surviving epics such as *Beowulf* may, if used with care, be of value: see, e.g., C. Clover, 'The Germanic context of the Unferþ episode', *Speculum* 55 (1980), pp. 444–68, for an important discussion of the political and social context of humour in heroic literature which retains its value whether or not one accepts the Germanic cultural genealogy proposed for certain motifs. I am grateful to Matthew Innes for these points and references.

[102] Thus Charlemagne forbade bishops from keeping *ioculatores*: *Duplex legationis edictum* (23 March 789), c. 31, *MGH Leges II. Capitularia regum francorum I*, ed. A. Boretius (Hanover, 1883).

better to emphasise control over emotions and the right to legitimate rule (and perhaps that these were *not* proper things for anyone else to say to the king or emperor) than by showing at best only mild, smiling amusement at these antics?

Another intriguing locus for humour, where professional entertainers were employed, was, at least on occasion, the funeral. Regino of Prüm concerned himself, disapprovingly, in his *De ecclesiasticis disciplinis* with people who sang, danced and told jokes around the tombs of the dead, as if the death of a brother was something to make merry about, rather than being something to be mourned.[103] This all suggests the characteristics of a wake, humour here being used as a way of releasing tension and helping the bereaved to cope with their loss.

Humour has many uses in social practice. As mentioned, it can be a means of negotiating social structures. An attempt to modify the norms of behaviour, if resisted and frowned upon, may be excused as humorous: 'I was only joking.' This can be a useful strategy because, just as authorities might claim the right to define what is or is not funny, and display power and authority by refusing to laugh, it is conversely sometimes unwise to seem to lack a sense of humour, and more often than not injudicious to overreact to something ostensibly intended as a joke. Humour can allow safe retreat from difficult situations.[104] Thus more subordinate parties in social relationships can use humour as a way of testing boundaries. Hence, one imagines, emperors faced with mocking jests from the crowd would be forced to take the abuse rather than show a loss of control.

Other possibilities exist and demand consideration but again lie beyond the reach of our evidence. Were there joking relationships in late antique and early medieval society, such as were famously discussed by the anthropologist A. R. Radcliffe-Brown?[105] Was joking and laughter more admissible in some social groups than others? Advice to a king could include the injunction to joke with the young men but to debate with their elders.[106] And what of female humour? The humour discussed

---

[103] Regino, *De Ecclesiasticis disciplinis et religione Christiana*, 1.398, *PL* 132, col. 185–400. *Medieval Handbooks of Penance: A Translation of the Principal Libri Poenitentiales*, trans. J. T. McNeill and H. M. Gamer (New York, 1990), pp. 318–19. Cf. *Capitula Trevirensia*, c. 11, which deals similarly with *saltatores* and *saltatrices* (tumblers) who sing, dance and joke around the bodies of the deceased.

[104] See G. Halsall, 'Social identities and social relationships in Merovingian Gaul', in *Franks and Alamanni in the Merovingian Period: An Ethnographic Perspective*, ed. I. N. Wood (Woodbridge, 1998), pp. 141–65, at p. 142.

[105] A. R. Radcliffe-Brown, 'On joking relationships', in his *Structure and Function in Primitive Society* (New York, 1965), pp. 90–104.

[106] Remigius of Rheims, Letter to Clovis. *Epistulae Austrasiacae* 2: *cum iuuenibus ioca, cum senibus tracta, si uis regnare, nobilis iudicare*, *CCSL* 117, ed. W. Gundlach (Turnhout, 1957), p. 409.

in this volume is unremittingly male in origin, even if sometimes about women. As Haldon notes, the humour of women – their side of the humorous use of gender – has been almost completely silenced. Hrotswitha of Gandersheim's *Dulcitius* is perhaps the first inkling that we have of this type of humour.[107]

Finally, though, one might wonder if we are not taking the literary analysis of texts too far if we read them very closely for instances that seem to offer irony and jest. Are we inscribing our interests, our characters and our social values on to past texts which were never written to be understood in that way? Might not future generations, by the same token, read the serious scholarly exegesis presented below in conjunction with what they might find out about the authors, and propose that this is itself a work of irony, a satire on the often too earnest pursuit of medieval studies? Might it be that the series of conference sessions at which these papers were first given originated in a light-hearted quest for a topic more entertaining than yet more discussion of the politics of priests and bishops? It might. It might not. But don't worry; I've got the key.[108]

---

[107] *Hrotsvithae opera*, ed. P. de Winterfield (Berlin, 1967), pp. 201–28; English translation by B. Hill, *Medieval Monarchy in Action* (London, 1967), pp. 118–37.

[108] In addition to thanking the authors of the following chapters for the inspiration they have provided, I should like to thank my colleague at Birkbeck College, Dr Emmanuele Curti, for help with the bibliography on ancient laughter. My thinking about the relationships between structure and agency benefited from discussion with Emma Campbell, who also excised some of the worst jokes from the original draft, something for which both author *and* readers should give thanks. For helping to germinate the original idea for this book, on an Intercity train between Leeds and London in July 1997, my profound thanks go to Paul Kershaw and Alan Thacker.

PART I

The fate of humorous writing

CHAPTER I

Laughter and humour in the early medieval Latin west

Danuta Shanzer

Few humorous writings from the period 500–800 spring to mind. The familiar biblical and liturgical parodies, comic lyrics and sequences such as adorn the *Cambridge Songs*, satires, Goliardic poetry, plays such as Hrotswitha's *Dulcitius*, animal fables, and innumerable items written in various vernaculars are all the products of a later period. Even Hucbald's *Ecloga de calvis* belongs to the tenth century. This study will in part reinforce prejudices about (lack of) early medieval humour by emphasising discontinuity with the rich humorous traditions of antiquity. But it will also discuss some examples of an unsympathetic type of early medieval humour that shows considerable continuity with the classical world, and analyse some little-known passages where a new type of humour may have been developing.

Studies that cut broad swathes must look for change. How much continuity is there between later Roman and early medieval humour, and how does one chart it? Where is it? Genre provides one convenient handle. 'Humour' (and its posher relative, 'wit') are messy, because they are often passing 'moments' that occur in many genres and literary forms where one *expects* them (for example in comedy, parody, satire, invective and epigram), as well as in genres where their presence is not a *sine qua non* of, or proper to, the genre. History, epistolography, biography and hagiography provide good examples.

DISCONTINUITY

There is indeed less humour in its standard homes in the early Middle Ages. Representatives of the comic genres either never existed or failed to survive: no early medieval comedy (unless one happens to find the *Querolus* amusing), few secular epigrams (Fortunatus, for example), no verse satire, no comic novels, few lampoons, no declamatory or comic invective.

Parodies or works with strong parodic elements

Literary histories, however, include various early medieval items that have plausibly been identified as parodies or extended spoofs.[1] Each parodies one of the serious areas of learning that occupied the early medievals. The *Epitomae* and *Epistolae* of Vergilius Maro Grammaticus seem to poke fun at grammarians. Aethicus Ister's *Cosmographia* has been considered a *Menippea* parodying encyclopaedic geography and ethnography.[2] A parody of the *Pactus legis salicae* is appended to a late eighth-century manuscript of it, concerning the possession of intoxicating substances.[3] Two other texts have been considered parodies of biblical scholarship: the *Cena Cypriani* (if it really *is* early medieval) and the *Ioca monachorum*, biblical catechisms organised as short questions and answers.[4]

One may entertain doubts about the latter. The earliest known form of the *Ioca*, that found in a seventh-century Schlettstadt uncial MS (no. 1093), seems an unlikely candidate for a humorous text. Some of the questions that may have struck people as amusing, such as '*Quis est mortuus et non est natus? Adam*' or '*Quis est natus et non est mortuos? Helias et Enoc*' (Who died but was never born? Adam. Who was born but never died? Elias and Enoch)[5] are really no funnier than the riddle of the Sphinx or Samson's riddle in Judges 14.14. Furthermore, 99 per cent of the text is straightforward factual material drawn primarily from Genesis and Exodus. Did the title alone, *Incipiunt ioca monachorum*, prompt people to consider these questions and answers humorous? *Ioca* may mean no more than 'jeux'.[6]

The same is not quite true of other later question-and-answer dialogues. By the ninth century many, such as the *Disputatio Pippini cum Albino*, go beyond factual questions. Many are reversed riddles, such as '*Quid est verbum? Proditor animae*' (What is a word? The betrayer of the soul),[7] and riddle-kennings, such as '*Vidi feminam volantem, rostrum habentem ferreum et*

---

[1] Parody subverts borrowed material, so some sort of knowledge of the purpose, nature and precise form of the original text is crucial for 'getting it'.

[2] P. Dronke, *Verse with Prose from Petronius to Dante: The Art and Scope of the Mixed Form* (Cambridge and London, 1994), pp. 14–19.

[3] See V. Väänänen, *Introduction au Latin Vulgaire* 3rd edn, Paris, 1981), pp. 198–9.

[4] See F. Brunhölzl, *Geschichte der lateinischen Literatur des Mittelalters*, vol. I (Munich, 1975), pp. 147 ff. and p. 527.

[5] See E. Wölfflin-Troll, '*Ioca monachorum*, ein Beitrag zur mittelalterlichen Räthselliteratur', *Monatsberichte der Königlichen preussischen Akademie der Wissenschaften zu Berlin* (1872), pp. 106–18 at p. 109.

[6] J. Le Goff, 'Le Rire dans les règles monastiques du haut moyen âge', in *Haut Moyen Age: culture, education et société. Etudes offerts à P. Riché*, ed. M. Sot (Nantes, 1990), pp. 93–103, at p. 103 seems to suggest that *ioca monachorum* means not 'monks' jokes', but 'jeux de moines', i.e. 'monks' games'.

[7] *Disputatio Pippini: Altercatio Hadriani Augusti et Epicteti Philosophi* (Illinois Studies in Language and Literature 24), ed. L. W. Daly and W. Suchier (Urbana, IL, 1939), pp. 137–43. See Bayless, below, pp. 157–78.

corpus ligneum et caudam pennatam, mortem portantem. – Socia est militum' (I saw a woman flying, with an iron beak and a wooden body and a feathered tail, carrying death. – That's a woman beloved of the soldiers).[8] Answer: *sagitta* (an arrow). A number now clearly contain familiar jokes. Take these two: '*Quis occidit hominem impune?*' (Who can kill a man and get away with it?) – '*Medicus*' (a doctor); and '*Quae mulieres maritis sunt utiliores?*' (Which women are the best to marry) – '*Divites quae cito moriuntur*'(Rich ones that die fast).[9] Both of these have clear and far more sophisticated analogues in Martial's epigrams. '*Nuper erat medicus, nunc est vispillo Diaulus: quod vispillo facit, fecerat et medicus*' (Recently he was a doctor. Now Diaulus is an undertaker. What he does as an undertaker he did as a doctor).[10] The doctor-turned-undertaker still buries his 'clients'. For the second riddle, compare Martial's tale of Gemellus' wooing of Maronilla. She is hideous, yet he begs and pleads. What is it about her that is so attractive? She coughs (*tussit*).[11] Enough said.[12]

The comic parallels the obscene

Outright humour seems only to occur in counterpoint with grammar, the encyclopaedic and legal traditions, and biblical scholarship. One sees a similar development in the fate of the obscene in the later Christian Latin west. Obscenity is certainly to be found in the west between the late fourth and the early sixth centuries, for example Ausonius' epigram on Eunus, the Syrian grammarian who practises cunnilingus, and sees different letters of the Greek alphabet in his mistresses' genitalia, a contorted and scholastic dirty joke.[13] In the sixth-century elegist Maximianus, Boethius is a panderer,[14] and a Constantinopolitan prostitute both laments over and prays to the authorial persona's *mentula* – surprisingly invoked as

---

[8] *Disputatio Pippini*, p. 142.

[9] *Altercatio Hadriani: Altercatio Hadriani Augusti et Epicteti Philosophi* (Illinois Studies in Language and Literature 24), ed. L. W. Daly and W. Suchier (Urbana, IL, 1939), p. 131.

[10] Martial, Epigram 1.47; also the variant at Epigram 1.30. *Martial Epigrams*, trans. W. C. A. Ker (2 vols., London and New York, 1919). For later, Byzantine jokes about doctors, see Haldon, below, pp. 63–4.

[11] Martial, Epigram 1.10, *Petit Gemellus nuptias Maronillae/et cupit et instat et precatur et donat./adeone pulchra est? immo foedius nil est. quid ergo in illa petitur et placet? tussit.*

[12] There is an even more cynical variant in which we hear that the coughing wife is merely leading her husband on: *blanditur, non moritur.* See Epigram 2.26, *Quod querulum spirat, quod acerbum Naevia tussit/inque tuos mittit sputa subinde sinus, iam te rem factam, Bithynice, credis habere? erras: blanditur Naevia, non moritur.*

[13] Epigram 87. See J. N. Adams, 'An epigram of Ausonius (87 p. 344 Peiper)', *Latomus* 42 (1983), pp. 95–109.

[14] Maximianus, *El.* 3, in *Massimiano elegie*, ed. T. Agozzino (Bologna, 1970), with D. R. Shanzer, 'Ennodius, Boethius, and the date and interpretation of Maximianus' *Elegia* III', *Rivista di filologia e di istruzione classica* 111 (1983), pp. 183–95.

such.[15] These poems contain explicit sexual material, but in both cases it is legitimised by reference to higher forms and is self-consciously clever. Maximianus parodies the philosophical hymn, Ausonius the pedantry of the teacher. Christianity introduced many new areas of social control that would temporarily squash the sexual and the obscene as acceptable literary topics for their own sakes. Something similar seems to have happened with the comic. To be permissible it had to be the reverse of something serious and scholarly.

CONTINUITY

Christian laughter

Latin literature 500–800 means Christian texts. While one can write books on 'Greek Comedy' or 'Roman Laughter', 'Christian Laughter' would hardly make a leaflet. All manner of things failed to amuse: scatology was out (except in a few isolated forms such as humiliation rituals in Germanic law – *Burgundian Law* 97, for example, which specifies kissing the posterior of a hound as punishment for stealing one – and a practical phrase in an Old High German traveller's phrasebook: '*Undes ars in tine naso*' ('A hound's arse up your nose')).[16] There are also echoes of permissible Roman and later Roman sub-scatology such as the death of the heretic or evil-doer on the latrine (Claudius and Arius) in the late seventh-century *Miracula Austrigisili* where the evil Warnarius, after being struck on the head through the posthumous agency of the saint, falls asleep in a privy, suffers a prolapse of his intestines through his anus and expires appropriately on a *sterquilinium*.[17] The pagan theatre was

---

[15] Maximianus, *El.* 5.87–106. At *El.* 5.110–52 the *puella* modulates into quasi-parody of a philosophical hymnic aretalogy.

[16] Burgundian law: *MGH Leges* 1.2.1, ed. L. De Salis (Hanover, 1892); *The Burgundian Code*, trans. K. F. Drew (Philadelphia, 1949; reprinted 1972). *PC* 42 in E. Steinmeyer and E. Sievers, *Die althochdeutsche Glossen* 5 (Berlin, 1879–1922), pp. 517–24. See also Kershaw, below, pp. 200–1.

[17] *Miracula Austrigisilis* 3, *MGH SRM* 4, ed. B. Krusch (Hanover, 1902), pp. 201–2: *pro secessu ventris intravit necessariam . . . omnia intestina vel iecora eius per posteriora de corpore evulsa sunt.* There is a parallel in Gregory of Tours – the death of Sidonius' wicked Arian priest at *Histories* 2.23: *ingressus autem in secessum suum, dum ventrem purgare nititur, spiritum exhalavit . . . Arrium illum, cui similiter in secessum fuerunt interna deposita per partis inferioris egestum*: *MGH SRM* 1.1, ed. B. Krusch and W. Levison (Hanover, 1951). Gregory knew of Arius' death story from Rufinus, *Historia Ecclesiastica* 10.13, in *Eusebius Werke. Bd. 2. Die Kirchengeschichte (Die griechischen christlichen Schriftsteller der ersten Jahrhunderte 9.2)*, ed. E. Schwartz (Berlin, 1908) (Rufinus' Latin text ed. T. Mommsen). For more on this point and on Gregory's comic treatment of such a death in *Gloria Martyrum* 79 (*MGH SRM* 1.2,

considered a home of unspeakable lusts and perversions.[18] The carnival-esque reversals of the *Saturnalia* fell into disfavour. Sex was out.

Laughter regarding learning, however, was clearly acceptable – this is evident from various parodies. But what other laughters were licit in the new Christian Latin world? One must start with laughter in the Bible. Old Testament examples of *ridere* almost all refer to *derision*.[19] Only two New Testament passages refer to laughter and both, significantly, are threatening prophecies: Luke 6.21, *beati qui nunc fletis quia ridebitis* (blessed are those that weep, for they shall laugh) and Luke 6.25, *vae vobis qui ridetis nunc quia lugebitis et flebitis* (woe to you who laugh now, for you shall mourn and weep).[20] Although the occasional saint could even expire *cum risu*,[21] Umberto Eco's sinister Brother Jorge (and many far earlier Christians) observed that Christ never laughed.[22] This observation clearly led the various prohibitions against laughter in early monastic rules.[23]

When Salvian described the *Romanus orbis* during the time of the fifth-century barbarian invasions, he said:

We play even while we live in dread of captivity, and laugh in fear of death. You would think that the whole Roman populace has somehow been imbued with Sardonic herbs: it dies, yet it laughs [*moritur et ridet*]. And for that reason, in almost all parts of the world, tears follow our laughter, and there has come upon us even now that saying of the Lord, 'Woe to you who laugh, for you shall weep.'[24]

Salvian's quotation is suggestive. The one New Testament passage that refers to laughter is used as the threat it is.

ed. B. Krusch and W. Levison (Hanover, 1969)), see D. R. Shanzer, 'History, romance, love, and sex in Gregory of Tours' *Decem libri historiarum*', in *Gregory of Tours*, ed. K. Mitchell and I. N. Wood (Brill, 2002).

[18] Salvian, *On the Governance of God* (*De gubernatione Dei*) 6.15–19, in *MGH Auctores Antiquissimi* 1.1, ed. C. Halm (Berlin, 1877).

[19] One partial exception appears in Genesis 18.10, Sarah's laughter when she hears that she is to have a child after menopause. Also Gen. 21.6. One genuine exception is Ecl. 3.4, *tempus ridendi* opposed to *tempus flendi*.

[20] See A. Rousselle, *Porneia* (Oxford, 1988), p. 121, citing Tertullian on the grim laughter of Christians contemplating the fate of pagans at the Last Judgement.

[21] The nun Disciola in Gregory of Tours, *Histories* 6.29.

[22] See *The Name of the Rose*, trans. W. Weaver (London, 1983), p. 130: 'Our Lord Jesus never told comedies or fables.' And p. 95: 'John Chrysostom said that Christ never laughed.' See also Innes, below, pp. 142–3.

[23] See Le Goff, 'Le Rire', pp. 93–103.

[24] *De gubernatione Dei* 7.1.6: *Nos et in metu captivitatis ludimus et positi in mortis timore ridemus. Sardonicis quodammodo herbis omnem Romanum populum putes esse saturatum: moritur et ridet. Et ideo in omnibus fere partibus mundi risus nostros lacrimae consequuntur ac venit etiam in praesenti super nos illud domini nostri dictum: vae vobis, qui ridetis, quoniam flebitis.* See also Halsall, below, p. 98.

Risus sardonicus

Sardonic humour,²⁵ connected to threatening behaviour, is a significant form of licit wit in the early Middle Ages.²⁶ Various manifestations of such humour appear in martyr-hagiography and historical texts.

In the *Acta Fructuosi Tarraconensis* there is the following exchange between the bishop and Aemilianus the *praeses* (258/9 under Valerian): ' "*Episcopus es?*" ' (Are you the bishop?) '*Fructuosus dixit: "Sum"* ' (I am). '*Aemilianus dixit: "Fuisti"* ' (You were) '*et iussit eos vivos ardere*' (and he ordered them to be burnt alive).²⁷ This section appears as proconsular *acta*, apparently strict transcriptions of the courtroom proceedings. Yet it contains an authentic grim joke. Prudentius in his *Peristefanon* worked from these *Acta*, and clearly interpreted Aemilianus' reply as humorous, for he recasts it as '*subridens ille ait: "Iam fuisti"* ' (Smiling he said, 'You *were*').²⁸ The grammatical point lies in the macabre contrast in meaning between the *infectum* and the *perfectum* of *sum*. One remembers Cicero's announcement about the executed Catilinarian conspirators: *vixerunt*.²⁹ In the *Passio Perpetuae* the crowds in the amphitheatre at Carthage cried out '*Salvum lotum! Salvum lotum!*' ('Well washed!' – the salutation used in the public baths), when Saturus was bitten by a leopard and drenched in blood.³⁰ When a Roman judge held a hearing over Saint Hippolytus he said, 'What is he called?' They answered, 'Hippolytus.' 'Therefore let him *be* Hippo-lytus, and let him die torn by wild horses.'³¹ Cruel and unusual punishment

---

²⁵ See *Paulys Real-encyclopädie der classischen Altertumswissenschaft. Neue Bearbeitung . . .* , ed. A. F. v. Pauly, G. Wissowa, W. Kroll and K. Witte (Stuttgart, 1894), 'Sardinia' 2495 for the somewhat obscure origins of the term. It cites Homer, *Odyssey* 2.302 with Eustathius *ad loc.* Aeschylus. Fr. 455 Nauck, Sophocles Fr. 163 Nauck. Plato, *Republic* 1.337, in *Plato. The Republic*, trans. P. Shorey (2 vols., London 1930, 1935). For the Sardinian herb, see Livy, *Histories* 17.14, in *Livy*, ed. and trans. F. G. Moore, E. T. Sage and A. C. Schlesinger (London, 1919–59); Vergil, *Bucolics*, 7.41; Pliny, *Natural History* 20.116, in *Pliny. Natural History*, ed. and trans. H. Rackham (London, 1938–63); Isidore, *Etymologies* 4.6.40, in *Isidori Hispalensis episcopi Etymologiarvm sive Originvm*, ed. W. M. Lindsay (2 vols., Oxford, 1911). See also Saloman Reinach, 'Le Rire rituel', in his *Cultes, Mythes et Religions*, vol. IV (Paris, 1912), pp. 109–29 and Eugen Fehrle, 'Das Lachen im Glauben der Voelker', *Zeitschrift für Volkskunde*, n.s., 2 (1930), pp. 1–5.
²⁶ Vladimir Propp, 'Ritual laughter in folklore', in *Theory and History of Folklore*, ed. A. Liberman (Minneapolis, 1984), pp. 124–46, at pp. 134–5 discusses alleged examples of ritual laughter accompanying death and killing, all involving groups. These he characterises as sardonic laughter.
²⁷ *Acta Fructuosi Tarraconensis* 2.8–9 in H. Musurillo, *The Acts of the Christian Martyrs* (Oxford, 1972).
²⁸ Prudentius' *Peristephanon* 6.47–48, *CCSL* 126, ed. M. Cunningham (Turnhout, 1966).
²⁹ For Cicero's laconic announcement, Ἔζησαν, rendering *vixerunt*, see Plutarch, *Life of Cicero* 22.2, in *Plutarch's Lives*, vol. VII, ed. and trans. B. Perrin (11 vols., London, 1919).
³⁰ *Passio Perpetuae* 21.2. See Musurillo, *Acts of the Christian Martyrs*, p. 131, n. 21 for the use of the phrase as greetings in the bath. He cites H. Dessau, *Inscriptiones Latinae selectae* (Berlin, 1892), 5725: *Bene Lava!* and *Salvum lotum!*
³¹ Prudentius, *Peristefanon* 11.85–7: '*Quis inquit/dicitur?' adfirmant dicier Hippolytum./'Ergo sit Hippolytus, quatiet turbetque iugales,/intereat feris dilaceratus equis.*'

originates in a judge's grim pun. The name of the saint determines his martyrdom: 'hippo-lytos', 'horse-torn'. Such jokes characterise evil persecutors.[32]

Le roi s'amuse

Examples can be found in historiography. In Gregory of Tours' *Histories* (2.27) the still pagan Clovis had plundered a Christian church and made off with an *urceus* of great size and beauty. The bishop begged, and Clovis agreed to return it. When Clovis asked for the vase 'in addition to his share', most were obliging, but one soldier struck the vase with his battle-axe: Clovis was not to get anything beyond his fair share. The vase must have stayed intact, because Clovis gave it to the bishop and nursed his injured *amour propre*. A year later at weapons inspection, he told the soldier, *urcei percussorem* ('vase-murderer'), that his arms were not in good trim, and knocked his battle-axe out of his hand. As he bent over, Clovis imbedded his own axe in his head. '*Sic, inquid, tu Sexonas in urceo illo fecisti*' – 'This is what *you* did at Soissons to that vase.'

Walter Goffart sees here (and in the two other places in book 2 where Clovis employs the *securis*) some ethnic typecasting: 'There is supposed to be something definitely Frankish about axes cleaving skulls, especially from behind. Gregory makes the point as a grim joke, by repetition.'[33] But the first episode is a grim joke in and of itself. One exulted over vanquished enemies, to be sure, and the typology of such speeches is already found in Homer.[34] But this story is not told as an epic vaunt: 'Go, sleep with the fishes. . . ' Instead, Gregory presents it as an enacted joke with a verbal punch line. It is preceded by narrative with no direct speech at all; Clovis' speech, with its emphatic 'tu' and telling 'sic', is highlighted.[35] The joke depends on a perversion of the *lex talionis*, repayment in kind, an eye for an eye, a pot for a pot. Or a man who insists on fair shares gets his fair share.

A similar type of repayment appears in Paul the Deacon's *Historia Langobardorum* (4.37). Romilda had betrayed Friuli to the Kagan of the

---

[32] K. M. Coleman, 'Fatal charades: Roman executions staged as mythological enactments', *Journal of Roman Studies* 80 (1990), pp. 44–93, reminds us that such executions were not a purely literary extravagance.

[33] W. Goffart, *Narrators of Barbarian History A.D. 550–800* (Princeton, 1988), pp. 212–13. The three passages are: Gregory of Tours, *Histories* 2.27, 2.40 and 2.42 (all associated with Clovis).

[34] For more on such speeches, see H. Pelliccia, *Mind, Body, and Speech in Homer and Pindar* (Göttingen, 1995), pp. 150–61, esp. pp. 158–9, which gives the standard rhetorical pattern. There are nice latter-day parallels in Prudentius' *Psychomachia* (e.g. 53 ff., 155 ff., 285 ff., 427 ff.).

[35] Cf. the state of Virginia's motto: *Sic semper tyrannis!*

Avars on condition that he marry her. Once the town had been captured, the Kagan spent the promised night with her,[36] but on the morrow turned her over to twelve of his men to gang-rape. When she finally was impaled, the men said, '*Talem te dignum est maritum habere*' ('This is the husband you deserve'). The *palus* (stake) is a deadly substitute for the *phallus*, and *talem* points the *talio*. There are parallels for similar bitter *taliones* by *barbaroi* in ancient historiography: Tomyris sated Cyrus I's thirst for slaughter by immersing his severed head in a sack of blood,[37] and the Parthians filled the dead Crassus' mouth with gold in ironic token of his greed.[38] A productive Vulgar Latin word for head was *testa*, properly 'pot',[39] and the exchange of dented head for dented pot makes a certain barbaric sense.

What are the generic origins of this sort of humour? In his *Narrators of Barbarian History*, Goffart argued that Gregory of Tours is a satirist.[40] His pessimistic, honest, straightforward voice, his dislike of ostentatious rhetoric, his alleged *rusticitas* and simple moral code are all said to constitute a satirical voice. Mishmash (*satura*) is found, we are told, in Gregory's lack of cohesive plot, in his piling-on of incidents. Goffart does not, however, explain the generic source of Gregory's satire, though he implies an argument like this: since Fortunatus knew Horace and Martial (the latter not, in fact, a satirist), he could have known Juvenal, and because Fortunatus was Gregory's friend one might have expected them to share reading.[41] This is too conjectural.

No Latin hexameter satire survives from later than Juvenal. Down to the fourth century (and beyond, if one believes Sidonius Apollinaris), satire (other than the *Menippea*) was a verse genre, and one in which writers wrote very self-consciously with deliberate allusions both to the genre itself and to their predecessors. Juvenal was revived in the late fourth century. However, at the same time satire entered *history*, and

---

[36] Paul the Deacon, *Historia Langobardorum* 4.37, *MGH Scriptores Rerum Langobardicarum et Italicarum*, ed. L. Bethman and G. Waitz (Hanover, 1878): *Romildam vero quae totius malitiae caput exstitit, rex Avarum propter iusiurandum, sicut ei spoponderat, nocte una quasi in matrimonium habuit, novissime vero duodecim Avaribus tradidit, qui eam per totam noctem vicibus sibi succendentes libidine vexarent.*

[37] Herodotus, *Histories* 1.214.4 ff. The exemplum was known to Sidonius Apollinaris – *Carmina* 9.29, 2.117, 9.30–7: *MGH Auctores Antiquissimi* 8, ed. C. Luetjohann (Berlin, 1887).

[38] Dio Cassius, *Roman History* 40.27, in *Dio's Roman History*, ed. and trans. E. Cary and H. B. Foster (London, 1914). The theme lived on in hagiography; see Gregory of Tours, *Gloria martyrum* 105, in *Gregory of Tours: Glory of the Martyrs*, trans. R. Van Dam (Liverpool, 1988), for an avaricious dead woman whose mouth was found full of molten gold with sulphurous flames.

[39] Väänänen, *Introduction au Latin Vulgaire*, p. 78. Also Gregory of Tours, *Gloria martyrum* 105, although M. Bonnet, *Le Latin de Grégoire de Tours* (Paris, 1890), p. 354 notes that the neuter is not normally used for the head. He gives examples of *testa* and *testum* side-by-side.

[40] Goffart, *Narrators*, pp. 197–203.   [41] Ibid., p. 200.

re-emerged as a prose form in two formal satirical excursus on the vices of Rome in Ammianus Marcellinus.[42] Jerome uses both satirists and satirical techniques throughout his writings.[43] The same could be said of Arnobius and Augustine,[44] and especially of the latter's treatment of pagan religion in the *City of God*.[45] It is argued elsewhere that it is the church fathers who become the new satirists.[46] No satirical self-consciousness and no generic markers appear in Gregory, because he was not writing satire. He never used the term.

One could propose a different genealogy for episodes such as the vase of Soissons or Clovis' purge of his relatives. The biographical tradition revelled in 'bons mots' and 'famous last words' delivered by the hero, witness Suetonius.[47] In the later Roman period, biography began to exercise more and more influence on history.[48] Even Ammianus Marcellinus, who professed to deplore imperial biography and Marius Maximus and his ilk,[49] was influenced by it within an annalistic structure. His treatment of Valentinian I provides a good analogy for Gregory on Clovis, even down to the following grim joke at *Res Gestae* 29.3.6. One of Valentinian's officials had asked for a new posting to a different province. The emperor said *subagresti verbo* (using unrefined speech): '*muta ei caput, qui sibi mutari provinciam cupit*' ('This bloke wants his province changed for him. Change his head'); he had the man beheaded. Grammar again lies near the heart of this joke: a play on the varying syntax of the dative: disadvantage versus advantage. Ammianus subsequently introduces another grim pleasantry: Valentinian kept two man-eating pet she-bears, *Mica Aurea* (Goldflake) and *Innocentia* (Unharming). The latter, *Innocentia*, after she had torn many men to bits, was 'honourably discharged'[50] and allowed to return to the woods *innoxiam*. The proper

---

[42] Amm. Marc. 28.4.1–35; see also *Scholia in Juvenalem* 4.53, in *Scholia in Iuvenalem vetustiora*, ed. P. Wessner (Leipzig, 1931). On Ammianus, see also Halsall, below, pp. 97–9.

[43] D. S. Wiesen, *St. Jerome as Satirist* (Ithaca, NY, 1964). A. de Voguë, *Histoire littéraire du mouvement monastique dans l'antiquité* (Paris, 1993) vol. I, pt 1, '356–385', pp. 259–60 links Jerome's penchant for satire with Tertullian. For satire in prose, see Wiesen, *St. Jerome as Satirist*, p. 249.

[44] In the *Confessions* Augustine criticised the Manichees exploiting Persius' recondite language. See *Confessions* 4.1.1, *nobis in officina aqualiculi sui fabricarent angelos et deos*, echoing Persius, *Satires*, 1.56. *St Augustine's Confessions*, ed. and trans. W. Watts (2 vols., London, 1912). The word *aqualiculus* was also picked up by Tertullian, *Ieiun.* 16: *deus ... tibi venter est ... et aqualiculus altare* and by Jerome, Epigram 66.5; 38.5; 107.10: *Sancti Eusebii Hieronymi epistulae*, *CSEL* 14–16, ed. I. Hilberg and M. Kamptner, (Vienna, 1996); *Commentariorun in Jeremiam Prophetan Libri* VI, *PL* 24, cols. 679–900.

[45] The same applies to sections of Prudentius' theological polemics, such as the *Contra Symmachum*.

[46] See my forthcoming 'Obscenity in the later Latin west'.

[47] For some examples, see Suetonius, *Life of Vespasian* 23.

[48] F. Leo, *Die griechisch-römische Biographie nach ihrer literarischen Form* (Hildesheim, 1965), pp. 234–40.

[49] Amm. Marc. 28.4.14.   [50] Amm. Marc. 29.3.9, *ut bene meritam*.

meaning *of innoxiam* was *active* – 'unharming' – but it was here used *passive* as 'unpunished', or 'unharmed'.[51] The *figura etymologica* of the *lucus a non lucendo* type emphasises the paradoxical nature of the 'pet'. Here several short but not sweet incidents depict the terrifying wit of Valentinian. They are true evidence of his character and of his *propositum cruentum*,[52] but none of them detracts from his performance as an emperor.[53] Deadly jokes and witty anecdotes had crept into history[54] by the later fourth century.[55] And it is from *there* that they come to Gregory, whose grim humour is not 'satirical'. Grimly humorous ethopoieic anecdotes are not incompatible with admiring attitudes towards one's subjects.[56]

Gregory would, however, also use such humour in more sinister and hostile contexts. He used a variant of an ancient bitter joke in *Histories* 2.42: in Macrobius' *Saturnalia* (2.2.2–3; copied from Gellius 5.5.1–7), Antiochus showed his army to Hannibal and asked *'putasne satis esse Romanis haec omnia?'* ('Do you think these will do for the Romans?'). Hannibal looks at the lazy and luxuriously outfitted soldiers and says *'plane satis esse credo Romanis haec, et si avarissimi sunt'* ('Yes, I think they will certainly do for the Romans, although the Romans can do with quite a lot'). In Gregory's version the protagonists are the wicked Ragnacharius and his 'filthy' *consiliarius* Farro. Whenever anyone brought the king some food or a gift he would say that it would 'do nicely for his Farro and

---

[51] See Servius, *In Aen.* 10.302: *innocuus est cui non nocetur, innoxius qui non novit nocere*, in *G. Servii Grammatici qui ferunter in Vergilii carmina commentarii*, ed. G. Thilo and H. Hagen (Leipzig, 1881). See *Thesaurus Linguae Latinae* (7 vols., Leipzig, 1900–99), s.v. 'innoxius' 1721.73–6 for Ammianus' usages.

[52] Amm. Marc. 29.3.9, *morum eius et propositi cruenti sunt documenta verissima.*

[53] Amm. Marc. 29.4.1, *Sollertiae vero circa rem publicam usquam digredientis nemo eum vel obtrectator pervicax incusabit* ... For Valentinian, see also Humphries, below, p. 78.

[54] Indeed even into chronicles. Take, for example, Theodoric's jokes cited in Anonymus Valesianus 61: *Aus der Zeit Theoderichs des Grossen* , ed. I. König (Darmstadt, 1997). Or, indeed, his grim mot after killing Odoacer: below, n. 56.

[55] See Suetonius, *Caligula* 29 for a catalogue of Caligula's threats and verbal outrages: *Immanissima facta augebat atrocitate verborum* ... In *Caligula* 32 his threats to Apelles and his girlfriends are introduced by *inter varios iocos.*

[56] Theodoric was witty both in an urbane and in an alarming fashion. See Anon. Vales. 61 and John of Antioch fr. 214a for his murder of Odoacer; *Fragmenta historicorum Graecorum*, vol v, ed. C. Müller (Paris 1851 and 1870), p. 29: Θεοδώριχος προσδραμὼν παίει τῷ ξίφει αὐτὸν κατὰ τὴν κλεῖδα, εἰπόντα δέ 'Ποῦ ὁ θεός;' ἀμείβεται· 'τοῦτό ἐστιν ὃ καὶ σὺ τοὺς ἐμοὺς ἔδρασας.' Τῆς δε πληγῆς καιρίας καὶ μέχρι τῆς ὀσφύος διελθούσης τὸ 'Οδοάκρου σῶμα, εἰπεῖν φασι Θεοδώριχον, ὡς τάχα οὐδὲ ὀστοῦν ἦν τῷ κακῷ τούτῳ· 'Theodoric rushed forward and struck him [Odoacer] with his sword on the collarbone while he was saying "Where is God?" Theoderic answered, "This is what you did to my men." As the timely blow pierced Odoacer's body all the way down to the crotch, they say that Theodoric remarked that the evil man probably had no bone.'

for himself' '(*hoc **suo sibi** Farroni sufficer*)'. When Clovis attacked him and he asked how large the rival force was, the bitter, rhyming chiastic answer came: '*tibi tuoque** Farroni est maximum supplimentum*' ('There's the biggest bonus for you and your Farro'). There is also the obedient and obliging Chlothar in *Histories* 4.3. He 'obeys' his partner Ingund, who asked him to find an *utilem atque habentem virum* (an able and wealthy husband) for her sister, Aregundis. Chlothar, after meeting the girl, said that he had not been able to find one wealthier and wiser than – himself! He suited action to word with an incestuous marriage.

Taking control: victims' jokes and cheek

The Epicurean sage could maintain *ataraxia* even on the rack.[57] Philosophical detachment before death, however, rapidly turned into vivid anecdote. A Praetorian Guards officer had been sentenced to execution by Nero.[58] After rebuking the emperor, he watched his own grave being dug – and badly.[59] '*Ne hoc quidem ex disciplina*', he commented: 'not even this is done properly'. When he was asked to stretch out his neck bravely (*fortiter*) for the axe, his *ultima verba* were: '*Utinam tu tam fortiter ferias!*' ('May you strike as bravely!') The pagan had no reward for his courage.[60] But when a grim joke was used by an oppressor in a Christian text, a reversal would follow: either in this world or the next, laughter would turn to a 'wailing and gnashing of teeth'. The victim might feel the Olympian detachment of Saint Agnes who laughed at the vanities of the world after her death.[61] Grim humour fortified living victims too, not just oppressors. Even though Pope Damasus clearly did not know how Saint Laurence was martyred,[62] Prudentius' *Peristefanon* (2.401–9) tells us he was grilled to death.

'Turn over the side of my body that has been burnt sufficiently long, and test what your Vulcan has done with his burning.' The prefect ordered him to be

---

[57] Diogenes Laertius 10.118. The Stoic wise man can likewise be happy even while being burnt in the bull of Phalaris; H. von Arnim, *Stoicorum Veterum fragmenta*, vol. III (Leipzig, 1903), fr. 586.

[58] Subrius Flavus in Tacitus, *Annales* 15.67, in *Tacitus: Histories and Annals*, trans. C. H. Moore and J. Jackson (4 vols., London, 1925–37).

[59] *Humilem et angustam.*

[60] The soldier, who had needed two blows to behead Subrius Flavus, boasted that he had done it with 'a blow and a half' (*sesquiplaga*).

[61] Prudentius, *Peristefanon* 14.95, *ridetque* (and she laughed).

[62] Damasus, Epigram 14 (33 F); *verbera carnifices, flammas tormenta catenae*, etc., in *Damasi epigrammata*, ed. M. Ihm (Leipzig, 1895).

turned over. 'It's cooked now, set to, and see whether it's more juicy raw or cooked.' So he jokingly spoke.[63]

Here Laurence's cheeky invitation matches his profile as the trickster saint who managed to give away the treasures of the church in Rome to avoid surrendering them.[64] Source criticism helps here, because the joke about being 'done' is not unique to the extravagant Prudentius. Ambrose used it, too, both in the *De officiis ministrorum*[65] and in his hymn for Saint Laurence.[66] It continued to amuse Aelfric.[67]

Clever cheek saved a potential victim in Paul the Deacon's *Historia Langobardorum* (1.20). A Herul lookout had been threatened by his king with death if he announced a Lombard victory. By saying '*Ve tibi misera Herolia!*' ('Woe to you, sorry Herulia') he got the king to say, '*Numquid fugiunt Heroli mei?*' ('Are my Heruls fleeing?'), to which he says, '*Non hoc ego, sed tu rex ipse dixisti*' ('You said so, O King, not me'). This 'you said it, not I' motif[68] has been identified as Germanic. Goffart points out that the story is very much like one in the Talmud.[69] This is unlikely,[70] but a different Jewish source is not out of the question: Jesus before Pilate:[71] '*Tu es rex Judaeorum?*' *Dicit illi Iesus*: '*Tu dicis*' ('Are you the King of the Jews?' Jesus said to him 'You said it'). Jesus had been known to get himself out of

---

[63] *Converte partem corporis / satis crematum iugiter / et fac periclum quid tuus / Vulcanus ardens egerit. / Praefectus inverti iubet / Tunc ille: 'Coctum est devora / et experimentum cape / sit crudum an assum suavius.' / Haec ludibundus dixerat . . .*

[64] His ruse in Prudentius *Peristefanon*, 2, 293–312 where he produces the repulsive poor of Rome as the *nummi, gemmae, monilia* and *talenta* of the church is not unlike the witticism of Cornelia, mother of the Gracchi, who said that her two sons were her ornaments. See Valerius Maximus 4.4 praef.: '*haec,*' inquit '*ornamenta sunt mea*', and J. Briscoe, *Facta et dicta memorabilia* (Stuttgart, 1998). There is a later, but parallel, story told of a ruse of Anicia Juliana to fool Justinian in Gregory of Tours, *Gloria confessorum* 102, *MGH SRM* 1.2, ed. B. Krusch and W. Levison (Hanover, 1969).

[65] *De officiis ministrorum* 1.207 in *Les devoirs / Saint Ambroise*, ed. M. Testard (2 vols., Paris, 1984–92) '*Assum est, inquit, versa et manduca*'.

[66] Ambrose, *Hymn* 13.31, in *Ambroise de Milan: Hymnes*, ed. J. Fontaine and J.-L. Charlet (Paris, 1992): *Versate me, martyr vocat / Vorate, si coctum est, iubet.* A similar suggestion is attributed to the Julianic martyrs of Merum in Socrates' *Historia Ecclesiastica* 3.15, in *Sokrates Kirchengeschichte*, ed. G. C. Hansen (Berlin, 1995).

[67] *Aelfric's Catholic Homilies: The First Series* (Early English Texts Society, s.s. 17), ed. P. Clemoes (Oxford, 1997), no. 29, lines 210–11. S. Horner, ' "Why do you speak so much foolishness?" Gender, humor and discourse in Aelfric's *Lives of Saints*', in *Humour in Anglo-Saxon Literature*, ed. J. Wilcox (Woodbridge, 2000), pp. 127–36, esp. pp. 128–9.

[68] Stith Thompson, *Motif Index of Folk-literature*, no. J1675.2.1.

[69] Goffart, *Narrators*, p. 428, esp. n. 318.

[70] T. Zachariae, 'Ihr sagt er, nicht ich', *Zeitschrift für Volkskunde* 25 (1915), pp. 402–8 denies the possibility of any connection with the Talmud.

[71] Mt. 27.11; Lk. 23.3, and Mk. 15. 2. None of the Anchor Bible Commentaries takes this as a clever answer, but as a sort of half affirmative. Brother William in Eco's *The Name of the Rose*, p. 133, rightly cites these examples in addition to 'Render unto Caesar' and 'Tu es Petrus'.

tricky situations with such cleverness – witness the interpolated passage in John depicting the woman caught in adultery.[72]

A costly jest

A gruesome joke could backfire on the joker – an Herodotean act of hubris. The passage is in Paul the Deacon's *Historia Langobardorum* (1.27): 'In that battle Alboin killed Cunimundus, and made a drinking-cup out of his head once he had cut it off. This type of cup is called a "scala" by them, but in Latin a *patera*.'[73] Later, at *Historia Langobardorum* 2.28,

When he was more flown with wine [*laetus*] than was appropriate at a feast in Verona, he asked that wine be given to the queen [i.e. Rosemunda, the daughter of Cunimundus] to drink in the cup which he had made from the head of his father-in-law Cunimundus. He invited her to drink happily with her father ... Therefore when Rosemund found out about the matter, she conceived a deep pain in her heart that she was unable to quell. She burned to avenge the death of her father on her husband.

An inconcinnity seems to betray two sources. Rosamund *should* be outraged because she has been asked to drink from her own father's skull. Instead she felt uncontrollable pain in her heart first *ubi rem comperit* (when she found out about the facts). But what is the *res*? There is no hidden trick to Alboin's invitation – just a monstrous joke. Presumably in one version of the story was the verbal deadly joke, '*Bibe laeta cum patre!*' ('Be happy and drink with Daddy!'), said Alboin, holding out the skull-cup. In the other version she must have been tricked into drinking from a skull-cup without knowing whose the skull was. No verbal joke, but an evil prank. Cunimundus' trophy skull becomes the agent of Alboin's own destruction. Alboin was buried *sub cuiusdam scalae ascensu* (where a staircase ascended). Goffart wonders what to make of this.[74] A sick pun on the word *scala* perhaps?

CHANGE

Cruel jokes about death delivered by judges, a gruesome joke turned on his torturer by a victim, wit used to escape from tight spots, killing

---

[72] John 8.2–11.

[73] For the custom, see Paul the Deacon, *Historia Romana* 6.10, which is derived from Orosius 5.23.17: *Pauli historia Romana, MGH SRG* 79, ed. H. Droysen (Munich, 1978); *Pauli Orosii historiarvm adversvm paganos libri VII, CSEL*, ed. K. F. W. Zangemeister (Leipzig, 1889).

[74] Goffart, *Narrators*, p. 392: 'One does not know quite what to do with Paul's report.'

witticisms of great and alarming rulers, and a cruel jest, characterised as such, that brought retribution on the jester all show continuity with Graeco-Roman traditions. In gallows humour, jokes, like the intent to joke, are clear. They are marked by words such as *ludens, ludibundus* or *subridens*. They elicit a frisson, shock or outrage. The second topic is more elusive, namely the assessment of apparently comic elements in early medieval hagiographical texts. In some passages a truer comic muse may be at work, one who elicits a gentle smile instead.

Hagiographical humour

'The past is a foreign country, they do things differently there.'[75] Often quaintly. Undergraduates laugh at etymologies from Isidore and medieval bestiaries. Modern writers who poke fun at the Middle Ages or at medievalism have an easy time of it. Take Roger Peyrefitte's cardinal discoursing on multiple relics in *The Keys of Saint Peter*.[76] First it is the arms of various saints:

St. James the Less', St. James the Greater's, St. Peter Chrysologus', St. Spiridion's... the arm of St. Aurelian at S. Maria Maggiore, and the arm of Gregory the Great at San Gregorio on the Caelius, all these closely resemble the six arms of Jesuit saints that are the pride of the Church of Gesù, although I suspect the arms of the Jesuit saints of being rather longer... At one time indeed, they threatened rather, by their excessive number, to choke the Church to death in the embrace of a Titanic Briareus. St. Andrew ran to seventeen arms... A great many outré relics were destroyed during the religious wars or the French Revolution. Thus, for example, a sneeze of the Holy Ghost, a sigh uttered by St. Joseph while he was sawing wood, the bones of the fish that Christ multiplied, the tail of His ass...[77]

The passage contains obvious comic exaggerations: the sneeze and the sigh are over the top. Yet serious scholarship on the relic trade or a medieval primary source might well list items that were not totally dissimilar. This is precisely what one finds in, for example, the table of contents of Patrice Boussel's *Des Reliques et de leur bon usage*, or if one examines the list of relics acquired by Louis IX for the Sainte Chapelle.[78] 'Un peu de souffle de Jésus dans une bouteille', 'le saint nombril' and – worse still – 'le saint prépuce' are all attested in such sources.[79]

---

[75] L. P. Hartley, *The Go-between* (London, 1953), prologue.
[76] For Byzantine parallels, see Haldon, below, p. 69.
[77] R. Peyrefitte, *The Keys of Saint Peter*, trans. E. Hyams (New York, 1957) p. 31.
[78] See P. Boussel, *Des Reliques et de leur bon usage* (Paris, 1971), p. 55.
[79] See *Dictionnaire d'archéologie Chrétienne et de liturgie*, ed. F. Cabrol, H. Leclercq and H.-I. Marrou (15 vols., Paris, 1907–51), 'reliques', for the *praeputium* and the *umbilicus*.

Norman Douglas in *South Wind* quoted one 'Monsignor Perelli' on the *Antiquities of Nepenthe* (a.k.a. Capri).

The Fountain of Saint Calogero, described as one of the most famous, was lukewarm, of ammoniacal and alkaline flavour; a glassful of it produced the most violent retchings and vomitings. Properly applied, however, the water had been found to relieve the gout, the discomforts of child-bearing, leprosy, irritation of the mucous membrane of the nose, impetigo, strabismus and ophthalmia. If the patient observed care in his diet, avoiding articles of calorific nature such as fried fish and boiled lentils, he would find himself greatly benefited by its use in the case of cornucoptic hydrocephalus, flatulence, tympanitis and varicose veins. It was useful, furthermore, as a cure for the stings of scorpions and other venomous beasts.[80]

Here we see a northern insular response to Italian antiquarianism, valetudinarianism and credulity. One can tell that this is not a serious passage, but sections of it, appearing on a mineral-water label, might *just about* pass. Moderns find all of this funny, and it is meant to be so, but how does one evaluate material from the past, when laughter itself may have changed to a great extent?[81] Was Bede joking when he stated that almost everything from Ireland can cure snakebite, including *rasa codicum folia* (scraped leaves of manuscripts)?[82]

One smiles at much material in early medieval saints' lives. But was one intended to? As a narrow case-study, one could examine examples of three specialised types of miracles in some early medieval hagiographical texts. Literary clues based on literary conventions may help answer the question.

The furniture of hagiography

Saints have their landscape. Jerome's fictions lived in the quasi-magical desert[83] complete with lions and centaurs, so charmingly depicted by the

---

[80] Norman Douglas, *South Wind*, vol. I (2 vols., Chicago, 1929), p. 244. The catalogue of fountains goes on until p. 247.

[81] See Propp, 'Ritual laughter', p. 127: 'We do not laugh now as people once laughed. Therefore, it is hardly possible to give a general philosophical definition of the comic and of laughter: such a definition can only be historical.'

[82] *Historia Ecclesiastica* I.1, in *Bede's Ecclesiastical History of the English People*, ed. and trans. B. Colgrave and R. A. B. Mynors (Oxford, 1969): *nullum ibi reptile videri soleat, nullus vivere serpens valeat: nam saepe illo de Brittania adlati serpentes, mox ut proximante terris navigio, odore aeris illius adtacti fuerint, intereunt: quin potius omnia pene quae de eadem insula sunt contra venenum valent. Denique vidimus, quibusdam a serpente percussis, rasa folia codicum qui de Hibernia fuerant, et ipsam rasuram aquae immissam ac potui datam, talibus protinus totam vim veneni grassantis, totum inflati corporis absumsisse ac sedasse tumorem.*

[83] The settings are both Syrian and Egyptian.

Master of the Osservanza. Martyrs haunt courts and places of execution. Serious bishops such as Ambrose, Augustine and Fulgentius worked in urban settings with matter-of-fact or solemn props. Fairy tale and biography both had their say. But there may be a new development in early medieval saints' lives, namely mundane props of a sort last seen in Apuleius' *Metamorphoses*: tubs, goatskins, hair from the barber's shop, dogs that beg and fawn, pots and pans, bacon.[84] M. R. James in 'The malice of inanimate objects' lists some examples, 'beings such as the collar-stud, the inkstand, the fire, the razor'.[85] Two miracles illustrate this: in Cogitosus' life Bridget, soaked in the rain, rushes home, and inadvertently hangs her dress up to dry on an obliging ray of sunshine.[86] In Gregory the Great's *Dialogues* a priest carelessly calls for his servant, saying, 'Come, you devil, and take my shoes off!' Immediately the laces begin to undo themselves: the devil is at work. The priest is terrified, and tells the devil to go away. This he does, leaving the shoes half unfastened.[87] Ultra-ordinary props endowed with preternatural life show the operation of the holy with unpromising material. This is not like the development of technicolour epic martyr-acts or big Renaissance classicising canvasses. It is a Dutch interior: something ordinary observed – only the ordinary has gone sour.[88]

In the *De doctrina Christiana* Augustine attacked the 'utterly inane' observations of so-called prodigies by superstitious pagans. He cited a witticism attributed to Cato the Elder, who had been asked whether it was a *monstrum* if mice ate one's slippers. He answered, 'no', but that it would

---

[84] For Saint Bridget feeding her dog bacon: Cogitosus, *Vita Brigidae*, *PL* 72, col. 779B: *Nam cum illa aliquando in caldario lardum advenientibus hospitibus coxerat, cani adulanti ac flagitanti misericorditer eam eam tradidit.* The dog reappears in *PL* 72, col. 781C behaving himself by not gobbling the bacon while Bridget is praying.

[85] M. R. James, *Casting the Runes and Other Ghost Stories* (Oxford, 1987), p. 288.

[86] Cogitosus, *Vita Brigidae*, *PL* 72, col. 779D–80A: *Nam haec ... largitate nimia pluviarum profusa, humidis vestibus domum rediit. Et cum umbra solaris per foramina domum intrinsecus intraret, illam umbram obtusa oculorum acie, arborem fuisse transversam et fixam putans, ac desuper complutam ponens tamquam in arbore grandi et firma, in ipsa tenui solari umbra vestis pependit. Et cum ipsius domus habitatores vicini hoc ingenti miraculo fuissent perculsi, hanc incomparabilem dignis laudibus extollebant.* Umbra seems to be used here as a 'reflection of the sun'.

[87] Gregory the Great, *Dialogues* 3.20 (*PL* 77) for the tale of Stephanus the Priest: *Qui quadam die de itinere domum regressus, mancipio suo negligenter loquens praecepit, dicens: Veni, diabole, discalcea me. Ad cujus vocem mox coeperunt se caligarum corrigiae in summa velocitate dissolvere, ut aperte constaret quod ei qui nominatus fuerat ad extrahendas diabolus caligas oboedisset. Quod mox ut presbyter vidit, vehementer expavit, magnisque vocibus clamare coepit, dicens: Recede, miser, recede; non enim tibi, sed mancipio meo locutus sum. Ad cuius vocem protinus recessit, et ita ut inventae sunt, magna iam ex parte dissolutae, corrigiae remanserunt.*

[88] For an interesting parallel and the cautionary implications of the usual turned unusual, see James, *Casting the Runes*, p. 292: 'Do they not ... suggest that when this malice begins to show itself we should be very particular to examine and if possible rectify any obliquities in our recent conduct?'

have to be considered to be a *monstrum* had the slippers eaten the mice.[89] Both here and in the previous examples cited the possible comedy lies in the triviality of props and 'prodigies'. Lowly stolen gloves[90] and shoes,[91] boots,[92] and footstools,[93] and even (it would seem) purloined underwear[94] are scattered throughout early medieval lives. In many of the miracles the conventions are all low – and hence comic.

There are reasons for the changes in convention. If one takes women saints alone, their social position shifts: initially they are often middle- or upper-class later Roman martyrs, in the *paterna domus* until haled before the magistrate (Perpetua, Agnes, Eulalia);[95] subsequently there are female monastic saints who, whatever their rank, often fight the battles of asceticism against food and flesh in more mundane and often rural settings. Predilection for *humilitas* also affects the props: for example, even a princess like Radegund must be seen to welcome the broom and the kitchen[96] and Sadalberga's nuns engage in epic exploits with two washing-coppers and chains, a fire and a *cella officinae*.[97] Hagiography from a monastic milieu, though it may link its protagonists to the greater historical canvas, must also depict the monastery and its surroundings.

---

[89] Augustine, *De doctrina Christiana* 2.20.31, ed. J. Martin, *CCSL* 32 (Turnhout, 1962): *Unde illud eleganter dictum est Catonis qui cum esse consultus a quodam, qui sibi a soricibus erosas caligas diceret, respondet non esse illud monstrum, sed vere monstrum habendum fuisse si sorices a caligis roderentur.*

[90] *Vita Bethari* 9, *MGH SRM* 3, ed. B. Krusch (Hanover, 1896), p. 617. A barbarian tries to steal the saint's *manicae quod vulgo 'wantos' vocant* and is punished by being made to eat his own hands by a demon. For socks, see Gregory of Tours, *Vita Patrum* 8.8, *MGH SRM* 1.2, ed. Krusch and Levison, pp. 211–94; *Gregory of Tours, Life of the Fathers*, trans. E. James (2nd edn, Liverpool, 1991).

[91] See *Vita Genovefae* 24, *MGH SRM* 3, p. 225 for a *furuncula* struck blind for stealing Geneviève's *calciamenta*.

[92] See Gregory the Great, *Dial.* 1.2, *PL* 77, col. 160B–C for a *caligula* used for a resuscitation: *caligulam de sinu protulit, et super exstincti pueri pectus posuit.*

[93] For a *scabellum suppedaneum*, see Gregory the Great, *Dialogues*. 1.2, *PL* 77, 161C and 164A: *Cumque pro utilitate monasterii ad constitutionem causae egressus fuisset, multi viri noti ac nobiles qui eum valde honorabant, vehementer admirati, sollicite requirebant quidnam hoc esset, quod tam tumentem ac lividam haberet faciem. Quibus ille dicebat: Hesterno die sero, peccatis meis facientibus, in scabello suppedaneo impegi, atque hoc pertuli.*

[94] *Vita Caesarii* 2.13–15, *MGH SRM* 3, p. 488 for Agretia, wife of Liberius, who suffers from chronic menstrual flux and desires what seems to be a bit of Caesarius' underwear (*panni* that are warmed by the fire and laid on him when he is naked) to cure her. *Cum ad occursum eius venissem, illa familiariter dignabatur meam parvitatem, infirmitatem suam ac si cum verecundia matronali prodens, coepit sub obtestatione domini multis precibus exposcere a me, ut unum pannum de tesselis [= 'tasseau'] illius, quem a nudo sui corporis habuisset feminae deferrem.* When she gets the cloth she puts it to her breast, horripilates, and is cured.

[95] Jerome, Epigram 1.

[96] Fortunatus, *Vita Radegundis* 1.23 for housework; 1.24 for the kitchen: *quanto fervore ad coquinam concursitabat, suam faciens septimanam; MGH SRM* 2, ed. B. Krusch (Hanover, 1888).

[97] *Obitus Sadalbergae* 2.21, *MGH SRM* 5 (Hanover, 1910), p. 62: *subito magno cum sonitu cella officinae quasi casura e semet flectendo adicitur igni . . . videns cellam fragoribus nec dirutam, sed illaesam permanentem.*

Intoxicating beverages

In later Gallic episcopal letters about food, fish, feast and fast there is a strong continuity leading back to Roman comedy and satire, and festal and convivial epistolography.[98] Feasting is central to comedy and its often festal settings, but drink is also central. Hence it seemed to me interesting to examine alcoholic beverages in early medieval hagiography.

The prototype of all miraculous multiplications of drink was the marriage at Cana,[99] so at some level all drink miracles go back to John's Gospel, and exist in a biblical world, where the Holy Man attends a wedding-feast. The lives of Merovingian saints featured many variants on this sort of wine miracle, including Clovis' stirrup-cup for his anti-Arian campaign,[100] wine to sustain construction- and harvest-workers,[101] wine miraculously supplied for a bishop's feast,[102] wine to heal,[103] and other miscellaneous multiplications.[104]

But drinking had become a sensitive topic in the later Roman Empire, what with the influx of various large hairy individuals who either drank the wrong sort of drink or just plain drank too much. Some early medieval hagiographical texts seem to associate excess drinking with barbarians in a way that suggests a comic ethnic slur. In Gregory the Great's *Dialogues*

---

[98] D. R. Shanzer, 'Bishops, letters, fast, food, and feast in later Roman Gaul' in *Culture and Society in Later Roman Gaul: Revisiting the Sources*, ed. R. W. Mathisen and D. R. Shanzer (Aldershot, 2001), pp. 217–36.

[99] John 2.1–11.

[100] Hincmar, *Vita Remigii* 19, *MGH SRM* 3, p. 311: *plenum vas quod vulgaris consuetudo flasconem appellat de vino quod benedixit-sicut etiam fecerat, quando post baptismum contra Gundebaudum perrexerat-praecipiens illi ut tam longe ad bellum procederet, quandiu illi et suis, quibus inde dare vellet, illud vinum de praedicto flascone non deficeret.*

[101] For wine on site, see *Vita Eparchi reclusi Ecolismensis* 23, *MGH SRM* 4, p. 560: *Et illud praeterea silencio non transibo quod tonna vini, dum ad eius basilicam hedificandi dispensaretur et valde iam pervenisset ad imum, noctu redundavit expleta.* Also *Vita Genovefae* 21, *MGH SRM* 3, p. 224. Genovefa prays and replenishes the carpenters' drink. It lasts as long as there is work to do on the basilica. *Vita Austregisili* 6, *MGH SRM* 4, p. 195: a harvest miracle; one empty *cupa* is miraculously filled so that it runs over with *mustum*.

[102] *Vita Lupi* 7a, *MGH SRM* 4, pp. 180–1. The saint has only one *modius* of wine (Falernian) at his own feast and prays. A messenger from his mother comes to tell him that 500 *modii* on twenty wagons are near the city gate. This is not strictly a Cana-type miracle, but a prophecy.

[103] *Vita Desiderii Cadurcensis, MGH SRM* 4, p. 596. The saint, *post mortem*, produces not just miraculous wine, but Falernian to heal Bishop Aregius of Rouen.

[104] *Vita Fridolini* 10, *MGH SRM* 3, pp. 430–1 – another wine-miracle, a cask of plenty, a 'galida', some sort of *mensura vinaria*. *Vita Eligii* 18a, *MGH SRM* 4, p. 709: a man who had a little Falernian, *pauxillulum Falerni in cadum . . . erat autem praefato viro positum vas in cellario quod vulgo 'tunna' vocatur*, with only two or three *metretae* in it. In the *Vita Eligii* one survives, while three fall in mysterious *lacunae*: see the *capitula* that specify wine miracles in 1.25, 2.18, 2.40 and 2.44. Only 2.18 survived. On barbarians and drink, in the works of Sidonius and Procopius, see Halsall, below, pp. 93–6 and 106–8. On the use of accusations of drunkenness as a tool of ridicule, see Humphries, below, pp. 75–88.

two Goths came to see Boniface of Ferentina on their way to Ravenna. He gave them a wooden barrel to drink from until they got there. They drank it at Ferentina, all the way to Ravenna, and back. They returned to Boniface and never once stopped drinking, yet all the same they never lacked for wine. It was as if the wine was not *contained* in the barrel, but *produced* by it.[105] The cornucopia is not unfamiliar, but it has been adapted to fit national stereotypes of heavy drinkers. Gregory specified 'Goths', after all. In the *Dialogues* the quantity of drink was at issue and ethnic difference is duly noted. In other saints' lives it may not just be a question of how much is drunk, but also what, namely beer versus wine.

Spilt beer

In Jonas' *Vita Vedastis* the saint is invited to a feast during Chlothar's reign. There he sees vessels in the house of one Hocinus brimming with beer, some consecrated according to pagan rites and others with Christian ones.[106] He blesses all of them, whereupon the pagan-consecrated ones burst their hoops (*legaminibus*) and spill their contents all over the pavement. Vedast tells the king that demons have sought to seduce the hearts of infidels with beer, but failed. This time the treatment is more neutral than in Gregory (one does not see the pagans drinking), but the dramatis personae are Franks and ample drink. Was this miracle intended to appeal to Franks, or to inspire a smile in people who did not identify with the beer-swilling pagans? A parallel miracle occurs in the same author's *Vita Columbani* (1.27), where Columbanus finds Suevi at Bregenz sacrificing beer to Vodan (a.k.a. Mercurius), where again the scene is used to emphasise difference and ethnicity.

Unspilt beer

In the *Vita Columbani* (circa 642) an antithetical miracle shows beer that is not spilt. A kitchen-servant is sent to draw beer from a barrel into a *tiprus*. Recalled by Columbanus in the middle of the task, he leaves the beer flowing. He expects to find it emptied. Instead the liquid is miraculously contained, as if the vessel had expanded in height. God had seen to it that neither the zeal of the abbot nor the eagerness of the servant diminished the monastery's substance. This is all very well, but note the curiously

[105] Gregory the Great, *Dialogues* 1.9.196B–C, *PL* 77: *Sicque usque ad eumdem venerabilem patrem Ferentis reversi sunt, ut nullo die cessarent bibere, et tamen vinum eis ex illo vasculo numquam deesset, ac si in illo vase ligneo quod episcopus dederat, vinum non angeretur, sed nasceretur.*

[106] *MGH SRM* 3, p. 410.

pompous parenthetic footnote at the opening of the passage: 'beer is prepared from grain or barley; other than amongst the Scordisci and the Dardani, it is used above all by peoples who dwell near the ocean, in Gaul, Britain, Ireland, and Germany'. Is this a piece of condescending ethnography from a Piedmontese who headed north? Jonas elsewhere seemed ironically aware of his programmatic props in the envoi to the *Vita Columbani*: 'The rich rhetors have a tear of balsam from Engeddi and incense-flowers from Arabia; I barely have butter from Ireland to fatten [my speech].'[107]

Drink and women saints

Women have come a long way from Jerome's anorexic female aristo-crats and Augustine's mother Monica, defended in an excursus in the *Confessions* against charges of incipient alcoholism, being a *meribibula*. Several early medieval woman saints, ascetics at that, multiply wine for their friends and workers without scandal: for example Radegund[108] and Genovefa.[109] But at least two women perform beer miracles. First, Sadalberga:[110] her (baseline) miracle is accompanied by self-conscious snobbery about lack of Falernian and how she turned to what the western tribes make, the *ius tritici* or *hordei*, namely *cerevesa*, to save the day for a feast. One may contrast Sadalberga with Bridget, the mistress of the beasts[111] and the consecrator of household activities. Jonas specified that people drank beer in Ireland; Cogitosus went further. In the *Vita Brigidae* some lepers come to get beer. Although there is none, Bridget makes do with what is available and blesses some bathwater. She turns it not just into beer, but into **optima** *cervisia*.[112] A homey touch? A gentle joke? A conscious updating of Cana to fit a northern insular clime?

---

[107] *Vita Columbani* 2: *Illi dotes balsami lacrimam ex Engaddi floresque aromatum ex arabia; nobis ex Hibernia vix Butyrum pinguiscit*; MGH SRM 4, pp. 1–52. See below, p. 94, for another educated southerner sneering at butter as a substitute for more civilised substances.

[108] Baudonivia, *Vita Radegundis* 10: a *tonella* of *merum* that stays miraculously full. A *punto*, a 'species dolii', is also mentioned here: MGH SRM 2, pp. 378–95.

[109] *Vita Genovefae* 21: Genovefa prays and replenishes the carpenters' drink. It lasts as long as there is work to do on the basilica: MGH SRM 3, pp. 204–38.

[110] *Obitus Sadalbergae* 20: MGH SRM 5, pp. 40–66.

[111] See Cogitosus, *Vita Brigidae* 782D–783A, the story of the man who killed the king's pet fox and is condemned to death. Bridget summons one of her own wild foxes, which creeps under her dress (*sub receptaculum Brigidae vestis se constituens*) and sits *sobrie* with her in her chariot. It replaces the king's pet fox, but eventually escapes cunningly. At 783D, Bridget is a sort of *potnia theron*.

[112] *PL* 72, col. 780: *Mirabili quoque eventu ab hac venerabili Brigida leprosi cervisiam petentes, cum non haberet illa, videns aquam ad balnea paratam, cum virtute fidei benedicens, in optimam convertit cervisiam.*

Vernacularisation

Low-level props, contrasts between wine and beer, and other small adjustments show a sort of vernacularisation, moving the conventions north and west and down the social scale, but also demonstrate linguistic glossing and translation. All these lives of Merovingian saints specify not just the container or measure in which the miracle takes place – *modius, dolium, cupa*,[113] *galida, degancia, ampulla Apuliqua* – but what it is called – *vulgo*: *tiprus, tunna, benna, punto, flasco*. What is one to make of this? Distance between author, subject and audience? Condescension? A garrulous compulsion to convey what no one wants or needs to know? These features may merely be an inevitable artifact of cultures in contact, but their effect is to lower the niveau of the hagiography.

Warnings to women with gula

In two final miracles both style and language are crucial to the comedy. A noble nun in the *Vita Columbani* (2.22) used to satisfy her greed (*gula*), stealing food undetected until God exacted vengeance. She was suddenly unable to eat permitted foods and, like Nebuchadnezzar,[114] only hungered after bran husks, leaves and field grasses. Once when she was at a meal she beheld a boar eating next to her, snuffling (*ventilans*) its food and grunting like a great filthy swine. She was frightened and asked what it was (*quid esset*). '"It is I," said the boar. "All the food that you ate illegally *I* ate with you [in you]. Know that from now onwards for a year you will have *this* food [i.e. the fodder]."' The heightened contrasts of the Circean transformation are comic: the noble girl descending to the boar; the fine food and the fodder. God's method for showing her true alter ego to her is both comic and surreal, a parody of the downfall of a mighty Babylonian ruler. Talking beasts, if not in fable, belong in low genres; Jonas' language reflects this – particularly the use of the low and onomatopoeic *grunnio*, 'grunt'. One cannot but remember that figure in classical satire, M. Grunnius Corocotta (the piglet).[115]

Nuns and lettuces

Should 'lettuce' make one laugh? One summer's day Sadalberga was walking in her garden and saw her *hortulanus*, Landefridus, cutting the

---

[113] *Vita Genovefae* 21, p. 224.   [114] Daniel 4.33.
[115] *Testamentum Porcelli*, in *Petronii Saturae*, ed. F. Buecheler (Berlin, 1904). See also Kershaw, below, p. 179.

grass. She was, allegedly, four stades or more away from him, but whispered: '*Defer nobis ex latucis, frater Landefrede!*' ('Bring me some lettuce, brother Lantfred!') The sound carried miraculously so that he heard his abbess's command as if it were spoken to him face to face.[116] What is the point of this story? To show how the saint used her power for everyday purposes? To show how she did not have to raise her voice? To show how even a sudden craving did not involve any forbidden foodstuff? It sounds quaint, to be sure, but one cannot make a sound case that it was intended to be comic.

One may, however, contrast a case with similar props in Gregory's *Dialogues* (1.4.165D) discussed (rather cursorily) by Erich Auerbach. A nun went out to the monastery garden, caught sight of a lettuce and longed for it. She forgot to bless it, bit it greedily, and was seized by a devil and collapsed in a fit. When Father Equitius exorcised the demon, it piped up from the nun's mouth in self-justification, 'What have *I* done? What have *I* done? I was having myself a nice sit on the lettuce. That woman came and bit me.' The man of God told him to leave, and naturally he did. A warning to greedy women, the situation is a burlesque of Eve's desire for the apple in Genesis and Adam's self-exculpation. If such conventions were found in genuinely unsophisticated writers, one would be more inclined to read them straight. In Gregory's case, however, the content suggests deliberate folksiness or implicit condescension rather than real naïveté.[117] If one be tempted to anthropologise and assume that earnest early medievals seriously envisaged miniature demons on lettuces, one must consider the devil's language.[118] The style of the rest of the passage is straightforward, but Gregory characterises his devil with a plaintive emphatic repeated pronoun *ego* and, above all, the very colloquial dative of advantage, *sedebam mihi*. The devil was not just sitting, but is characterised as an aggrieved victim who 'was having himself a nice sit'[119] – minding his own business, no doubt, too; all injured innocence![120]

---

[116] *Obitus Sadalbergae* 22, *MGH SRM* 5, pp. 62–3. Note how the voice threatens the lazy archdeacon with a beating. Here a miraculously large fish is provided for Sadalberga for her to cook.

[117] See E. Auerbach, *Literary Language and its Public in Late Latin Antiquity and in the Middle Ages* (Bollingen, 1965), p. 96: 'The dialogues disclose an almost childlike fairy-tale world'; p. 97: 'Many of the stories are extremely naïve'; p. 98: 'grotesque humour', 'These devils are comical goblins.' Auerbach, however, never quite made it clear whether he thought Gregory was telling these stories with a straight face or not. The comic linguistic features are not reflected in the Greek translation.

[118] There are close analogies to ancient Greek studies and the controversies about whether organs spoke in Homer. See Pelliccia, *Mind, Body, and Speech*, pp. 15–27.

[119] Or 'sitting by myself'.

[120] Gregory the Great, *Dialogues* 1.4, *PL* 77, 165D: *Quadam die una Dei famula monasterio virginum hortum ingressa est: quae latucam conspiciens concupivit, eamque signo crucis benedicere oblita, avide*

CONCLUSION

Many humorous genres seem to decline or vanish in the early Middle Ages for fairly obvious reasons. Education and the urbane audience required for sophisticated risqué traditional Latin epigrams are lacking. The controls of the church account for the unacceptability of the obscene. Parody that inverted learned or authoritative genres, however, did continue in a limited way. Pedantry and *Fachsprache* continued to amuse people. But humour appeared in other genres. Christian laughter inverted the fate of derisor and derisee. Grim jokes inherited from the biographical tradition through later Roman historiography enlivened the portrayal of strong rulers. Those are all continuities. What of discontinuities? The 'pillow principle' – 'suppress it here and it swells up elsewhere' – seems to be operating. Just as obscenity improved the pornodeaths of later Roman female martyrs, so too in some instances one can see the comic in hagiographical texts. The human animal could not survive without smiling. Finally, there seems to be a change in the furniture of saints' lives, a predilection for gentle comic touches, low objects, talking beasts, vernacular demons and such like.[121] All of this may signal a change in milieu (the monastery), attitude (tweeness), a change in audience (beer vats for those who swill it) or a newly emphasised message about how the workings of God permeate even the humblest events and objects of everyday life – the stuff of comedy.[122]

---

momordit; sed arrepta a diabolo protinus cecidit. Cumque vexaretur, eidem patri Equitio sub celeritate nuntiatum est, ut veniret concitus, et orando succurreret. Moxque hortum idem pater ut ingressus est, coepit ex eius ore quasi satisfaciens ipse qui hanc arripuerat diabolus clamare, dicens: *'Ego quid feci, ego quid feci? Sedebam mihi super latucam; venit illa, et momordit me.'* Cui cum gravi indignatione vir dei praecepit ut discederet, et locum in omnipotentis dei famula non haberet. Qui protinus abscessit, nec eam ultra contingere praevaluit. See Auerbach, *Literary Language and its Public*, pp. 98–9.

[121] My conclusions about the furniture of early medieval saints' lives are in disagreement with P. Brown, 'Enjoying the saints in late antiquity', *EME* 9 (2000), pp. 1–24, at pp. 16–17 on inimitableness and distance in later Roman and early medieval hagiography.

[122] My heartfelt special thanks to Sam Barnish, Andreas Schwarcz and Roger Tomlin, all of whom helped with the raw material.

CHAPTER 2

Humour and the everyday in Byzantium

John Haldon

In its simplest form, humour can be defined as a stimulus that generally produces what psychologists and physiologists call 'the laughter reflex', although the picture is actually more complex than this.[1] However, there are as many different cultural forms of this stimulus as there are human societies. Furthermore, there are several paradoxes to be confronted when considering the nature of humour and laughter. One is quite simply that the so-called laughter reflex has no apparent biological purpose: its only generally agreed function is to provide relief from tension (although one could count this as a biological function, too) – and the point about humour, of course, is that it consists precisely in the deliberate or accidental creation of a context in which tension of one sort or another can be built up and then dissipated. This can be done quickly, through the format of the standard joke; or at length, in the form of satire or parody; or a combination. Another paradox about laughter is that it is a very complex physiological response – it actually involves the co-ordinated contraction of some fifteen facial muscles as well as altered respiratory patterns – but has no obvious physiological origin: telling an amusing story, and generating *humour*, is a *cultural* phenomenon. On the other hand, the success of the story can be gauged by the response, and the nature of the response can tell us something about cultural values and attitudes: the knowledge and understanding of the listeners, their assumptions, and the degree to which the teller of the tale and the listeners share a common standpoint within the same culture.[2] Like that of any society, Byzantine humour can help the modern reader understand a little more about that culture.

[1] See M. Lafrance, 'Felt versus feigned funniness: issues in coding smiling and laughing', in *Handbook of Humor Research*, vol. 1, *Basic Issues*, ed. P. E. McGhee and J. H. Goldstein (New York, 1983), pp. 1–12.

[2] See esp. C. P. Wilson, *Jokes: Form, Content, Use and Function* (London, 1979), pp. 41–3.

It seems appropriate to start with some lines from a twelfth-century Constantinopolitan satire about the economic hardships of life as a scholar.

> Ever since I was a young boy my father used to tell me,
> Learn your letters, my boy, and there'll be no one like you;
> My boy, see Mr so-and-so? he used to go on foot,
> He now rides a fat mule with double leather straps;
> While he was learning he had no shoes,
> But now you see him in his winklepickers;
> While he was learning, he never combed his hair,
> But now he's so proud of his coiffure.
> And he never used to glimpse the doors of a public bath house;
> Now he bathes – three times a week!
> His clothes used to be filled with lice the size of almonds –
> Now they're stuffed full with the emperor's gold.
> So learn your letters, take heed of the words of your old father,
> and there'll be no one like you!

The essence of the son's reply, which takes up the remaining 280 or so lines of the poem, is summarised in the next five or six. He did learn grammar, he tells us, but he curses the day he was sent to school. For look at him now:

> If they'd made me a craftsman . . .
> and had I learnt [a] craft . . .
> I could have opened my pantry to find it full of bread,
> copious wine and cooked tunny, slices of tunny, dried tunny, mackerel;
> instead, I open it now and I see nothing but empty shelves;
> files and files of parchment;
> I open my bag to find a piece of bread, and I find another, smaller, file;
> I put my hand in my pockets, feel around for my purse,
> search for a coin, and even it's full of bits of parchment . . .

Two things strike the reader straight away about these lines. The first and most obvious is that they retain still much of their humour, even for us; and it is worth asking why. The second is that they clearly depend on caricature and exaggeration for their full effect; and therefore, even if we do still find them funny in some senses, we cannot appreciate the full irony of the poet's words because we – or perhaps you – do not know about the details of twelfth-century life and contemporary attitudes and values in this particular major medieval town.

A superficial answer to the question posed above – why do *we* find these lines amusing still – is not too difficult to suggest: in the poem we recognise certain characteristics and values found in parts of our own society (the rather silly notion that learning and education are both superior to, and better earners than, the trades and skills of the simple craftsman, for example); more importantly, and at a much more general level, the opposition between a father's good advice and the son's experience of life; or the envy in observing others' good fortune and comparing it with one's own situation. Perhaps most pertinently for us, the complaint of the scholar that all his learning and intellect bring him no solid financial rewards is nearer the mark! In fact, the same writer almost certainly wrote a number of other diatribes about the poor financial rewards for the scholar, bemoaning the preferential treatment shown to the uneducated wealthy; he even wrote a Homeric pastiche lamenting the low prestige of learning, in which the poorly paid scholar bids adieu to his books, since he would be better off watching street-theatre or actors.[3]

Fully to appreciate the barbs of this twelfth-century satirist, however, these generic common elements are not enough. One needs to know a great deal more about the day-to-day existence of Constantinopolitans in the twelfth century: that a mule was an extremely expensive beast of burden, for example, more so indeed than a horse; that leather harness had a particular significance in the socially competitive and highly individualistic world of the Byzantine bourgeoisie;[4] that pointed shoes (called 'long-snouts' in the colloquial Greek of the text) were a western European trend, and considered therefore rather barbarous – but at the same time fashionable. The rest of the poem is full of reflections and satirical observations just as dependent upon an insider's knowledge of the society the writer is commenting on. On the other hand, one should also know that parchment was actually fairly expensive – to make a book of about 200 quarto-size pages, one would have to pay out a sum corresponding roughly to one-third of the yearly salary of a middling state official: only eight pages were to be obtained from each animal hide, so that at least twenty-five animals would have to be slaughtered, their hides treated with lime, cured, dried, oiled, stretched and pressed, cut to shape and sewn.

---

[3] See R. Beaton, 'The rhetoric of poverty: the lives and opinions of Theodore Prodromos', *Byzantine & Modern Greek Studies* 11 (1987), pp. 1–28, at pp. 3–4; text is to be found at *PG* 33, pp. 1419 ff. (from which the quotes above are taken).

[4] On Byzantine 'individualism' and social competitiveness, see P. Magdalino, 'Byzantine snobbery', in *The Byzantine Aristocracy, IX to XIII centuries* (British Archaeological Reports, International Ser., 221), ed. M. Angold, (Oxford, 1984), p. 62; and in general, A. Kazhdan and G. Constable, *People and Power in Byzantium: An Introduction to Modern Byzantine Studies* (Washington, DC, 1982).

The satire actually contains quite a few contradictions or paradoxes of this sort, designed, of course, to alert the reader to the intermediate position of the chief character – the author's complaints are actually written for the imperial court; and although the description he gives in this and three other similar satires offers a very useful caricature of life in the imperial capital, the purpose is both to lampoon some features of that life and at the same time to impress his patron, the emperor, with his literary skills and wit, thereby gaining imperial favour. In addition, in choosing to compose the satires in a form of the spoken Greek of the time, rather than the classicising and archaic literary language usual in works of literature, the writer makes excellent use of the fact that there existed a very marked diglossy in Byzantine society: the cultural élite wrote in a formal literary language akin to the classical Attic dialect of the fifth and fourth centuries BC (in other words, some 1,500 years earlier), whereas the spoken language of the mass of the ordinary populace had already evolved a long way towards what is now standard spoken Modern Greek. The chasm between the spoken demotic language and the learned style of the élite was marked enough, for example, for the early twelfth-century imperial princess Anna Comnena to affect the need to translate a soldiers' ditty into the élite language for the benefit of her cultured readers.[5] This diglossy also, in itself, of course, functioned symbolically, evoking for each particular observer different facets of their cultural experience, some shared, others part of the personal world of the individual.

The name Byzantium is a convenient convention, coined during the seventeenth century to describe the Roman Empire in the east after the fifth and sixth centuries AD, in other words, after the western Roman Empire had become the various barbarian successor kingdoms of the Franks, Visigoths and Ostrogoths, Burgundi and so forth. But when exactly 'Byzantine' begins and 'late Roman' ends is a moot point. Some prefer to use Byzantine for the eastern part of the Roman Empire from the time of Constantine I, that is to say, from the 320s and 330s; others apply it to the eastern empire from the later fifth or sixth century, especially from the reign of Justinian (from 527 until 565). In any case, the term Byzantine legitimately covers the period commencing with the late

5 *Anne Comnène, Aléxiade*, ed. B. Leib (3 vols., Paris, 1937, 1943, and 1945); index P. Gautier (Paris, 1976), ii, 4.9 (English trans. *The Alexiad of the Princess Anna Comnena*, trans. E. R. A. Sewter (Harmondsworth, 1969), pp. 82–3); A. Kazhdan and A. W. Epstein, *Change in Byzantine Culture in the Eleventh and Twelfth Centuries* (Berkeley, Los Angeles and London, 1985), p. 84. For some introductory discussion on diglossy and its social and psychological aspects, see C. A. Ferguson, 'Diglossy', in *Language and Social Context*, ed. P. P. Giglioli (Harmondsworth, 1972), pp. 232–51; and H. and R. Kahane, and R. L. Ward, *Spoken Greek* (Washington, DC, 1945).

Roman era and is used to describe the history of the politics, society and culture of the medieval east Roman Empire until its demise at the hands of the Ottomans in the fifteenth century. It was a society of contrasts: a mass of rural and provincial peasant producers, perhaps 90 per cent of the total population for most of its history, and a few major urban centres, of which Constantinople itself (the Queen of Cities, the second Rome) was by far the largest and wealthiest, the seat of emperors, the focal point of literacy and élite culture. It was a sophisticated state, with a complex fiscal system supporting an army, navy and administrative bureaucracy which was able to preserve the basic forms of the late ancient state well into the high Middle Ages. It was also, of course, the heartland of the Orthodox church and, from the ninth century, the centre of a far-flung Christian cultural commonwealth and of copy-cat state forms stretching from the Balkans to the Russian principalities. Its history covers a very long period, and it must be obvious that considerable changes in state organisation, as well as in social and cultural values, took place over that time; indeed, while there are enough constants and continuities to make the use of one term for the whole social formation entirely legitimate, it is also true to say that in several respects the state and society of the fifteenth century bear little relationship to those of the sixth. This is particularly true of the social and economic relationships in Byzantine society and the vocabulary through which they were understood; it is even more so in the case of many of the state's key administrative apparatuses.

But the 'Byzantines' actually called themselves Romans, and if they did use the words Byzantium or Byzantine, it was used (illustrative of the connections that learned Byzantines drew between their own culture and that of the ancient world) to describe the capital city of their empire, Constantinople, ancient Byzantion. The hallmarks of this culture were that it was Christian, that the language of the state and the dominant élite was Greek, and that its political ideology was founded on its identity with the Christian Roman Empire of Constantine the Great. Much more importantly from the perspective of cultural self-identity, the literate Byzantine élite from the later eighth and ninth centuries located its roots in the late Roman world, and saw the classical inheritance, in learning and literature especially (in a suitably Christian guise, of course), as its own. The élite used this cultural capital to differentiate itself both from the foreigner, barbarian or outsider, as well as within Byzantine society, to distinguish itself from the semi-literate or illiterate masses of rural and townsfolk. Fortunately, we have moved a long way from the days when a historian like William Lecky could write, in 1869, the following:

Of that Byzantine empire, the universal verdict of history is that it constitutes, without a single exception, the most thoroughly base and despicable form that civilisation has yet assumed. There has been no other enduring civilisation so absolutely destitute of all forms and elements of greatness, and none to which the epithet *mean* may be so emphatically applied . . . The history of the empire is a monotonous story of the intrigues of priests, eunuchs, and women, of poisonings, of conspiracies, of uniform ingratitude.[6]

This image, which was hardly even typical of the historiography of the east Roman world in its own time, lives on, of course, in some popular ideas about the Byzantine world, a combination of Victorian moralising with Crusaders' prejudices; and in the use of the adjective 'Byzantine' in a pejorative sense. There are some modern scholars who have, consciously or not, transferred these prejudices to the world of contemporary scholarship. Indeed, a recent major study of medieval east Roman economic history included in its index entries such as 'Byzantinists (curious obsession of)' and even 'Byzantinists (dotty and antiquarian pursuits of)'.[7]

Given our present knowledge of the structures of belief of medieval Orthodoxy, of Byzantine administrative and institutional practices and their evolution, of Byzantine literary and historiographical concerns, it is not difficult to get some idea of what constituted the everyday at different times in the Byzantine or east Roman world. On the other hand, trying to relate what Byzantines did – as this is reflected through our various types of source material – and what they thought (or better still, what they thought they were doing[8]) is much more difficult, and indeed represents one of the most basic problems of history writing, as such.

There has been for many years an ongoing debate about this issue in terms of the narrative construction of the past through the historiographical appropriation and interpretation of sources, and especially written sources. In its most recent form, this debate has been revived by those who are working from what one might very broadly call a post-modernist approach. Somewhat crudely, this view denies the possibility of any sort

---

[6] W. E. H. Lecky, *A History of European Morals from Augustus to Charlemagne* (2 vols., London 1869), pp. 2, 13–14.

[7] M. F. Hendy, *Studies in the Byzantine Monetary Economy c. 300–1450* (Cambridge, 1985).

[8] Of course, in asserting the relevance of intentions as a fundamental element in human consciousness and practice, I am not thereby assuming either that intentions can ever be identified or located, or – more importantly – that the intentions ascribed to actions by the actors, or by other commentators, are necessarily true. Indeed, Marx's comment at the beginning of his *The Eighteenth Brumaire of Louis Bonaparte* is a useful reminder of this: 'Men make their own history, but they do not make it just as they please; they do not make it under circumstances chosen by themselves, but under circumstances directly encountered, given and transmitted from the past' (Karl Marx and Frederick Engels, *Selected Works* (London, 1968), p. 96).

of objective account of the past, and insists on the entirely relative and discursively constructed nature of historical knowledge. In contrast, there exists a range of alternative views which, again very broadly, seek to establish the possibility of an account of the past based on the notion that the past possessed an objective reality for those who occupied it; and that human beings in the past acted meaningfully and intentionally in respect of their own perceptions and social/cultural context. Thus the structures and sets of relationships that both determined and were determined by the ways in which these individuals and groups acted can, at least in part, be redescribed in ways which both reflect their significance – as products of social action – for the people of the period themselves and are also meaningful for the historian. As literary artifacts, narratives must of course have a different form from the actions, contexts, motives and causes which they describe and connect (in the same way that a sentence may have a different form from the statement it is used to make). But this is perfectly consonant with their acting also as means of describing relationships which had a reality and significance in terms of the direction in which a particular past situation evolved. This is a complex debate, and there is not space here to pursue it in detail.[9] While this does not banish the problem of discursive relativity, with which I have a certain sympathy, the fact that human beings act both with intentions, and on the basis of socially determined patterns and codes, does permit us to redescribe the results of their actions in a way that, while being selective and determined by the purpose and ideological context of the questions we want to ask, is nevertheless useful for us in trying to see how a particular society was able to function and to reproduce itself.

One approach to this that is worth pursuing is provided by looking at Byzantine attitudes to what would today be termed social values and, more narrowly, at how these were embedded and reflected in particular forms of Byzantine behaviour. Humour appears to me to be an appropriate subject of study because, whether the product of deliberation (as in telling a story or joke) or the spontaneous result of observing a particular situation, humour reveals a considerable amount about how people perceived their own personal world and the context they inhabited. Just like

---

[9] For some introductory literature and discussion representing both sides of the argument, see I. Hasan, *The Postmodern Turn: Essays in Postmodern Theory and Culture* (Cleveland, OH, 1987); and the various essays in *The New Cultural History*, ed. L. Hunt (Berkeley, 1989); *Modern European Intellectual History: Reappraisals and New Perspectives* ed. D. LaCapra and S. L. Kaplan (Cambridge, 1982). For some critical comments on 'post-modernism' – admittedly a very loose formulation, which has a very broad applicability, see K. Soper, 'Postmodernism, subjectivity and the question of value', *New Left Review* 186 (March–April 1991), pp. 120–8.

members of any society, Byzantines were born into an already-given set of norms of behaviour, of explanatory and legitimating practices about the world, its physical properties, its inhabitants and what might be expected of them within the context or place they are assigned. Patterns of behaviour, the expression of emotions such as love, anger or pity are already laid out and are subsequently both inculcated and absorbed by the recipient in a variety of subtle and less subtle ways: in the modalities through which parents or guardians in different social strata or groups care for the newly born; through the ways in which the young observe their elders communicate their desires and feelings (or fail to do so); and through the conscious and felt demands made of people by progressively increasing circles of social contact – parents, siblings, family, village, district and so on. Human beings need to make sense of their experience in order to survive – they possess a need for culture, in its most basic sense, in terms of what Clifford Geertz called a 'web of meaning'.[10] Humour appears universally to be one of the instruments through which this is achieved.

Humour is one of the most subversive elements of human social discourse, whether in its written or its oral form. It appears to be inseparable from the human condition, so that its universal presence can be assumed to represent at the very least a social, if not an obviously physiological, function. A moment's reflection will confirm that humour is used on an everyday basis in all sorts of social situations – as a means of reaffirming intimacy or attempting to establish a relationship, as a means of diffusing anger or frustration, or of displaying contempt – as well as a way of negotiating complex or difficult social moments.[11] The forms taken by humour thus vary according to the context and the ends to which it is deployed – when those ends are conscious, of course (irony, satire, slapstick, caricature, for example). In addition, one can seek or discover humour in all sorts of situations which were in themselves not amusing, at least for the people involved in them, and this is, of course, the basis of the sick joke. In addition to these aspects we can also find situations that *we* are in spontaneously funny or humorous, adding a further dimension to humour as a means of social exchange.[12] There has been a great deal of work done in these fields by both psychologists and

---

[10] C. Geertz, *The Interpretation of Cultures* (London, 1975), pp. 5–7.

[11] For some useful introductory studies, with further literature, see esp. A. C. Zijderveld, 'The sociology of humour and laughter', *Current Sociology* 31(3) (1983), pp. 1–103; *Handbook of Humor Research*, vol. I, *Basic Issues*, ed. McGhee and Goldstein; and Wilson, *Jokes*.

[12] See M. Mulkay, *On Humour: Its Nature and its Place in Modern Society* (Oxford, 1988), pp. 52–4.

anthropologists, and in recent years increasingly also by sociologists, and various theoretical approaches have been evolved, which have attempted to get to grips with the psychological and social stimuli and functions of the phenomenon, and to move on from some of the first theories proposed by earlier thinkers: Thomas Hobbes,[13] for example, or early in the twentieth century, Freud, who suggested that humour (or what he termed 'joke-work') was a parallel phenomenon to the dream, and could be interpreted, whatever the degree of sophistication of the humour in question, to throw light on the individual's unconscious.[14] The explosive respiratory reaction to successful humour, he contended, was the effect of the orgasmic release of unconscious stimuli, both aggressive as well as sexual. Henri Bergson propounded a theory of laughter which was grounded in the perceived contrasts between human intellectual aspirations and the restrictive physical contexts they inhabit.[15] Also, one must not forget that the ancients also evolved theories of humour.[16] Since A. R. Radcliffe-Brown and other anthropologists started to analyse humour as a medium of social relationships,[17] a vast amount of empirical material has been collected from both 'traditional' as well as more intensively industrialised societies. The importance of humour for a whole range of forms of social practice has become apparent: Radcliffe-Brown's fundamental 1920s article on the 'joking relationship' is still a good place to start.[18]

One of the most important facets of humour is that, for it to function effectively, it must bring two independent but internally consistent frames of reference into play. In serious exchange, a unitary mode of discourse is employed, which takes for granted the existence of *one* real world, in the context of which ambiguity, contradiction, inconsistency or semantic uncertainty present serious problems. But humour depends on the creation of interpretative *pluralism*: in telling a story, for example, by presenting a narrative based on the listeners' assumptions about one frame of reference, and then by inverting the expectations by introducing

---

[13] See D. Heyd, 'The place of laughter in Hobbes' theory of emotions', *Journal of the History of Ideas* 43(2) (1982), pp. 285–96.

[14] See S. Freud, *Wit and its Relation to the Unconscious* (London, 1916); and the discussion in R. Wollheim, *Freud* (London and Glasgow, 1971), pp. 96–105.

[15] H. Bergson, *Laughter* (London, 1911 2nd edn 1937).

[16] See G. Soyter, *Griechischer Humor* (Berlin, 1959).

[17] A. R. Radcliffe-Brown, 'On joking relationships', in his *Structure and Function in Primitive Society* (New York, 1965), pp. 90–104.

[18] For a brief survey, see M. L. Apte, 'Humor research, methodology and theory in anthropology', in *Handbook of Humor Research*, vol. I, *Basic Issues*, ed. McGhee and Goldstein, pp. 183–212.

a resolution to the narrative through the introduction of values that normally accompany a very different set of assumptions.[19] The simplest example is that in which two quite separate contexts clash: a bad joke from a fifth-century collection provides a good illustration. The doctor visits an ill-tempered patient: 'You are sweating *very* badly,' says the doctor. 'I'm doing my best,' says the tetchy patient, 'can you do any better?'[20] The answer is perfectly logical, except that it belongs to a different set of assumptions from those assumed in the opening statement about the relationships between certain concepts in the sentence. Precisely because of the break caused by the answer to the expected course of the narrative, the surprise and accompanying relief of tension induces the physiological signs of amusement alluded to already – laughter, smiles and so on (or, as perhaps in this case, groans).

The nature of social behaviour, and the spectrum of what is acceptable within a particular social context or across a whole society, obviously vary enormously from culture to culture. What people find amusing provides a useful way into this network of values. An examination of a culture's humour – or what we can perceive of it – can thus provide useful insights into the taken-for-granteds, the day-to-day norms expected of the characters in the stories and the situations described, whether the humour in question is of the coarsest and simplest or the most refined and intellectually complex variety, whether it depends on the simple scatology of children (and some adults) or on a much more complex body of cultural capital and attitudes to particular sorts of knowledge and their deployment in social life. I give some examples of both below. But one of the results of some of the research into humour as a social phenomenon has been to suggest that humour that takes place inside relatively formal social institutional structures – kinship relationships, for example – is at the same time implicated in the contradictions built into those structures. Humour can thus be used to challenge patterns of social relations and power; but in situations of social equilibrium it is generally employed in accordance with the dominant values and power relationships.[21] A study of a culture's humour can provide a great deal of information about the way in which people coped with the multiple realities of daily life, with its potentially conflicting experiences and perceptions that have, somehow,

---

[19] See Halsall, below, pp. 89–90.

[20] B. Baldwin, *The Philogelos or Laughter-lover* (Amsterdam, 1983), p. 35, no. 186; *Philogelos, der Lachfreund von Hierokles und Philagrios*, ed. A. Thierfelder (Munich, 1968).

[21] The most useful survey of these arguments can be found in Mulkay, *On Humour*.

to be reconciled. Humour is one of the strategies all human societies employ to do this.[22]

Humour is also one of the most basic of all cultural tools for reaffirming a common identity, whether across very broad cultural boundaries, in terms of a national or ethnic identity, or inside a society, within discrete or self-defining and exclusive groups whose amusement at the behaviour of those outside their group is designed to maintain their own identity, and at the same time to justify their continued 'differentness'.[23] In both cases, humour directed against one's own group can be just as valuable an affirmation of the positive attributes one would prefer to ascribe to it.[24] Some of the most amusing jokes for Byzantines related to the strange characteristics of foreigners or, if you were a Constantinopolitan, provincials. Tales of the natural fecklessness and laziness of Armenians[25] or the hot temper of Cilicians,[26] the stupidity of Cappadocians (the country bumpkins of Byzantium), the treachery and fickleness of Turks and all those whom the Byzantines archaisingly referred to as 'Scythians' (the various peoples of the Russian steppe),[27] of the ignorance of Paphlagonians (even though – and perhaps partly because – many persons of Paphlagonian origin rose

---

[22] See in particular G. H. Mead, *Mind, Self and Society* (Chicago, 1934), pp. 206–8; and P. Berger and Th. Luckmann, *The Social Construction of Reality* (Harmondsworth, 1967); A. Schütz, *Der sinnhafte Aufbau der sozialen Welt* (Vienna, 1960).

[23] I. D. Rinder, 'A note on humor as an index of minority group morale', *Phylon* 26 (1965), pp. 117–21; W. Zenner, 'Joking and ethnic stereotyping', *Anthropological Quarterly* 43 (1970), pp. 93–113; Zijderveld, 'The sociology of humour and laughter', pp. 47–52.

[24] See Wilson, *Jokes*, pp. 189–220.

[25] See *Le Traité sur la Guérilla (de velitatione) de l'empereur Nicéphore Phocas (963–969)*, ed. and trans. G. Dagron and H. Mihaescu (with commentary by G. Dagron) (Paris, 1986), § ii (note the author's gloss on his own description of Armenian incompetence: 'for, after all, they are still Armenians'); for an English translation, see also *Skirmishing*, in *Three Byzantine Military Treatises* (Corpus Fontium Historiae Byzantinae 25 = Dumbarton Oaks Texts 9), ed. and trans. G. T. Dennis (Washington, DC, 1985), see chs. 152–3.

[26] *Miracula S. Artemii*, in *Varia Graeca Sacra*, ed. A. Papadopoulos-Kerameus (St Petersburg, 1909), Mir. 26 (p. 37.15–17); *The Miracles of Saint Artemios: Translation, Commentary and Analysis*, trans. J. Nesbitt and V. Crysafulli (Dumbarton Oaks, Washington, DC, 1995), p. 149.

[27] See, for example, Maurice's *Strategikon* 11.1 (Persians are wicked, dissembling, servile, but also patriotic and obedient); 11.2 (Avars are superstitious, treacherous, foul, faithless, greedy): *Das Strategikon des Maurikios* (Corpus Fontium Historiae Byzantinae 17), ed. G. T. Dennis and trans. E. Gamillscheg, (Vienna, 1981); *Maurice's Strategikon: Handbook of Byzantine Military Strategy*, trans. G. T. Dennis, (Philadelphia, 1984); cf. Theophylact Simocatta, *Historiae* 7.7 on the Avars: *Theophylacti Simocattae Historia*, ed. C. de Boor (Leipzig, 1887; revised and emended edn P. Wirth, Stuttgart, 1972); and *Nikephoros Patriarch of Constantinople, Short History* (Corpus Fontium Historiae Byzantinae 13, ser. Wash.), ed. C. Mango (Washington, DC, 1990), §§ 35–6 on the Bulgars). For a summary of Byzantine 'ethnology', see *The Oxford Dictionary of Byzantium*, ed. A. Kazhdan (New York and Oxford, 1991), vol. II, p. 734, with literature, and M. Maas, 'Terms of inclusion: Christianity and classical ethnography from Justinian to Heraclius', in *The Byzantine and Early Islamic Near East: Patterns of Communal Identity*, ed. L. I. Conrad (forthcoming).

to high positions at court and in government),[28] or of the impetuosity of westerners (referred to as the 'light-haired peoples', later as the Latins) – such tales abounded, although we have only a few pale reflections of the wealth of this material in the chronicles and hagiographical literature of the time. Foreigners came in for particularly crude stereotyping: according to writers of the twelfth century, following the opinions of the street, westerners were snot-nosed, catarrh-ridden[29] and short-tempered, always ready to pull out their swords; public drunkenness was normal among them; their eating habits were grotesque, gulping down chines of beef boiled in great cauldrons, eating smoked pork with, of all things, peas, or even sharp sauces with garlic; casual violence was usual among them.[30] Their style of warfare came in for particular criticism, although in fact we know that some of the Crusader leaders were capable and intelligent field-commanders who quickly adapted to the new conditions with which they were confronted.[31] This was a society in which bishops rode to battle on warhorses and fought alongside the knights and lords (who were often, of course, their close kin). Yet behind the criticism lies a certain envy of Latin military prowess and success – western mercenaries had been a regular feature in Byzantine armies since the tenth century.

Even more disparagingly, Theophylact of Ohrid, archbishop of Bulgaria in the late eleventh and early twelfth centuries, refers lovingly to his flock as 'mindless toads, barbarians reeking of sheepskins';[32] and although he represents a very small and highly educated literate élite, such opinions seem to have been shared by the majority of ordinary folk. Having said this, it is also worth noting that there is a clear evolution in Byzantine attitudes to non-Romans – foreigners – from the late Roman period through to the twelfth century and after: a greater degree of sophistication in distinguishing 'good' from 'bad' foreigners, a greater potential for individualising people is permitted, a development

---

[28] See P. Magdalino, 'Paphlagonians in Byzantine high society', in *Byzantine Asia Minor (6ᵗʰ–12ᵗʰ Centuries)*, ed. N. Oikonomidès (Athens, 1998), pp. 141–50.

[29] See B. Baldwin, 'Bohemond's breathing', *Byzantine & Modern Greek Studies* 15 (1991), pp. 314–16. For earlier views of gluttonous barbarians, see Halsall, below, pp. 93–4; for the western rejoinder, see Balzaretti, below, p. 123.

[30] *Das Strategikon des Maurikios*, 3 (the 'light-haired peoples' – Franks, Lombards, etc. – are bold, undaunted in battle, proud, impetuous and undisciplined). They are also destructively loquacious. See also *Alexiad* 10.9.3; 14.4.5 (Sewter's translation, pp. 322, 450–1). For humour and ethnic stereotyping, particularly referring to diet and military affairs, see also Halsall, below, pp. 89–113 and Shanzer, above, pp. 42–4.

[31] See, for example, R. C. Smail (ed. C. Marshall), *Crusading Warfare, 1097–1193* (Cambridge, 1995), pp. 168–74.

[32] Kazhdan and Epstein, *Change*, p. 169. For other examples of humour based upon inappropriate behaviour, especially with regard to foreigners, see Halsall, below, pp. 96–113.

that reflects both the increasing political and cultural independence and importance of the medieval west and its greater penetration, socially, culturally and economically, of the east Roman sphere.

What was amusing for Byzantines in the appearance or behaviour of foreigners was not simply their Otherness; it was the absurdity of their behaviour or inappropriateness of their dress in situations where a Byzantine would have behaved quite differently. Humour was particularly located in the absurd or improper, whether an old man behaving in the manner of a younger man, a priest acting like a soldier, or a human being resembling or behaving like (from the perspective of Byzantine prejudice, of course) an animal. Byzantine satire and parody, as well as personal and religious invective, all used this means of poking fun at, and making ridiculous, their targets.[33]

Attitudes to laughter varied over the Byzantine period (although it is obvious that what was regarded as acceptable behaviour by social élites or religious institutions did not always hold across society as a whole). The traditional attitude to laughter typified in classical literature was part of the taken-for-granted culture of the late Roman world. Laughter induced by humorous tales was thought of as a virtue, a quality bestowed on individuals by divine providence and favour, and a number of writers collected jokes and amusing stories which were ascribed to a variety of famous persons. In classical times, a famous group of sixty wits had used to meet at a temple in the Athens of Demosthenes, and their jokes were so popular that the father of Alexander the Great, Philip II, paid a considerable sum for a copy of their work. Nearly 800 years later – sometime about 400 AD – an unknown compiler produced a collection of witticisms and tales known as the *Philogelos*, the 'Laughter-lover', a collection of mostly pretty mediocre jokes, which was copied again and again in Byzantium. But with the progressive Christianisation of Roman society and the state from the reign of Constantine I in the 320s and 330s, things become more complex. Traditional attitudes began to be transformed among some elements of society as Christian morality and ethics gained in influence. Laughter was frowned upon, for it intruded upon and sullied the joy proper to a true believer, a joy resulting from the knowledge that Good had triumphed over Evil; tears of contrition, sympathy and a gentle smile were praised as the qualities of a good Christian. Christian thinkers of the early church evolved, in fact, a fairly elaborate theory of divinely inspired jubilation and joy, and a corresponding idea of a

---

[33] Cf. the brief entry in *The Oxford Dictionary of Byzantium*, vol. II, p. 956 and the examples given.

specifically Christian sense of humour, a theory which eventually produced, among other things, the rather sharp dialectical humour of the Danish philosopher Kierkegaard. However, the fact that the qualities to which I have just referred – contrition, sympathy and so on – were also among the chief characteristics desirable in a holy man and ascetic, whose life, it was generally recognised, could be emulated only by very few, suggests that few actually attained such a refined spiritual state.[34]

This was only the 'official' line; although no doubt very many churchmen, devout believers and members of the monastic communities that proliferated in the later Roman and Byzantine world adhered as far as they were able to this model, it is also very apparent that the church struggled in vain across the whole period of the existence of the Byzantine state – and, indeed, beyond – to prevent displays of spiritual levity. The so-called Quinisext council held at Constantinople in 692 (to confirm the acts of the fifth and sixth ccumenical councils held carlier, hence its name) issued 102 canons regulating issues of concern to the eastern church; among them, canons 71 and 76 prohibited the traditional jokes and theatrical performances organised by law students in Constantinople as inducing licentious behaviour and encouraging the devil's interference in man's affairs. Dressing up in foreign clothes was proscribed, as was any sort of charivari.[35] Many of these proscriptions were repeated in the acts of later councils or in commentaries on canon law; but the very fact that these ordinances had to be repeated, as well as a great deal of other evidence, suggests that neither the court nor the mass of the ordinary population paid them much attention. Indeed, the church historian Socrates, writing in the early fifth century AD, refers to a collection of theological jokes compiled by Bishop Sisinnios, most of which depended for their effect upon a fairly intimate knowledge of Christological debates, the membership and characteristics of various heretical groups, and the personalities of leading public figures of the day;[36] and

---

[34] Cf. *Anastasius Sinaites, Interrogationes et Responsiones*, ed. J. Gretser, in *PG* 89, cols. 311–824, *Question* 6; 15; 93. For discussion of the complex tradition behind this text, see J. F. Haldon, 'The works of Anastasius of Sinai: a key source for the history of seventh-century east Mediterranean society and belief', in *The Byzantine and Early Islamic Near East*, vol. I, ed. A. Cameron and L. Conrad (Princeton, NJ, 1992), pp. 107–47. The original collection of 103 questions and their answers was reconstituted by M. Richard, 'Les Véritables "Questions et réponses" d'Anastase le Sinaïte', *Bulletin de l'Institut de Recherches et d'Histoire des textes* 15 (1967–8), pp. 39–56 (= M. Richard, *Opera Minora* 3, no. 64, and App. iv–v). For western Christian views of laughter see Innes, below, pp. 142–3.

[35] See *Sacrorum Conciliorum nova et amplissima Collectio*, ed. J. D. Mansi (53 vols., Florence and Venice, 1759–98; repr. Paris and Leipzig, 1901–27), vol. XI, 972A–C.

[36] Socrates, *Historia Ecclesiastica*, in *PG* 67, cols. 33–841, see § 6.22.

the twelfth-century canonist Balsamon condemned the great carnivals that took place in association with saint's day celebrations, with their buffoonery, transvestism and carousing – pious women were forced to flee from such ostensibly holy events because of the lecherous and bawdy behaviour and language of the participants.[37] Thus, although it is true that the church succeeded in bringing about the abandonment and conversion to different uses of theatre buildings as such, popular festivals continued to involve mimes and jesters as well as satirical performances aimed at persons of note; in addition, the literary genre of satire itself, although eclipsed in the period from the seventh to eleventh centuries, experienced a revival thereafter.[38] Street theatre certainly had a continuous existence, whatever the attitude of the ecclesiastical authorities: in the late tenth century the verse epitaph for Emperor John I makes him proclaim: 'I, whose victories were once celebrated with the lyre, am now, alas, mocked in theatrical displays.'[39]

The humour of the day-to-day was largely unaffected by church pronouncements on morals, therefore, and there is plenty of evidence for the deployment of various types of humour, both on the streets of Constantinople as well as in literature, to give some idea of how people responded to difficult situations, ranging from problems with paying the rent to the results of a political *coup d'état*. The variety of Byzantine humour is as wide as our own, although its emphases were often somewhat different. It was, moreover, used in both religious/moral as well as secular, day-to-day contexts, with as much effect. Indeed, one of the most effective devices used by Christian apologists against nonbelievers, doubters and all those who treated their faith without due respect was precisely to make fun of *their* beliefs and to cast aspersions on *their* integrity. In the later seventh century, and some years after the successful Islamic conquest of the region, the wandering preacher and theologian Anastasius of Sinai wrote a scathing denunciation ridiculing the behaviour of many Christians in the towns and village communities of Syria and Palestine. If the priest speaks at length, many members of the congregation yawn loudly and make a pretence of falling asleep; they

---

37 For Balsamon, see K. Rhalles and M. Potles, *Syntagma tôn theiôn kai hierôn kanonôn* (4 vols., Athens, 1852–9), vol. II, comm. to Quinisext canon 62 (p. 452); Kazhdan and Epstein, *Change*, pp. 82–3.

38 See H.-G. Beck, *Geschichte der byzantinischen Volksliteratur* (Handbuch d. Altertumswiss. 12, 2.3 = *Byzantinisches Handbuch* 2, 3, Munich, 1971) pp. 25–7 and 101–5, 193–6; H. F. Tozer, 'Byzantine satire', *Journal of Hellenic Studies* 2 (1881), pp. 233–70; B. Baldwin, 'A talent to abuse: some aspects of Byzantine satire', *Byzantinische Forschung* 8 (1982), pp. 19–28.

39 See R. Morris, 'The two faces of Nikephoros Phokas', *Byzantine & Modern Greek Studies* 12 (1988), pp. 83–115, at p. 114.

rush from the church 'as though from the courthouse'. Some arrive only in time to take communion, rushing into church 'like dogs', gulping down the sacraments and rushing out again. Many spend the service chattering and gossiping, standing around ogling the women in the gallery, thinking only of the pleasures of the flesh. The picture is exaggerated, but by turning ordinary churchgoers into figures of fun, Anastasius was warning his readers and listeners to mend their ways.[40]

Jokes at the expense of doubters and those who were thought to be not quite orthodox were commonplace. There is an excellent example from a collection of the miracles of Saint Artemios, a healing saint who cured by incubation, dating to about the same time. Clients went to the church where the saint's remains were interred, and slept in the colonnade around the associated hospital, or in the main building itself, often camping out for several days. There, they would dream that they were visited by the saint – often in the guise of a doctor, but one guided by divine wisdom, of course – who cured them in one of a variety of ways. Artemios was particularly adept at curing hernias and problems connected with the genital region, and on this particular occasion a wealthy young man suffering from a rather nasty hernia was persuaded to visit the saint and stay in the church overnight. He was accompanied by an Alexandrian wit who was in Constantinople at the time, and who kept on making sceptical remarks about the whole business. The watchmen insisted on locking the two in for the night; but the Alexandrian unfortunately needed to relieve himself and, not being able to get out, decided to urinate against one of the columns in the church. This turned out to be a big mistake. He was immediately rewarded by feeling an agonising pain in his lower abdomen and, on reaching down to see what the matter was, exclaimed: 'By God and Saint Menas, both you and this saint are fakes; woe, woe, he's sent me your hernia!' The humorous point of the story, with the twist in the tale – a saint who can hurt people – was no doubt clear enough to contemporaries.[41]

The writer of the miracles of Artemios, it should be noted, frequently emphasises the incompetence and greed of doctors in comparison with the efficacy of his saint; faith was more important than rational science. The Byzantine curse 'may you fall into the hands of doctors' (and part of a long anti-medical tradition in Hellenistic and Roman culture) was not just an indication of distrust or fear of doctors; it evoked at the same

---

[40] *PG* 89, cols. 825A–849C; Haldon, 'Anastasius of Sinai', p. 133, n. 48. For a possible fifth-century parallel, see Halsall, below, p. 98.
[41] *Miracles of Saint Artemios*, 112/113.

time the notion that doctors, who depended for their skills on human rather than divine powers, were an impious bunch of charlatans at the best of times.[42]

Unfortunately, the existing examples of Byzantine humour, whether of a visual or verbal/literal sort, are for the most part limited to what the literate élite composed, or thought worth passing on for posterity. Examples of the day-to-day banter that mediates most normative social relationships, as well as moments of tension and crisis, in virtually all the societies that I know about – between husband and wife, parents and children, workmates and colleagues, friends as well as strangers of the same and of the opposite sex – are virtually non-existent, for by its very nature such banter was hardly ever written down. A couple of examples of casual irony referring to everyday experience will have to suffice: the Byzantine proverb 'One man does things honestly; the other writes it down' is a joking reference to the notorious corruption of notaries; or 'Hey, your house is on fire!', 'Don't worry, I've got the key' – roughly the equivalent of 'Mind your own business!'[43]

Humour was often, again as in many societies, a safe vehicle through which to address rulers or to make criticisms of those in power. Just as importantly, it was also a very effective way of rapidly communicating popular criticisms of an established order or a particular policy. Popular rhymes and catcalls, often fairly coarse, and thus the more readily understood, were shouted by passers-by during public imperial occasions. For example:

> You've drunk too much again,
> pissed out of your mind again . . .

ran the first two lines of a popular song aimed at the usurper Phocas in the early seventh century. Such humour was, naturally, heavily context-bound. Compare the, to us, apparently unamusing quip yelled at the same emperor:

> Get up and learn about the situation;
> Maurice [the deposed ruler] isn't
> dead yet.[44]

---

[42] J. F. Haldon, 'The miracles of Artemios and contemporary attitudes: context and significance', in *The Miracles of Saint Artemios: Translation, Commentary and Analysis*, ed. J. Nesbitt and V. Crysafulli (Dumbarton Oaks, Washington, DC, 1995) pp. 33–73, at pp. 44–6. For western jokes about doctors, see Shanzer, above, p. 27.

[43] H.-G. Beck, *Byzantinisches Lesebuch* (Munich, 1982), pp. 377–8.

[44] See P. Maas, 'Metrische Akklamationen der Byzantiner', *Byzantinische Zeitschrift* 34 (1912), pp. 28–51, at pp. 35–6.

Its humour for contemporaries lay in a simple pun, for the Greek word for 'situation' (*katastasis*) also happens to be the technical term for imperial ceremonial,[45] thus evoking for contemporaries the well-known fact that Phocas, a former junior officer in the army, was relatively ignorant about court precedence and ritual, or the ways of a big city; at the same time, it reminded the new emperor of his lowly provincial origins, a fact that was in itself a source for humour for the streetwise Constantinopolitan. There are several similar examples.

The simplest humour is often, of course, very cruel: practical jokes involving the physical debunking of an important (or self-important) person; public derision and scorn founded on an individual's failure to fulfil others' expectations; and so on. Emperor Constantine IX, a fun-loving fellow according to his biographer, the eleventh-century philosopher Michael Psellos, used to invite people to feasts in his mansion gardens, in which he would beforehand have pits dug into which the unsuspecting guests might tumble – Psellos, an intellectual, regards this as perfectly reasonable fun![46] In classical antiquity, as in many traditional societies, physical deformity in particular was a source of amusement, an attitude which, although frowned upon by Christian thinkers, certainly had a continuous history throughout the Byzantine period, and often recurs in satirical works. The twelfth-century satirist quoted already frequently made his leading characters ludicrous by placing them in situations which, while ostensibly reflecting their actual social situation or station in life, and the dress and habits due to them, actually made them grotesque: the overweight abbot on his skinny mule, for example, or the large nagging wife and the puny browbeaten husband, and so on. Literary accounts of bad or evil rulers regularly included (usually fictional) elaborations on their physical malformation or, especially, the hideous way in which they died.[47]

Here one may pause for a moment to consider a somewhat paradoxical point, namely that there is a close connection between the medieval Byzantine method of disqualifying individuals from imperial power and this attitude towards deformity as laughable or ridiculous. The standard

---

[45] See *The Oxford Dictionary of Byzantium*, vol. I, pp. 400–1.

[46] *Michael Psellos, Chronographia*, trans. E. R. A. Sewter (New Haven, 1953), 2.34, 2.39–40.

[47] Thus Constantine V, the iconoclastic emperor of the eighth century (741–75) was described in later iconophile texts in the most lurid terms. See P. Speck, *Ich bin's nicht, Kaiser Konstsantin ist es gewesen. Die Legenden vom Einfluß des Teufels, des Juden und des Moslem auf den Ikonoklasmus* (Poikila Byzantina 10) (Bonn, 1990). For the late Roman precursors of this thinking, see Humphries, below, pp. 82–3; for Christian treatment of the theme of the ludicrous deaths of evil-doers, see Shanzer, above, p. 28.

means of punishing those who had been ousted from power or who had threatened the position of the reigning emperor was to mutilate them: a number of possibilities existed: apart from the chopping off of hands, putting out the eyes was a favourite, but slitting the nose and cutting out the tongue were also popular. An emperor, appointed by God, should be a perfect physical specimen, at least in theory; mutilation automatically disqualified one from the imperial position. Such punishments were favoured above execution (although that was also employed), according to the occasional commentary on the subject, because their use displayed the exercise of *philanthropia*, love of one's fellow men: taking a life was God's prerogative. In practice, this approach was riddled with contradictions, and there was actually no really coherent approach. Indeed, Emperor Justinian II, who was deposed and mutilated in 695, made his return to power with the assistance of the Bulgar Khan in 705 and succeeded in recovering his throne. But it is generally forgotten in discussions of Byzantine penal practice that deformity was also *laughable*, and by deliberately mutilating an individual who had threatened the status quo, that individual (and those who associated with him) was rendered absurd, ridiculous. He was, in effect, made harmless through the loss of his former dignity and pride, becoming instead the butt of popular derision: a fairly effective means, in fact, of disabling a political opponent.[48]

Parody and satire retained their popularity throughout the Byzantine era, regardless of their fate as acceptable forms of literary activity. Fragments of popular rhymes about the late sixth-century emperor Maurice likened the emperor to a priapic rooster and portrayed him strutting about with no care for his subjects; tenth-century popular verse about the empress Theophano presented her as an ageing whore who would do anything to please her new lover;[49] when the emperor Alexios I lost a battle to the Turkic Pechenegs in the Balkans in 1088, but managed successfully to withdraw very rapidly back to his base at Goloê, the people of the town are reported to have greeted him with sarcastic comments on the efficiency of his military marches.[50] All three become figures of fun; they thereby lose their imperial and authoritative aspect, so that the humour here acts as both a challenge to their fitness to rule and

---

[48] See E. Patlagean, 'Byance et le blason pénal du corps', *Sodalitas* 6 (1984), pp. 405–26. See also Introduction, above, p. 18.

[49] Maas, 'Metrische Akklamationen der Byzantiner', p. 34; see M. J. Kyriakis, 'Satire and slapstick in seventh- and twelfth-century Byzantium', *Byzantina* 5 (1973), pp. 291–306, at pp. 291 ff.

[50] Anna Comnena, *Alexiad* 7.3.12 (Sewter's translation, p. 227 and n. 23; the comment is only in the Vatican Epitome: see *Anna Comnène*, ed. Leib, vol. II, 101, note to lines 20–1).

a reminder that 'the people' also have a voice; the latter represented a crucially important element in the relations of political power in the imperial capital, which no emperor could afford to ignore.

Satire, whether in literary or oral form, functioned perhaps most effectively as a form of criticism in Byzantine society and politics. In literature, it took several forms, including both parody and allegory; and its real target was often concealed in a timeless garb of classical allusion, easily penetrated by contemporaries, but also functioning as a demonstration of the learning and knowledge of the composer. In this way Byzantine satirists wrote in the form of Platonic dialogues or the satirical allegories of Lucian. Theodore Prodromos, who almost certainly wrote the satirical poem quoted from at the beginning of this chapter,[51] also wrote a poem called the *Katomyomachia*, or 'the war between the cat and the mice', a parody on classical tragedy and at the same time a satire in which the mouse 'cheese-stealer' describes the terrible lives of the mice who live in fear of the predator cats, the whole being an allegory on relations within Byzantine society. Theodore also wrote parodies poking fun at aspects of everyday life: illiteracy, lewd behaviour or – always a popular motif – the helpless situation of a patient in the hands of a bad dentist.

Literary activity also reflects and is part of the broader social and cultural picture, and it is important to note that the sort of acerbic satire this writer produced reflected the rise during the eleventh century of a new element in middle-Byzantine urban society, a class of professional writers from relatively modest origins, whose expectations were never met by the social realities of their lives, and whose frustration and anger was directed both at representatives of the old élite – people who happened to write because that was what members of their class were expected to do, rather than because they needed to earn a living from it – and at the people who had encouraged them to take up this profession, their aspiring parents.[52] The very fact of this shift in emphasis and expansion of a genre tells much about patterns of social structure in Constantinople at this time.

Even the most serious of political or theological issues could be made fun of, and with a serious intent. In the late fourth century the churchman and theologian Gregory of Nyssa satirised the divisive Christological

---

[51] See M. Alexiou, 'The poverty of ecriture and the craft of writing: towards a reappraisal of the Prodromic poems', *Byzantine & Modern Greek Studies* 10 (1986), pp. 1–40; R. Beaton, 'The rhetoric of poverty: the lives and opinions of Theodore Prodromos', *Byzantine & Modern Greek Studies* 11 (1987), pp. 1–28; and A. Kazhdan, *Studies on Byzantine Literature of the Eleventh and Twelfth Centuries* (Cambridge, 1984), pp. 87–114.

[52] See the discussion, with further literature, in Beaton, 'The rhetoric of poverty', pp. 4–6.

debates of his day: 'If you ask for your change, the shopkeeper phil-
osophises to you about the Begotten and the Unbegotten; if you ask about
the price of a loaf, the answer is: "The Father is Greater than the Son";
and if you say "Is the bath ready?", the attendant affirms that the Son is
of Nothing!'[53]

Gregory's comments refer to the final stages of the controversy over
Arianism, a doctrine that challenged the established 'orthodox' definition
of the relationships between the different elements of the Trinity. Such
debates today might seem at the best arid, and at the worst entirely
trivial. But people took them in deadly earnest, for correct belief was
crucial to correct practice, in other words, to as sinless a life as possible;
in turn, it was well known that if some elements of the Christian flock
erred from the path of righteousness, then God might punish them all –
with a plague, a war, earthquakes and other calamities. This is summed
up very nicely in a mid-seventh-century story about a certain abbot, to
whom God appeared in a dream. 'Is it true that all rulers are appointed
by heavenly command?' he asked. The answer was positive. 'Then why,
O Lord, did you send the wicked tyrant Phocas to rule the Roman
people?' 'Because', came the stern reply, 'I could find no one worse.' I
hardly need to add that this was not taken as amusing by those who were
told the story![54]

Belief and practice were directly related to causal sequences, and
everyone felt strongly about this. The fact that, as other contemporary
commentators make quite clear, the ordinary 'person in the street' did not
have a clue about the theological and philosophical subtleties involved
was neither here nor there; just as today we argue about economics and
inflation, even though most of us do not have much idea of the complexities of theories of price and value. Gregory's humorous remarks –
designed to arouse the sympathy of his audience and readers – thus tell
quite a bit about the relationship between beliefs and why people responded to particular situations in the ways in which, according to other
sources, they did.

The eleventh-century intellectual Michael Psellos wrote a number of
prose satires denouncing the ignorance of some of the clergy, the preten-
tiousness of some of his visitors in Constantinople, and the mercenary
values and superficial culture of the new class of professional writers, to
be represented by men such as Theodore Prodromos in the following

---

[53] A. H. M. Jones, *The Later Roman Empire: A Social, Economic and Administrative Survey* (Oxford, 1964),
    p. 964.
[54] Anastasius Sinaites, *Interrogationes et Responsiones*, Qu. 16.

century.[55] However, he was himself subjected to the hostility of the military magnates of the provinces. 'Do not wish to be a city gent' (in other words, involved in Constantinopolitan and court politics), says the eleventh-century general, Kekaumenos, in a book of advice to his son, a military officer: 'You can't be a clown and a general at the same time.'[56] Psellos' criticism of some of the clergy was mirrored in a scathing satire about a collector of relics, penned by Psellos' contemporary, the imperial official Christopher of Mytilene.[57] This man, the monk Andrew, had assembled a quite remarkable collection of holy bits and pieces: some ten hands of the martyr Prokopios, eight legs of Saint Nestor, twelve forearms of Saint Demetrios, five breasts of Saint Barbara, fifteen jaws of Saint Theodora and no fewer than four heads of Saint George! He has managed thus, says Christopher, to metamorphose a holy warrior into an octopus and a hermit into a hydra; and to drive home his point he goes on to offer Andrew objects for his collection – how about Saint Elias' buttocks or a piece of Gabriel's wing?[58] A century later the theme of monastic and priestly corruption is taken up, from a slightly different social angle, by Theodore Prodromos, in a poem in which he lampooned the abbot and leading members of a Constantinopolitan monastic house. But the satires of 'Poor Prodromos', as he was called, not only attacked public institutions such as monasteries, popular attitudes to classical learning and literature, and the cultural exclusivism of the aristocratic élite; they also satirised family life and domestic cares, in the process telling a great deal about the private aspect of urban society, the household, diet and relationships between husbands and wives. Although Prodromos' satires are often very sophisticated, they also include a considerable amount of pretty coarse, ribald wit about sex and physical relationships. Indeed, the author uses the universal parallel between food and its preparation and consumption, on the one hand, and sexual activities of various sorts on the other, to great effect: 'Come and have some of my frothy white stuff, ladies!', says the yoghurt-seller in the hearing of the impoverished, frustrated and single scholar; while the butcher's wife who, we are assured, tempts him with her breast-meat and belly-fat (lamb and pork), rejects him when he admits he cannot afford her price. He cannot even afford

55 Psellos, *Chronographia*, 1.30.

56 Kekaumenos, *Strategikon* 20.19–20, in *Cecaumeni: Strategicon et incerti scriptoris de officiis regiis libellus*, ed. B. Wassiliewsky and V. Jernstedt (St Petersburg, 1896 and Amsterdam, 1965).

57 See E. Follieri, 'Le poesie di Cristoforo Mitilineo come fonte storica', *Zbornik Radova Vizantoloshkog Instituta* 8(2) (1964), pp. 133–48.

58 *Die Gedichte*, ed. E. Kurtz (Leipzig 1903; corr. C. Crimi, in *Bollettino della Badia Greca di Grottaferrata* 39 (1985), pp. 231–42), no. 114. For parallels, see Shanzer, above, pp. 38–9.

a well-greased sausage, the connotations of which hardly need further elaboration.[59]

Humour of varying sorts was inevitably, as one would expect, part and parcel of any social gathering. Accounts from a wide range of literary sources, from hagiographies describing the mealtimes of soldiers or peasants, to descriptions of imperial feasts, make it clear that jokes and amusing stories were a regular means through which common values and beliefs were reaffirmed. Round the campfire somewhere in northern Palestine, in a soldiers' bivouac in the early seventh century, we can read how troopers from a cavalry unit argued about the respective merits of their own personal saints, scoffing and satirising each others' claims.[60] At the imperial table the quality of the humour covered the whole range: in the later twelfth century, wisecracks and puns were certainly expected of the diners: on one occasion, when the emperor Isaac asked for the salt, one of the guests replied, gesturing at the bevy of attractive female guests in the emperor's personal retinue, 'Would you first taste of these, and then order others to be brought in.' The guests fell about laughing. The humour is apparent only when one understands the pun: the Greek word for salt is *alâs*, and for 'other women' *âllas*.[61]

Various degrees of social solidarity or group identity were similarly thus highlighted: jokes based on gender solidarity or group and status identities are a particularly obvious category.[62] There survive a substantial number of jokes about nagging wives, for example – Prodromos' first satire deals with the theme of the hen-pecked husband married above his class, while the second deals with the woes of an impoverished father of thirteen and identifies with the oppressed patriarch struggling to pay his bills and keep his head above water. Jokes or stories expressing similar sentiments from women hardly exist in written form, but there is every reason to suppose that women's attitudes to men, however conscious or not they may have been of the nature of their social situation, were just as strongly represented, in an oral tradition. This tension could be transferred into the religious sphere, too: there is a nice story from a sixth/seventh-century collection of tales about the monastic life (many of them demonstrating a good deal of wry humour) of a monk walking

---

[59] See Alexiou, 'The poverty of ecriture', pp. 16–18.

[60] *Saint Anastase le Perse et l'histoire de la Palestine au début du VIIe siècle*, vol. I, *Les Textes*; vol. II, *Le Commentaire*, ed. B. Flusin (Paris, 1992), vol. I, miracles 13.15–18.

[61] Niketas Choniates, *Historia*, 441.23–6, in *Niketas Choniates: Historia* (Corpus Fontium Historiae Byzantinae 11), ed. J. A. van Dieten (New York and Berlin, 1975).

[62] See Mulkay, *On Humour*, pp. 134–6. For a discussion of humour and gender relationships, see also Balzaretti, below, pp. 114–28.

along a road, who spies some nuns coming towards him. Like any good monk, he crosses to the other side of the track to distance himself from these sources of temptation. Says the abbess leading the nuns: 'If you were a proper monk, you wouldn't even have noticed that we were women!'[63] The story was not intended to be humorous, of course, but given what is now known about the Byzantine sense of the amusing, there is equally no reason to suppose that those who heard or read the story were not able to glimpse the humorous element embedded in the narrative.

Occasionally, a literate and privileged female writer, such as the early twelfth-century princess, Anna Comnena, or the early ninth-century noblewoman and nun, Kassia, did give vent to their feelings about men in writing; but this rarely involves the sort of ribald and crude humour of the sort found in men's joke-telling (and probably in women's oral joke-telling). Kassia's humour includes parodic debunking of young men of noble birth who think they know everything; but her violent antipathy towards Armenians who, in her time, were particularly prominent in the state establishment and at court, reflects Byzantine prejudices at large: 'Unbelieving Armenians are mean and ignorant; when they become believers they are even meaner and more ignorant,' she avers.[64]

It must by now be fairly clear that, for the most part, the genres of Byzantine humour are not very different from those of our own culture; and that it is not difficult to extract from them a good deal of information about the social psychology of writers or groups in a variety of different social and intellectual contexts. It is obvious that much of this humour is so embedded in the culture which produced it, with values in many respects so very different from our own, that it takes some considerable effort to appreciate its function and the nature of the response it elicited. But the effort is worthwhile, for it represents a valuable way of situating literary activity in the context of the social practice that engendered it, and a fruitful means of trying to look at those practices to see how they were perceived by the people, both individuals and groups, who lived them on a day-to-day basis.

---

[63] Beck, *Byzantinisches Lesebuch*, p. 319.
[64] Ed. K. Krumbacher, in *Sitzungsberichte der philos.-philolog. und der historischen Classe der K. bayer. Akad. der Wiss. zu München* 1 (1897), pp. 347–9, see B. Baldwin, *An Anthology of Byzantine Poetry* (Amsterdam, 1985), pp. 155–6. On Kassia, see I. Rochow, *Studien zu der Person, den Werken und dem Nachleben der Dichterin Kassia* (Berlin, 1967).

PART II

Humour and the politics of difference

CHAPTER 3

The lexicon of abuse:
drunkenness and political illegitimacy
in the late Roman world

Mark Humphries

INTRODUCTION

In the anonymous, mid-fourth-century narrative known as the *Origo Constantini imperatoris* (The origin of the emperor Constantine), several apparently remarkable statements are made about the moral fibre – or, more precisely, the lack of it – of the enemies of the emperor Constantine.[1] Prominent among these villains are Galerius, Augustus of the eastern empire (305–11), and his short-lived associate as western emperor, Severus (Caesar, 305–6; Augustus, 306–7). The relationship between the two men, so our anonymous author has it, was based on their shared propensity to heavy drinking: 'Severus Caesar was ignoble both by character and by birth; he was a heavy drinker [*ebriosus*] and for this reason he was a friend of Galerius.'[2] Galerius' own fondness for drink and its deleterious effects are soon described: 'Galerius was such a heavy drinker [*ebriosus*] that, when he was intoxicated, he gave orders such as should not be implemented.'[3]

This chapter will explain why it is significant that an emperor should be characterised as an *ebriosus*.[4] It will show that emperors described in this fashion were not 'mere' heavy drinkers, but that allegations of drunkenness were employed to undermine the very legitimacy of their rule.

---

[1] Text in *Origo Constantini: Anonymus Valesianus*, vol. 1, *Text und Kommentar* (Trierer Historische Forschungen 11), ed. I. König (Trier, 1987). For a recent discussion, see *From Constantine to Julian: Pagan and Byzantine Views*, ed. S. N. C. Lieu and D. Montserrat (London, 1996), pp. 39–42.
[2] *Origo* 4.9.   [3] *Origo* 4.11.
[4] Throughout I will either translate *ebriosus* as 'heavy drinker' or leave it untranslated. It is inappropriate to translate it as 'alcoholic' (as, for example, J. Stevenson in her translation of *Origo* 4.9 and 11, in *From Constantine to Julian*, ed. Lieu and Montserrat, p. 44), since modern views of alcoholism characterise it as a disease: P. Antze, 'Symbolic action in Alcoholics Anonymous', in *Constructive Drinking: Perspectives on Drink from Anthropology*, ed. M. Douglas (Cambridge, 1987), pp. 149–81, esp. pp. 154–8. In antiquity, by contrast, heavy drinking was seen primarily as a moral failing: J. H. D'Arms, 'Heavy drinking and drunkenness in the Roman world: four questions for historians', in *In Vino Veritas*, ed. O. Murray and M. Tecusan (London, 1995), pp. 304–17 at pp. 315–17.

The discussion here focusses primarily on texts dealing with emperors of
the tetrarchy established by Diocletian and the succeeding Constantinian
dynasty, so that the material will cover both the political and religious
rivalries of the late third and early fourth centuries AD. It will emerge that
no single religious group monopolised this particular vituperative technique, and that the connection between drunkenness and illegitimacy
was drawn equally by pagans and Christians.

DRUNKENNESS AND THE CONSTRUCTION OF ILLEGITMACY

First, why should drunkenness be considered a defect in an emperor?
The reason is to be sought in the place drunkenness occupied in Roman
moral topography, particularly its opposition to the valued quality of
decorum, which meant proper and dignified behaviour that kept inherent
vices in check.[5] In Cicero's *De officiis* – the best surviving guide to Roman
political morality – the conduct of a good servant of the state was marked
by the display of *decorum* both in private and in public.[6] For Cicero, *decorum*
was essential to the proper exercise of *honestas* (honourableness), and thus
it was one of the foremost qualities that served to distinguish mankind
from all other animals.[7] This distinction between men and beasts was
epitomised by their diverging attitudes towards and reactions to lusts
and pleasures. Animals, being governed by the appetites of their bodies,
easily succumbed to sensual temptations; but men, who were characterised by reason, ought to be able to shun them.[8] Such attitudes to lusts
and pleasures had profound implications for the conduct of politicians.
Because of the heavy responsibilities of government, the behaviour of
men holding political office should be characterised by the same qualities as might be found in a state's laws.[9] In other words, statesmen took
on the characteristics of the state, and as such they ought to embody its
virtues.[10] It was precisely their possession of these virtues that legitimated

---

[5] For what follows: D'Arms, 'Heavy drinking and drunkenness', pp. 306–8; also E. Gowers,
The Loaded Table: Representations of Food in Roman Literature (Oxford, 1993), pp. 19–21.

[6] Text: *M. Tullii Ciceronis De officiis ad Marcum filium libri tres*, ed. O. Heine (Berlin, 1885). A helpful
study of the *De officiis* may be found in *Cicero: On Duties*, ed. M. T. Griffin and E. M. Atkins
(Cambridge, 1991), esp. pp. xxi–xxviii.

[7] Cicero, *De officiis* 1.11 and 96 (differences between men and beasts); and 1.93–5 (relationship of
decorum to *honestas*).

[8] Cicero, *De officiis* 1.11; see Aulus Gellius, *Noctes Atticae*, 19.2 in *A. Gellii Noctes Atticae*, ed. P. K.
Marshall (2 vols., Oxford, 1968).

[9] Thus the implications of Cicero, *De officiis* 1.92 discussing the acquisition and disposal of wealth.

[10] Explicitly at Cicero, *De officiis* 1.124: *est igitur proprium munus magistratus intellegere se gerere personam
ciuitatis debereque eius dignitatem et decus sustinere.*

their hold on power; consequently, to compromise these values by suc-
cumbing to base passions would have had the effect of undermining a
statesman's authority.[11]

The idea that a statesman should embody the virtues of the state
was given a new focus with the advent of the Augustan principate:
now it was the emperor, above all others, who should personify political *decorum*.[12] Inscriptions and coin legends disseminated this message of imperial virtue throughout Italy and the provinces, advertising
the emperor as the upholder of personal and political rectitude.[13] The
force of this association was apparent from the outset in the character of
Augustus' moral reforms, which explicitly sought to undo the excesses
of the late Republic.[14] Moreover, the identification of emperors from
Augustus onwards with qualities such as *clementia*, *libertas* and *moderatio*
advertised not only their adherence to ancestral values, but also their
devotion to good government in keeping with the rules of *decorum*, as
well as with the expectations of their subjects.[15] In this system, any emperor who did not show self-control was considered to be deficient in
imperial virtues. This was precisely the point of the damning portrait of
the emperor Claudius painted in Seneca's satire, the *Apocolocyntosis*: not
only does the Claudius presented there explicitly lack certain virtues, he
also possesses an abundance of manifest vices.[16]

These ideas continued to prevail in the late empire. For example, incidents of extreme rage – such as Theodosius I's massacre of civilians at
Thessalonica in 390 – still required ostentatious displays of *clementia* and
moderatio to calm the uneasiness of the emperor's subjects.[17] Lapses into
anger, after all, suggested a bestial nature quite unbecoming in a civilised

---

[11] See C. Edwards, *The Politics of Immorality in Ancient Rome* (Cambridge, 1993), pp. 196–7, esp. p. 197:
'Self-control legitimated the power of the elite in a way that wealth alone could never do.'

[12] A. Wallace-Hadrill, '*Civilis Princeps*: between citizen and king', *Journal of Roman Studies* 72 (1982),
pp. 32–48; see also his *Suetonius: The Scholar and his Caesars* (London, 1983), pp. 142–74. For the
Carolingian elaboration on this theme, see Innes, below, pp. 137–42.

[13] The exhaustive treatment of this ideological interrelationship is J. R. Fears, 'The cult of the
virtues and Roman imperial ideology', *ANRW* 2.17.2 (1981), pp. 827–948.

[14] See most recently K. Galinsky, *Augustan Culture* (Princeton, 1996), esp. pp. 80–90, 128–40.

[15] For a comprehensive survey of the *virtutes* with which emperors associated themselves: Fears,
'Cult of the virtues', pp. 889–948. For the expectations of subjects: S. M. Braund, 'Praise and
protreptic in early imperial panegyric: Cicero, Seneca, Pliny', in *The Propaganda of Power: The Role
of Panegyric in Late Antiquity*, ed. M. Whitby (Leiden, 1998), pp. 53–76, esp. pp. 65–74.

[16] S. M. Braund, 'Paradigms of power: Roman emperors in Roman satire', in *Humour and History*,
ed. K. Cameron (Oxford, 1993), pp. 56–69, esp. pp. 62–8; cf. *Seneca: Apocolocyntosis*, ed. P. T. Eden
(Cambridge, 1984), pp. 8–12.

[17] P. Brown, *Power and Persuasion in Late Antiquity* (Madison, MI, 1992), pp. 48–61 (on anger and
deportment), and pp. 109–13 (on Theodosius).

man, hinting that he was descending to the level of a barbarian.[18] Ammianus Marcellinus, writing at the end of the fourth century, was critical of the excessive and unpredictable behaviour of Valentinian I (western Augustus, 364–75).[19] The emperor's short temper showed, so Ammianus complained, that 'he had surely forgotten that rulers ought to avoid all excesses [*omnia nimia*], just as if they were precipitous cliffs'.[20] Valentinian was no heavy drinker (as, indeed, Ammianus points out),[21] but a propensity to drunkenness would have made such losses of self-control altogether more likely. Elsewhere in his history, Ammianus described the fabled bibulousness of the Gauls in precisely these terms: among this race, he remarks, 'the senses are weakened by continual intoxication, which in Cato's view is a voluntary kind of madness [*furoris uoluntarium speciem*]'.[22] Here Ammianus is picking up on the common assertion that drunkenness loosened all those restraints by which vices might be held in check.[23] In other words, the dangers posed by drunkenness were precisely those posed by a lack of *decorum*. Any emperor who, like Galerius or Severus, was an *ebriosus* did not – indeed, could not – embody these virtues as he should. Rather, a drunken emperor was one whose vices lacked restraint, and who was susceptible, therefore, to extreme acts of bestial and barbaric wickedness.

The Roman polemical tradition had long drawn a connection between private immorality and public disgrace. Just as virtues could provide material for praise, so vice could be seized upon for the purposes of invective.[24] In terms of drunkenness, Cicero himself exploited the

---

[18] T. E. J. Wiedemann, 'Between men and beasts: barbarians in Ammianus Marcellinus', in *Past Perspectives: Studies in Greek and Roman Historical Writing*, ed. I Moxon, J. D. Smart and A. J. Woodman (Cambridge, 1986), pp. 189–201; see R. C. Blockley, *Ammianus Marcellinus: A Study of his Historiography and Political Thought* (Brussels, 1975), pp. 183–4. See also Halsall, below, pp. 91–3.

[19] M. Humphries, '*Nec metu nec adulandi foeditate constricta*: the image of Valentinian I from Symmachus to Ammianus', in *The Late Roman World and its Historian: Interpreting Ammianus Marcellinus*, ed. J. W. Drijvers and E. D. Hunt (London, 1999), pp. 117–26. For Valentinian's murderous sense of humour, see Shanzer, above, pp. 33–4.

[20] Amm. Marc. 30.8.2. On Ammianus' moral universe, see esp. R. Seager, *Ammianus Marcellinus: Seven Studies in his Language and Thought* (Columbia, NY, 1986).

[21] Amm. Marc. 30.9.2.

[22] Amm. Marc. 15.12.4, a relatively common trope: M. B. Lançon, '*Vinolentia*: l'ivrognerie en Gaule à le fin de l'Antiquité d'après les sources littéraires', in *Archéologie de la vigne et du vin (Caesarodunum 24)* (Paris, 1990), pp. 155–61.

[23] Eloquently expressed by the younger Seneca in his essay on drunkenness: '*Omne uitium ebrietas et incendit et detegit, obstantem malis conatibus uerecundiam remouet*' in *Epistulae Morales*, 83.19, ed. L. D. Reynolds (2 vols., Oxford, 1965), vol. I, pp. 278–84.

[24] The point is made most clearly by Quintilian, *Institutio Oratoria* 3.7.15 and 19, in *Quintilian: Institutionis oratoriae libri duodecim*, ed. M. Winterbottom (2 vols., Oxford, 1970).

opportunities quite mercilessly in his invectives against Mark Antony. In his second *Philippic*, for example, Cicero remarks that Antony's excessive drinking at a friend's wedding party would have been bad enough as a private vice; what made it worse, however, was that the morning after, when he was addressing the Roman assembly, he vomited all over himself and the platform from which he was speaking.[25] For vituperative purposes, then, it was easy to draw a connection between private drinking and allegations of public incapacity, and when applied to a character like Antony, it impugned the validity of his political authority. This was a moral paradigm destined to have a long history: at the very end of antiquity, a collection of moral exempla from Gaul includes the reproof from a father to his drunken son that 'A man who advises others ought to be able to control himself.'[26] As for emperors, Ammianus had noted that Valentinian I's short-lived predecessor Jovian (Augustus, 363–4) had been a glutton, too fond of wine and sex – but the historian hoped that Jovian, in recognition of his imperial status, would have abandoned such vices had he ruled for longer.[27] Moreover, such condemnations could provide opportunities for scathing humour. Cicero's account of Antony's vices, including his heavy drinking, seems to have been constructed quite deliberately to provoke laughter by appealing to certain comic archetypes.[28] Indeed, in his treatise on oratorical technique, Cicero recommended the polemical use of humour to diminish an opponent in the eyes of the audience.[29] In particular, he designated whatever was morally reprehensible (*turpitudo*) as a target for humorous invective.[30] By directing attacks on such instances of deviant behaviour, humour could be used to reinforce a polemicist's ideal of the social order.[31] Accusations of drunkenness, then, had the effect of making their targets appear at once ridiculous and loathsome.

---

[25] Cicero, *Philippica* 2.63: '*tantum uini in Hippiae nuptiis exhauseras, ut tibi necesse in populi Romani conspectu uomere postridie*'. in *M. Tulli Ciceronis Orationes*, ed. A. C. Clark (2nd edn, 6 vols., Oxford, 1901–18), vol. II, pp. 109–55. For commentary: Edwards, *Politics of Immorality*, pp. 190–5.

[26] A. C. Dionisotti, 'From Ausonius' schooldays? A schoolbook and its relatives', *JRS* 72 (1982), pp. 83–125, at p. 103, lines 66–7.

[27] Amm. Marc. 25.10.15.

[28] L. A. Sussman, 'Antony as *Miles Gloriosus* in Cicero's *Second Philippic*', *Scholia* 3 (1994), pp. 53–83, esp. pp. 79–80 on Antony's drunkenness.

[29] Cicero, *De oratore* 2.336 (see 2.216), in Cicero, *De oratore*, ed. K. W. Pederit, revised O. Harnecker (3 vols., Leipzig, 1889), vol. II. For other instances of Ciceronian humour, cf. K. A. Geffcken, *Comedy in the Pro Caelio* (Leiden, 1973).

[30] Cicero, *De oratore* 2.236. Ugliness (*deformitas*) was also fair game, since it would have provided an outward manifestation of inner baseness: T. S. Barton, *Power and Knowledge: Astrology, Physiognomics, and Medicine under the Roman Empire* (Ann Arbor, MI, 1994), pp. 95–131, esp. pp. 110–15.

[31] See A. Corbeill, *Controlling Laughter: Political Humor in the Late Roman Republic* (Princeton, 1996), p. 6.

This was precisely the strategy employed by the anonymous author of the *Origo Constantini imperatoris* when he asserted that Galerius and Severus were heavy drinkers. By ridiculing them as repositories of vice when, as emperors, they ought to have been paragons of virtue, he sought to impugn the very legitimacy of their tenure of the throne. One can begin now to appreciate why this author should have claimed that Severus was a friend of Galerius because he was an *ebriosus*. This was a judgement on the moral character of the two emperors and, by extension, of their régimes. In similar fashion, the Christian rhetor Lactantius, author of the vitriolic pamphlet *De mortibus persecutorum* (on the deaths of the persecutors), explains how Diocletian (Galerius' predecessor) and his co-emperor Maximian were drawn together: 'Maximian was not unlike Diocletian; for they could not have joined in such faithful friendship had not the one mind, the same way of thinking, as well as equal resolve and identical opinion been found in them both.'[32] Yet this was a meeting of minds of the worst possible kind, since Lactantius portrays both Diocletian and Maximian as men guilty of the most atrocious breaches of *decorum*. Diocletian was a man of 'insatiable greed', while Maximian's extraordinary appetites extended to sexual excesses with men and women alike.[33] This is precisely how the author of the *Origo* made the association between Galerius and Severus hinge upon their fondness for drink: like Diocletian and Maximian, they were men drawn together by a shared taste for debauchery.[34]

The effect of such imagery is driven home by the stark contrast that Lactantius draws between the persecutors and their Christian adversaries. A glimmer of the *Origo*'s drunken Galerius can be seen in Lactantius' characterisation of that emperor's mother. She is portrayed as a semi-barbarian Pied Piper, leading her neighbours down the road of debauchery and excess. Lactantius remarks how she was 'an extremely superstitious woman who worshipped the gods of the mountains [*deorum montium cultrix*]', in whose honour 'she held sacrificial feasts almost daily, and gave banquets for her neighbours'.[35] How different were the local

---

[32] Lactantius, *De mortibus persecutorum* [*DMP*] 8.1, in *Lactantius: De Mortibus Persecutorum*, ed. and trans. J. L. Creed (Oxford, 1984).

[33] Lactantius, *DMP* 7.5 (on Diocletian) and 8.5 (on Maximian).

[34] The opposite was also held to be true: according to Aurelius Victor, *Caesares* 41.2, in *Aurelius Victor: Livre des Césars*, ed. and trans. P. Dufrraigne (Paris, 1975), Constantine and Licinius failed to secure a lasting alliance *ob diuersos mores*. For associations according to similar virtues, see, esp. R. Rees, 'The private lives of public figures in Latin prose panegyric', in *Propaganda of Power*, ed. Whitby, pp. 77–101.

[35] Lactantius, *DMP* 11.1. It is probable that Lactantius' assertion that she was a *deorum montium cultrix* was intended to portray her as a woman outside the boundaries of civilised urban society, and

Christians who refused to succumb to such temptations, and who, while these pagan festivities were in full swing, would devote themselves to fasting and prayer.[36] But Lactantius' most successful deployment of such rhetoric is used to extol Constantine's virtues. When the time comes, at the abdication of Diocletian and Maximian, to choose new Caesars to join the tetrarchy, Constantine would seem to embody all those qualities most needed in an emperor. He was:

> a young man of the greatest integrity, and the most deserving of imperial rank, whose remarkable physical presence, together with his upright habits [*decoru habitu*], military industry, moral probity [*probis moribus*] and incomparable affability, meant that he was loved by all the troops, as well as being favoured by the citizens.[37]

In appalling counterpoint to this paragon of excellence stands the character of Severus, the man chosen as Caesar in Constantine's stead. Like the author of the *Origo*, Lactantius presents him as an *ebriosus*, who drinks so heavily that for him 'night is as day and day is as night'.[38]

CONSTRUCTED DRINKING

So far we have seen the enemies of Constantine presented as men given over to excess, and that this is frequently symbolised by their propensity to drunkenness. One might suspect that this is a partisan perspective reflecting the prejudices of pro-Constantinian sources, especially when Constantine himself emerges, as he does in Lactantius, as a model of *decorum*. Suspicions ought to be aroused further by reflecting on the significance attached to drinking in the Roman literature of praise and invective. Furthermore, in late antiquity, as in earlier periods of Roman history, the rituals of drinking assumed enormous social importance, particularly in the lives of the élite. 'Drinking', as Mary Douglas has noted, 'is essentially a social act, performed in a recognized social context', and that in most societies there are 'rules about where, when, and what to

---

hence a suitable mother for the bestial, barbaric monster that was Galerius (cf. *DMP* 9.2). The trope has a lengthy pedigree; see, amongst others, R. Buxton, *Imaginary Greece: The Contexts of Mythology* (Cambridge, 1994), pp. 88–92; E. Dench, *From Barbarians to New Men: Greek, Roman, and Modern Perceptions of Peoples from the Central Apennines* (Oxford, 1995), esp. pp. 126–9 and 166–73; and (of course) F. Braudel, *The Mediterranean and the Mediterranean World in the Age of Philip the Second* (2 vols., London, 1972), vol. I, pp. 35–8.

[36] Lactantius, *DMP* 11.1.   [37] Lactantius, *DMP* 18.10.

[38] Lactantius, *DMP* 18.12. The image is an old one – see Cicero, *De finibus* 2.23: '*qui solem, ut aiunt, nec occidentem umquam uiderint nec orientem*', in M. *Tullius Cicero: De finibus bonorum et malorum*, ed. and trans. H. Rackham (Cambridge, MA, 1931).

drink, and in whose company'.[39] Recent work on drinking in antiquity has stressed similar patterns.[40] When Cicero portrayed Antony spewing all over himself and the speaker's platform, he did so to an audience who accepted that drinking belonged to the elaborate social rituals of aristocratic society, whether at banquets (*conuiuia*, *epulae*) or at religious celebrations (such as Saturnalia). Yet the same audience accepted that, for the purposes of political ridicule, heavy drinkers such as Antony could be portrayed as having breached the rules that circumscribed social drinking.[41] So, too, the accusations of drunkenness levelled against Constantine's enemies were made against a background where social drinking remained a norm for the social élite. Sumptuously appointed dining rooms (*triclinia*) in villas and townhouses throughout the empire show in spectacular fashion how such structured drinking rituals persisted into late antiquity.[42]

Drunkenness, like any value-laden concept, was elastic, and could be manipulated to suit particular polemical contexts. The portrayal of Constantine's enemies as illegitimate debauchees was a finely modelled one, exploiting the worst possible interpretations of specific characteristics. For example, both Lactantius and the ecclesiastical historian Eusebius of Caesarea describe Galerius' immense physique as a grotesque manifestation of his moral depravity. Lactantius is particularly eloquent on this score, describing how the emperor's 'body imitated his morals [*corpus moribus congruens*]', with his 'vast fleshy expanses extended and bloated to horrendous immensity'.[43] Lactantius prefaces this description of Galerius' obesity with a sketch of the fundamental flaws in the emperor's character: he was a man of bestial and barbaric nature, possessed of a savageness alien to Roman ways.[44] Hence Galerius'

---

[39] M. Douglas, 'A distinctive anthropological perspective', in *Constructive Drinking*, ed. Douglas, pp. 3–15, at p. 4. For other early medieval assumptions about proper drinking, see Shanzer, above, pp. 42–4.

[40] For classical Greek drinking, not considered here, see the lively appraisal of J. N. Davidson, *Courtesans and Fishcakes: The Consuming Passions of Classical Athens* (London, 1997), pp. 36–69.

[41] D'Arms, 'Heavy drinking and drunkenness', esp. pp. 307–8; see also Edwards, *Politics of Immorality*, pp. 198–204.

[42] L. Bek, '*Quaestiones conuiuiales*: the idea of the triclinium and the staging of convivial ceremony from Rome to Byzantium', *Analecta Romana Instituti Danici* 12 (1983), pp. 81–107; K. M. D. Dunbabin, 'Scenes from the Roman *convivium*', in *In Vino Veritas*, ed. Murray and Tecusan, pp. 252–65; S. P. Ellis, 'Power, architecture, and decor: how the late Roman aristocrat appeared to his guests', in *Roman Art in the Private Sphere*, ed. E. K. Gazda (Ann Arbor, MI, 1991), pp. 117–34.

[43] Lactantius, *DMP* 9.3; cf. Eusebius, *Historia Ecclesiastica* [*HE*] 8.16.4, in *Eusebius Werke II, Die Kirchengeschichte*, vol. II, ed. E. Schwartz (Leipzig, 1908).

[44] Lactantius, *DMP* 9.2: '*Inerat huic bestiae naturalis barbaries, efferitas a Romano sanguine aliena*'. See n. 35, above, for the relationship of barbarity to bestiality. For Byzantine linkage of physical deformity with the inability to rule legitimately, see Haldon, above, pp. 65–6.

horrifying girth symbolised not only his personal depravity; it was, above all, an outward sign of his unsuitability to the position of emperor.

Yet this was not the only possible interpretation of Galerius' physique, in that corpulence could be considered as a sign of good qualities in an emperor. Certain portraits that have been identified as Constantine's erstwhile ally, the eastern Augustus Licinius (308–24), show him as fat-faced and heavy jowled, with a jaunty smile playing across his lips. This image may have been designed to emphasise Licinius' energy, strength and power, as well as his jovial amenability.[45] So the corpulence that Lactantius and Eusebius interpreted as an outward sign of Galerius' inner depravity was used by Licinius to assert his imperial virtues. On the face of it, this seems a startling contradiction, but it accords well with ancient physiognomical practice. It was not corpulence itself that was bad so much as the quality of the expansive flesh: if it was solid, thick and dry, it could represent power and strength; but if it was soft, flabby and moist, then it reflected inner depravity.[46]

In time, however, Licinius too was excoriated as a villain and, in typical fashion, the traits that he had once stressed as signs of his virtue were now twisted to become symbols of his wickedness. While Eusebius would condemn him in rather stock fashion for his depraved lust,[47] the *History of Constantine* by the Athenian author Praxagoras – now lost, and known only though a Byzantine summary – hit rather closer to the heart of Licinius' own image, making an issue of how he had 'masked his cruelty beneath a kindly appearance' (ἔκρυπτε... τὴν ὠμότητα φιλανθρωπίας προσχήματι).[48] So much for the jaunty smile shown in Licinius' portraits: if for Licinius it was representative of his benevolence, in Praxagoras' hands it became an emblem of a tyrant's cruel dissimulation.[49] As I show below, this malleability of imperial public images in the hands of polemicists was a fate which was to befall even Constantine himself, as disgruntled

---

[45] R. R. R. Smith, 'The public image of Licinius I: portrait sculpture and imperial ideology in the early fourth century', *JRS* 87 (1997), pp. 170–202, esp. pp. 191–3. For Carolingian rulers' use of the smile, see Innes, below, pp. 137–42.

[46] See, for example, Pseudo-Aristotle, *Physiognōmonika* 807A–B, also 813B, in *Aristotle: Minor Works*, ed. and trans. W. S. Hett (Cambridge, MA, 1936), pp. 84–137. See Barton, *Power and Knowledge*, p. 111, for similar examples. See more generally, M. W. Gleason, *Making Men: Sophists and Self-representation in Ancient Rome* (Princeton, 1995), esp. pp. 55–81.

[47] Eusebius, *HE* 10.8.5–9.

[48] Photius, *Bibliotheca* [*Bibl.*] codex 62, *Fragmente der griechischen Historiker*, ed. F. Jacoby (Leiden, 1923–), 219. *Photius: Bibliotheca*, ed. and trans. R. Henry (1959); see Lieu and Montserrat, *From Constantine to Julian*, pp. 7–9.

[49] Cf. Pseudo-Aristotle, *Physiognōmonika*, 805A: 'the brave man [ἀνδρεῖος] and the shameful man [ἀναιδής] have the same facial expression'.

pagan authors after the mid-fourth century began to look to him as
the source of the empire's ills. Once again, images of drunkenness were
evoked, this time to ridicule the emperor whom Lactantius had upheld
as the embodiment of imperial *decorum*.

THE EXCESSES OF CONSTANTINE

The most complete pagan narrative of Constantine's reign is contained in the late fifth-century *New History* by Zosimus. In this account,
Constantine is described as a bastard son of a harlot; a man whose moral
laxity led him to weaken the empire's defences; and a coward whose only
reason for converting to Christianity was to gain absolution for his murder of his son Crispus and the empress Fausta.[50] According to the ninth-
century Byzantine patriarch and bibliophile Photius, Zosimus' narrative
was essentially plagiarised from the earlier (and now fragmentary) *History
after Dexippus*, written by the militant pagan Eunapius of Sardis in the early
fifth century.[51] Eunapius' *History*, however, has not survived the censor-
ship of Byzantine editors, who were shocked by its hostile assessments
of Christian emperors, especially Constantine.[52] Indeed, even within his
own lifetime, Eunapius had been forced to revise the work and excise
from it many of his most pungent anti-Christian jibes.[53]

Very little about Constantine is to be found in the scraps of Eunapius'
History that have come down to us, but a glimpse of what it might
have said can be gleaned from his extant work on the *Vitae Sophistarum*
(Lives of the philosophers and Sophists). In the *Vitae*, Constantine is portrayed as a venal and inept emperor who, among many other crimes,
allows himself to be seduced by his wicked praetorian prefect, Ablabius,
into condemning to death the pagan sage Sopater.[54] Sopater himself
is likened by Eunapius to the classical philosopher Socrates, whom the
Athenians considered the 'walking image of wisdom', and whom they

---

[50] Zosimus, *Historia Nova*, 2.8.2 (low birth); 2.29.2–5 (conversion); 2.32–4 (weakening the empire),
in *Zosimus: Historia Nova*, ed. L. Mendelssohn (Leipzig, 1887).

[51] Photius, *Bibl.* codex 98. Of course, Photius' assertion is not accurate for all of Zosimus' history,
but it holds good for the Constantinian period.

[52] The Byzantine lexicon known as the *Suda* remarks that 'Eunapius wrote rubbish about him':
Eunapius, fr. 9.1 in *The Fragmentary Classicizing Historians of the Later Roman Empire*, ed. and trans.
R. C. Blockley (Liverpool, 1981).

[53] Photius, *Bibl.* codex 77.

[54] Eunapius, *Vitae Sophistarum* [*VS*] 464, in *Philostratus and Eunapius: The Lives of the Sophists*, ed. and
trans. W. C. Wright (Cambridge, MA, 1921), pp. 342–565. For commentary, R. J. Penella, *Greek
Philosophers and Sophists in the Fourth Century AD: Studies in Eunapius of Sardis* (Leeds, 1990), pp. 52–3,
126–7 and 129–30.

should not have condemned to death had they not been corrupted by drunkenness, madness and licence at the festival of Dionysus, the god of wine.[55] So, too, Sopater's condemnation was the product of a régime blighted by drunkenness. First, Eunapius describes in bleak terms how the new capital of the empire, Constantinople, was filled with 'the intoxicated multitude [τὸν μεθύοντα . . . δῆμον] that Constantine had transported to Byzantium by emptying other cities . . . because he loved to be applauded in the theatres by men overwhelmed by debauchery [παραβλυζόντων κραιπάλης ἀνθρώπων].[56] Later on, when a shortage of grain supplies threatened famine on the city, Constantine was faced by an abrupt cessation of this drunken approval (σπάνις ἦν τοῦ μεθύοντος ἐπαίνου). The emperor panicked, and Ablabius seized this opportunity to persuade Constantine that Sopater had induced the crisis. The sage had cast a magic spell, so Ablabius claimed, which had obstructed the winds that brought the grain ships to Constantinople. It was enough to gain Sopater's condemnation.[57] Eunapius uses the drunken crowds of Constantinople as a device to undermine the legitimacy of Constantine's rule. The emperor's deplorable susceptibility to drunken adulation robbed him of the one man who by reasoned argument could have checked his intemperate policies. In the end, however, Constantine was left at the mercy of the dissipated Ablabius, who, far from influencing the emperor with reason, controlled him just as a demagogue might an unruly mob.[58] The implication is clear. Just as the drunkenness of the Athenians had prompted them to murder Socrates and so hasten the decline of their city and of Hellas as a whole,[59] so Constantine's pathetic vulnerability to the whims of his drunken subjects led him to condemn Sopater, and so undermine the security of the Roman Empire.

While Eunapius was particularly outspoken in his insinuations against Constantine's probity, he was not the first to deploy images of debauchery to deride the Christian emperor's reputation. That distinction went to the man who, because of his energetic efforts to restore paganism, seems to have been the hero of Eunapius' *History*: the emperor Julian (361–3).

---

[55] Eunapius, *VS* 462.   [56] Ibid.   [57] Ibid. 463.

[58] Contrast ibid. 462 on Sopater and 464 on Ablabius. A famous fragment of Eunapius' *History* directs a similar accusation against others who, like Constantine, put their faith in Christianity. Describing paintings set up at Rome, which showed the hand of God securing an imperial victory over the barbarians, he complained that such scenes were 'the rubbish of painters in their cups' (κωθωνιζομένων γραφέων φλήναφος): (Eunapius, fr. 68 Blockley = *Fragmenta Historicorum Graecorum*, ed. C. Müller (Paris, 1841–70), fr. 78).

[59] Thus Eunapius *VS* 462.

Among his surviving works is that commonly known as the *Caesares* (but actually entitled the *Symposion* or *Kronia*), a satire composed at Antioch in 362, which describes a banquet of the gods at which various Roman emperors, together with Julius Caesar and Alexander the Great, are called upon to compete against each other in virtue.[60] Because the gods also want to be amused by this contest, Zeus summons one further emperor to act as a comic stooge during the debates. The man chosen for this role is Constantine, and his efforts to defend his reputation are ridiculed at every turn.[61] That Constantine is Zeus' choice for this ludicrous spectacle has less to do with his cowardly qualities – although he is said to prefer bribing barbarians to fighting them – than with his devotion to a life of pleasure and enjoyment.[62] At the end, when the gods award the prize for virtue to Marcus Aurelius (no surprise there![63]), they command the defeated contestants to choose particular gods as guardians and guides.[64] This provides an opportunity to poke fun not just at Constantine, but at Christianity, too.[65] When the pathetic figure of Constantine cannot find any god whose morals match his own, he ends up running after Tryphē, the personification of decadence.[66] She takes pity on him, and leads him off to her friend Asōtia, the personification of dissoluteness. Constantine discovers that Asōtia is already embracing a partner of her own, none other than Jesus Christ, who invites all manner of reprobates to come to him and be washed with water – an obvious parody of baptism. At once, Constantine realises that this is the place for him.[67]

The function of this scathing satire is not difficult to divine. Although he was himself a scion of the Constantinian house, he had little affection for Constantine himself. After all, Constantine had shown by his conversion to Christianity that he was an enemy of the pagan gods whose worship Julian now sought to restore. By ridiculing Constantine and his religion, Julian plainly attacked his legitimacy as emperor. But equally,

---

[60] The major study is G. W. Bowersock, 'The emperor Julian on his predecessors', *Yale Classical Studies* 27 (1982), pp. 159–72. Bowersock, whose approach to the work is at times rather precious, refuses to find the work in the least bit funny, but his reserve has been challenged in a recent study of Julian's literary oeuvre: R. Smith, *Julian's Gods: Religion and Philosophy in the Thought and Action of Julian the Apostate* (London, 1991), pp. 13–14.

[61] Julian, *Caesares* 328D–329D and 335A–B, in *The Works of the Emperor Julian*, ed. and trans. W. C. Wright (3 vols., Cambridge, MA, 1913), vol. II, pp. 344–415.

[62] Julian, *Caesares* 317D; see also 329A.

[63] For Julian's admiration of Marcus: Smith, *Julian's Gods*, p. 42.

[64] Julian, *Caesares* 335C–D.

[65] See Bowersock, 'Julian on his predecessors', pp. 163–4.

[66] On *tryphē*, see Dench, *From Barbarians to New Men*, pp. 12 and 58–9.

[67] Julian, *Caesares* 336A–B.

by doing so, Julian risked undermining his own position as a descendant of Constantine, so he needed to find some way of rehabilitating the family's reputation. This he managed to achieve by emphasising the virtues of Claudius II (268–70), the emperor claimed to have been the progenitor of the house of Constantine, and of Constantius I (305–6), Constantine's father.[68] In the context of the satire, the ruse works, and it is only out of regard for such distinguished ancestors that the family is not utterly damned.[69] Of course, Julian stops short of making any explicit accusation of drunkenness against Constantine, but his emphasis on the first Christian emperor's addiction to pleasure and debauchery leaves the reader in no doubt as to Julian's belief in Constantine's moral degeneracy.[70] From here it was a comparatively small step for Eunapius to take when he embellished his account of Constantine's reign with images of drunkenness.

CONCLUSION

The image of Constantine as a slave to pleasure and debauchery is a disconcerting one to those versed in a Christian tradition that has tended to emphasise his virtues. It is a reminder, however, that the image of the emperor which has been handed on to posterity was produced in a polemical context, where the fine detail of what Constantine's achievements had been often counted for less than his reputation as religious innovator.[71] Lactantius, a Christian, had extolled Constantine as the embodiment of imperial *decorum*; the author of the *Origo* had implied it; both had buttressed the image by lampooning Constantine's enemies as debauchees, especially in terms of their immoderate drinking. These were caricatures, of course, but their deployment sought to make their authors' arguments more persuasive. In so doing, Lactantius and the anonymous author of the *Origo* appealed to archetypes of imperial behaviour, which taught that bad emperors were characterised by a propensity to drink heavily, an indulgence that made it difficult, indeed impossible, to control base passions as a good emperor should. It

[68] *Caesares* 313D; see Bowersock, 'Julian on his predecessors', p. 163 and nn. 27–9.
[69] Julian, *Caesares* 336B: διὰ τὸν Κλαύδιον καὶ Κωνστάντιον.
[70] See Gowers, *The Loaded Table*, pp. 15 and 18, for the moral topography to which Julian's portrait of Constantine appeals.
[71] There is now a large literature on this topic, for example: G. Fowden, 'Constantine's porphyry column: the earliest literary allusion', *JRS* 81 (1991), pp. 119–31; also his 'The last days of Constantine: oppositional versions and their influence', *JRS* 84 (1994), pp. 146–70; M. Humphries, '*In nomine patris*: Constantine the Great and Constantius II in Christological polemic', *Historia* 46 (1997), pp. 448–64; and the various essays in *New Constantines*, ed. P. Magdalino (Aldershot, 1994).

is hardly surprising, then, that those who wrote to defend Constantine and his religious beliefs should have chosen to portray his enemies as villainous reprobates with a fondness for booze. The picture could so easily have been different, and in the works of Julian, Eunapius and Zosimus we catch a glimpse of an opposing perspective. When mounting Christian intolerance undermined the social and cosmic order that had been upheld by devotion to Rome's ancestral gods, defensive pagans were forced to reassess the role in this process played by Constantine. In their turn, pagan zealots appealed to the same archetypes of drunkenness and illegitimacy as the pro-Constantinian sources had done previously. The images of emperors as good or bad men were largely contingent upon the aims of a particular polemicist. When emperors were labelled as heavy drinkers, or their reigns were stigmatised as being pervaded by a drunken atmosphere, these should not be mistaken for accounts of actual bibulousness. Rather, they served to locate those emperors and their régimes in the darkest and most foetid corners of the moral landscape of late antiquity.[72]

[72] This paper is revised from the version delivered in Leeds. Whatever virtues it may possess owe much to the perceptive criticisms of Guy Halsall (London), Susan Rosser (Manchester) and Roger Rees (Edinburgh), as well as those who participated in the discussion after its delivery at the conference. My thanks also to Christopher Kelly (Cambridge), who, apropos other matters, has encouraged me to pursue this enquiry into the parallels and interpenetrations between praise and invective. The fault for all remaining vices, however, rests solely with me.

CHAPTER 4

Funny foreigners: laughing with the barbarians in late antiquity

Guy Halsall

INCONGRUITY: THE HUMOUR OF THE INAPPROPRIATE

In the 1980s and 1990s, the cartoons of Gary Larson became very popular on both sides of the Atlantic; indeed Larson's work, 'The Far Side', has a special relevance to early medievalists, as Vikings were a favourite topic.[1] One thing that makes Larson's cartoons amusing is his knack of setting familiar things in inappropriate settings or circumstances. The people (or animals, or amoebas) are rarely saying or doing anything – in itself – especially amusing. What makes us laugh is, simply enough, the idea of serious, intellectually brilliant nuclear physicists playing school-yard pranks on each other, cows playing 'knock on the door and run' with the farmer, and so on. Similarly, in the earlier 1990s in Britain, whilst Larson's archaeological cartoons were being employed in the journal *Antiquity*, a startling, runaway success was scored by Rob Newman and David Baddiel's 'History Today' sketches. Here, two old Oxbridge historians in suits, ostensibly debating the origins of the Crimean War, rapidly ended up trading the sorts of insult that we associate with primary-school days. The humour was especially enhanced when this was sprinkled with phrases of academic language: 'I am familiar with her work.' The dialogue itself was, mostly, no funnier than if it had indeed been spoken by two eight-year-olds in a playground. What made it funny was *who* was speaking it.

Incongruity has always been central to humour theory. Much humour works by constructing a set of expectations that are then juxtaposed with an unexpected conclusion, or by the bringing together of anomalous components into the same event or image. 'Humor may ... depend on the combination in one object or event of attributes or lines of thought that are normally unrelated – incongruous juxtapositions of sights and

---

[1] See, for example, G. Larson, *The Far Side Gallery* (London, 1989). For Larson's own discussion of his work, see G. Larson, *The Prehistory of the Far Side* (London, 1990).

sounds (e.g. somebody well known in fancy dress or playing a role in a play that sharply contrasts with his normal character).'[2] Incongruity, however, presupposes congruity. As a humorous technique, therefore, it must be learnt.[3] This is especially pertinent to the historian of humour. If, as we shall be here, we are concerned less with deciding when something which *we* regard as funny was seen as humorous at the time[4] than with identifying instances which seem humourless today but which may have been funny in the past, we, like the small children analysed by psychologists, are involved in a process of learning codes.

This chapter therefore begins by establishing the code: what antique writers considered congruous in the image of the barbarian. As Jonathan Wilcox has recently argued, 'for the incongruity to seem funny, there must also be a level of humorous appropriateness'.[5] Thus a first case-study explores how the antique image of the barbarian could be used humorously without incongruity. Then, if incongruity is a frequent element of humour, not all incongruity is humorous. It has sometimes been argued that incongruity needs resolution in the form of a punch line or caption to be funny. This notion has been critiqued, however, and the example of Larson's cartoons, or the Newman and Baddiel sketches, underlines this. Here the punch lines or captions are themselves part of the incongruity. I shall sometimes show this below, although there are also instances wherein the incongruity is 'resolved'. It is perhaps more useful to look for 'cues', setting up the anecdote as humorous. This is important. In the sources discussed here, the frame cannot be simply that of genre; overtly comedic genres were few and far between in this period, so that humour had to retreat into genres which could include the comic, and humorous strategies, but were not humorous in themselves.[6] Not all such cues are such that they immediately create a frame that excludes other

---

[2] D. E. Berlyne, 'Humor and its kin', in *The Psychology of Humor: Theoretical Perspectives and Empirical Issues*, ed. J. H. Goldstein and P. E. McGhee (New York, 1972), pp. 43–60, at p. 45. See also Haldon, above, pp. 58–60.

[3] See, for example, the works of Paul E. McGhee: 'Cognitive development and children's comprehension of humor', *Child Development* 42 (1971), pp. 123–38; 'On the cognitive origins of incongruity humor: fantasy assimilation versus reality assimilation', in *The Psychology of Humor*, ed. Goldstein and McGhee, pp. 61–80; 'A model of the origins and early development of incongruity-based humour', in *It's a Funny Thing, Humour*, ed. A. J. Chapman and H. C. Foot (Oxford, 1977), pp. 27–36.

[4] As for example, with H. Magennis, 'A funny thing happened on the way to heaven: humorous incongruity in Old English saints' lives', in *Humour in Anglo-Saxon Literature*, ed. J. Wilcox (Woodbridge, 2000), pp. 137–57, esp. pp. 137–8.

[5] J. Wilcox, 'Introduction', in *Humour in Anglo-Saxon Literature*, ed. Wilcox, pp. 1–10, at p. 4.

[6] See Shanzer, above, pp. 25–47. For cues, see also Balzaretti, below, p. 117.

readings.[7] They do, however, mark out the episode, and especially, on occasion, its resolution, from the main thread of the narrative. The later case-studies below thus explore strategies of inversion. Most examples have been chosen precisely because historians have taken them far more seriously than seems ever to have been intended. That said, I do not think that any of these stories is now, or perhaps ever was, especially hilarious. Most represent learned, witty conceits. Here, especially, I am concerned with the evocation of wry smiles, not belly laughs.

THE FAR SIDE: IMAGES OF THE BARBARIAN

The difference between the civilised man and the barbarian was one of the most crucial binary divisions in classical literature. That the division was more rhetorical than factual is fairly readily apparent, but that in some ways strengthens its role within the writing of the period. In this chapter I concentrate on the differences between Romans and northern barbarians, or occasionally southern barbarians (Moors).[8] One key concept differentiated civilised men from barbarians – freedom. There were two dimensions to this, however: the spatial and the chronological. The barbarians were unfree because they were unable to live according to law and thus could not have true government. As the elder Pliny put it:

In the middle of the earth ... customs are gentle, senses clear, intellects fertile and able to grasp the whole of nature; and they also have governments, which the outer races never have possessed any more than they have ever been subject to the central races, being quite detached and solitary on account of the savagery of the nature which broods over those regions.[9]

Thus there were biological/geographical reasons for the barbarians' inability to live according to lawful government, which went back to the Hippocratic author of *Airs, Waters, Places*. Greek bio-geography put

---

[7] Here I differ from Berlyne, 'Humor and its kin', p. 54.

[8] For useful introductory studies of Graeco-Roman attitudes to the barbarians, see, for example: P. Geary, 'Barbarians and ethnicity', in *Late Antiquity: A Guide to the Postclassical World*, ed. G. Bowersock, P. R. L. Brown and O. Grabar (Cambridge, MA and London, 1999), pp. 107–29; P. Heather, 'The barbarian in late antiquity: image, reality and transformation', in *Construction of Identities in Late Antiquity*, ed. R. Miles (London, 1999), pp. 234–58; W. R. Jones, 'Images of the barbarian in medieval Europe', *Comparative Studies in Sociology and History* 13 (1971), pp. 376–407; G. B. Ladner, 'On Roman attitudes toward barbarians in late antiquity', *Viator* 7 (1976), pp. 1–26; P. Veyne, 'Humanitas: Romans and non-Romans', in *The Romans*, ed. A. Giardina (Chicago, 1993), pp. 342–69; G. Halsall, *Barbarian Migrations and the Roman West* (Cambridge, forthcoming), ch. 2.

[9] Pliny the Elder, *Natural History* 2.80.190, in *Pliny: The Natural History*, vol. II, ed. and trans. H. Rackham (London, 1942).

Greece in the middle of the world and explained the faults of foreigners by reference to their living too far to the east, west, north or south, and the superiority of the Greeks by the fact that they possessed examples of both of any two extremes. By the Roman period, changes had been made. In Roman ethnography or bio-geography, perhaps not surprisingly, the world was seen as more 'banded'. The barbarians' characteristics were explained by their living too close to, or too far from, the sun, with detrimental results for their biological make-up. Roman superiority derived from living mid-way between the two extremes, as the quote from Pliny illustrates.

The Germans, too far from the sun, had their blood drawn down through their body, making them tall, brave but rather stupid.[10] Moors, on the other hand, lived too close to the sun; the blood was drawn to their heads, making them cowardly but cunning. The Germanic barbarian was similar in characteristics to, though wilder than, the Gaul or Celt, to whom he was related.[11] They were numerous and tall (aspects to which I shall return),[12] wild and incautious, obeyed only blind fury and were emboldened by success.[13] They were ferocious, inconstant (another point to which I shall return) and mendacious.[14] Like the Gauls, they were prone to dramatic mood swings and easily discouraged.[15] The barbarians were slaves to their passions, and therefore doubly unfree: their rulers were tyrants rather than proper governments; they had no reason, and so were subject to the tyranny of their emotions.[16] Geographical factors only emphasised this, so that at the ends of the earth lived wild people such as Tacitus' Fenni,[17] with no religion, no government, no proper clothing or houses, and no fire. Beyond people like that came the truly weird and wonderful: man-eaters; amazons; people who could only squeak. These fantasies represent extreme departures from the proper norm of civilised life. Given that military affairs were a key element of classical ethnographic stereotyping, it is also noteworthy that these

---

[10] Pliny, *Natural History* 2.80.189. See also Vegetius, *Epitome* 1.2, in *Vegetius: Epitome of Military Science*, trans. N. P. Milner (2nd edn, Liverpool, 1996).

[11] Strabo, *Geography* 7.1.1–2; 4.4.2, in *The Geography of Strabo*, vol. III, ed. and trans. H. Leonard Jones (London, 1924).

[12] Dio Cassius 38.47.5, in *Dio's Roman History*, vol. III, ed. and trans. E. Cary (London, 1914).

[13] Tacitus, *Histories*, 2.22, 4.23, 4.29, in *Tacitus: Histories and Annals*, trans. C. H. Moore and J. Jackson (4 vols., London, 1925–37).

[14] Velleius Paterculus, *History* 2.118, in *Velleius Paterculus: Compendium of Roman History*, ed. and trans. F. W. Shipley (London, 1924).

[15] Dio Cassius, *Roman History* 38.48.5. See also 38.47.5, where the Germans are reckless and impetuous.

[16] See also Humphries, above, pp. 76–8.

[17] Tacitus, *Germania* 46, in *Tacitus: Germania*, trans. J. B. Rives (Oxford, 1999).

characteristics are very often displayed in accounts of barbarian fighting. Barbarians rush forward with unthinking bravery, displaying reckless but undisciplined courage and ferocity, but if they are stoutly resisted they soon give up and turn to flight. Needless to say, barbarians are typically useless at any 'scientific' warfare such as siege-craft.[18]

The chronological dimension to this was that the Romans were held to have left this state far behind in their past. In Lucretius' *De rerum natura* the earliest Romans are remarkably similar to other writers' descriptions of people living at the ends of the earth.[19] The point where the Romans left this stage behind was when they discovered law. The conceptual dividing line between civilised and barbarous was thus a clear one. The image of the barbarian was, however, rhetorical. It was a floating category, which could be deployed for a number of purposes in, it is worth remembering, dialogue *between Romans*, not between Romans and barbarians. Discourse is not concerned with 'us' being like this whereas 'you' are like that, but with 'us' being (or thinking we ought to be) like this because 'they' are like that. Thus the numerous aspects of the barbarian stereotype could be deployed to make any number of points, simply by virtue of being an Other. This makes it a mistake to discuss supposed 'contradictions' within authors' works in their views of the barbarians, or to try to track their changes in views of the barbarian. The Roman/barbarian dichotomy was always more blurred in reality. The category of the barbarian was, simply enough, in Claude Lévi-Strauss' formula, 'good to think with'. This made it, nevertheless, an important structuring principle, and thus one which played a big part in shaping people's views of how things ought to be. It was, therefore, readily available for rhetorical exaggeration and inversion

OVERTALL, OVERFED AND OVER HERE: SIDONIUS AND THE BURGUNDIANS

A well-known example may illustrate the late antique code concerning the barbarians, and one way in which it could be used humorously: Sidonius Apollinaris' account of having Burgundian soldiers billeted on him.[20] The senator Catullinus had asked Sidonius to compose a poem,

---

[18] For classic statements, see Tacitus, *Histories* 4.23; Cassius Dio, *History*, 56.22.2, in *Dio's Roman History*, vol. VII, ed. and trans. E. Cary (London, 1924). As Vegetius says (*Epitome* 4, Pref.), cities are what first distinguished early man from the beasts, so it is unsurprising that the barbarians should have been considered useless at their capture.

[19] Lucretius, *De rerum natura* 5.925–1090, in *Lucretius: De rerum natura*, ed. and trans. W. H. D. Rouse (London, 1924). At 5.958–9, Lucretius points out that early man did not know law.

[20] Sidonius, *Carmina* 12, in *Sidonius: Poems and Letters*, ed. and trans. W. B. Anderson (2 vols., London, 1936 and 1965).

an epithalamium; Sidonius pleaded his circumstances, with 'crowds' of barbarians living in his house, as an excuse for not complying. Sidonius wheels out all the stock features of the Germanic barbarian. First are his characteristic long hair and his language, two immediate signifiers of barbarism. That there are crowds of these barbarians also draws attention to a Roman ethnographic cliché: the sheer numbers of the northern barbarians. Then Sidonius attempts to acquire the reader's sympathy, by saying that he has to praise the songs of these interlopers, though claiming to do so 'with wry face'. Famously, he describes the 'gluttonous' Burgundians spreading rancid butter on their hair (*infundens acido comam butyro*), emphasising their northern origins: they use butter rather than oil to anoint themselves; something which, to Sidonius' audience, would be fairly amusing in itself. Gluttony is another archetypal barbarian trait, linked to the barbarian's inability to govern his passions.[21]

Then, as the poem's centrepiece, Sidonius puns on another well-known feature of the northern barbarian: his height. 'Do you want me to tell you what wrecks all poetry?' he asks. 'Driven away by barbarian thrumming, the Muse has spurned the six-footed exercise ever since she beheld these seven-foot patrons.' He proceeds to say that, whilst Catullinus' eyes and ears may be happy because, unlike his own, they do not have to bear the sight and sound of the Burgundians, they are nothing like as happy as his nose, which, unlike Sidonius', is spared the reek of the garlic and onions, upon which the barbarians feast at Sidonius' expense. The billeted warriors consume ten breakfasts a day, says Sidonius, revisiting the theme of their gluttony. He then returns to the Burgundians' numbers and height: 'so many and such big giants that not even the kitchens of Alcinous could support them'. Sidonius closes with an intimate joke shared between his reader and himself. Some time previously, he had found himself in trouble when it was suspected that an anonymous but vicious satire upon leading figures at the emperor Majorian's court was his work. The accusation arose when Catullinus was tricked into revealing that he knew and was amused by the satire, thus leading to the supposition that he must have learnt it from his friend Sidonius up in Clermont.[22] Consequently, Sidonius ends by saying that already his muse must be silent 'after only a few jesting hendecasyllables,

---

[21] On the implications of gluttony, see also Humphries, above, pp. 80–4. For Christian humour on the theme of gluttony, see Shanzer, above, pp. 45–6, and for Byzantine variations on this theme, see Haldon, above, p. 59.

[22] Sidonius, *Epistulae* 1.11.3. For the episode, see J. Harries, *Sidonius Apollinaris and the Fall of Rome* (Oxford, 1994), pp. 93–4.

lest anyone call them satire': a clear reference to the hot water into which the two of them had fallen.

Even without the joking conclusion, no one can doubt that Sidonius was intentionally being humorous, even if the humour deployed, for all its allusions, is mostly of a fairly base form, belonging to the same pedigree as racist jokes or jokes about minorities. Humour, however, unifies. Sidonius wants to beg Catullinus' forgiveness for not having written him an epithalamium (it is not the only occasion in Sidonius' oeuvre where he elaborately gets out of having to write something for someone). Thus he uses cruel humour to evince his sympathy, but he also does so by playing upon shared ideas about an out-group: the barbarians.[23] By laughing (if he did so), Catullinus is made complicit.[24] He recognises that he and Sidonius belong together in the same social group. As with many a racist joke, in the context of fifth-century Gaul, these jokes about barbarians were born of insecurity in a changing world.[25] As Rome, as a political unity, collapsed all around them, the Gallic aristocracy responded by stressing the other aspect of Roman identity: culture and learning. Not for nothing was this the golden age of Gallic letter-writing.[26] This cultural identity was deployed increasingly self-consciously in opposition to the 'barbarians' and their supporters who were fast coming to hold the real political and military power in Gaul. In this context, the construct of the barbarian must have become ever more visibly divorced from reality. As many recent studies have shown, many 'barbarians' were as 'Roman' by origin and language as Sidonius' circle.[27] Indeed, some of Sidonius' clique themselves saw which way the wind was blowing and took service with the Burgundian and Gothic kings.[28] Sidonius thus used the trope of the barbarian to draw Catullinus to himself. This was done by targeting

---

[23] Sidonius does exactly the same thing at *Epistulae* 8.3.2, where the rushed nature of the work he has sent to Leo is blamed partly on having to share lodgings with a couple of Gothic women.

[24] '[The joke] will further bribe the hearer with its yield of pleasure into taking sides with us without any very close investigation': S. Freud, *The Standard Edition of the Complete Works of Sigmund Freud*, vol. VIII, *Jokes and their Relation to the Unconscious*, ed. J. Strachey, with A. Freud, A. Strachey, A. Tyson and A. Richards (London, 1960), p. 103.

[25] See, e.g., D. Chiaro, *The Language of Jokes: Analysing Verbal Play* (London, 1992), p. 8. See also H. Martineau, 'A model of the social functions of humor', in *The Psychology of Humor*, ed. Goldstein and McGhee, pp. 101–25, at p. 119.

[26] I. N. Wood, 'Continuity and calamity; the constraints of literary models', in *Fifth-century Gaul: A Crisis of Identity?* ed. J. Drinkwater and H. Elton (Cambridge, 1992), pp. 9–18; also his *The Merovingian Kingdoms, 450–751* (London, 1994), pp. 20–2; R. Mathisen, *Roman Aristocrats in Barbarian Gaul: Strategies for Survival in an Age of Transition* (Austin, TX, 1993).

[27] See, especially, P. Amory, 'Names, ethnicity and community in fifth- and sixth-century Burgundy', *Viator* 25 (1994), pp. 1–30.

[28] E.g. *Epistulae* 4.22, 8.3 (Leo) and 8.6 (Namatius).

his laughter at an Other. At the very end of the letter, Sidonius makes use of the other alternative. His joke about the risks of being thought satirical also incorporates Catullinus, but this time by making him laugh at the pair of them together. Laughing at an out-group, especially an out-group perceived to be inferior, creates community, but an even greater sense of unity is created when people feel able to laugh at themselves.[29] Sidonius' is thus a clever strategy. First of all he ridicules a group which both he and Catullinus regard as base outsiders and parvenus. This places them both in the same social group. Then Sidonius ends by demonstrating that the two of them are not merely members of the same broad class, but very close associates, by joking about their shared unfortunate experience in the past. With all this, how could Catullinus fail to forgive him for not writing his epithalamium?

INCONGRUITY AGAIN: HOW TO SHOCK A SAVAGE

If, as shown above, the difference between the civilised and the barbarous was one of the most important structuring oppositions in antique thought, then to play with the stereotypical characteristics of the Roman or Greek and the barbarian must surely have been one of the most glaringly obvious strategies of satire or irony available to late antique authors. This was a strategy with a long pedigree. Edith Hall has discussed the ways in which the characteristics stereotypically associated with Hellenes and barbarians can, in Greek tragedy, be found displayed equally by both groups.[30] However, rather than simply showing that really there was not much to choose between the two, the barbarian Hellenes and the noble barbarians (Trojans, Persians and so on) represent satirical or ironic inversion. The inversion could, at least on occasion, serve not to blur the distinction but to reinforce it. They presuppose 'the invented ethnocentric world of tragedy', 'so fundamental a dogma as to produce striking rhetorical effects on being inverted'. 'They embody an ironic and sophistic reversal of the accepted premise that Greeks are superior to the rest of the world.'[31] A barbarian behaving like a Greek could, if perhaps not in the genre of tragedy, be more openly funny. To a public accustomed to repeated presentation of what distinguished the Hellene

---

[29] See the discussion of experiments in H. R. Pollio, 'What's so funny?', in *Not Work Alone: A Cross-cultural View of Activities Superfluous to Survival*, ed. J. Cherfas and R. Lewin (London, 1980), pp. 143–65, at pp. 151–2.

[30] E. Hall, *Inventing the Barbarian: Greek Self-definition through Tragedy* (Oxford, 1989).

[31] Ibid., pp. 222–3, 222 and 223.

from the barbarian, such an inversion was ludicrous, it was ridiculous, and it could be funny.

To take what might be regarded as a flippant, but is nevertheless an appropriate, modern example from Larson's work,[32] the line 'Oo! Goldfish, everyone! Goldfish!' is not in itself funny. Even if the line were spoken by someone crossing the drawbridge of a medieval castle it would only (at best) be mildly amusing. What makes this cartoon one of Larson's most popular is that the line is being spoken by a horned-helmeted, sword-wielding Viking (the archetypal 'barbarian' figure in modern western culture) as he and his torch-brandishing colleagues storm over the drawbridge into the castle, under heavy arrow-fire. At the risk of over-elaboration, we do not laugh because we see that the Viking can actually be a sensitive soul like ourselves, but because the *very idea* of a sensitive Viking, especially in battle, is funny. Thus conceptual *difference* is underlined. In the following examples this sort of image is very much in evidence, where a barbarian speaks or acts in quite the opposite way from that expected.

These examples thus employ a rather different, more subtle humorous usage of the barbarian image from that deployed by Sidonius. Although based upon the same shared knowledge of stereotypes, rather than using pun and exaggeration to create humour, it inverts the norms. The barbarian is placed in the situation of the Roman to create 'striking rhetorical effects'. This produces incongruity and the possibility of humour. In my first example, the most savage barbarians are out-savaged; the next selections highlight ludicrous situations wherein barbarians try to act like Romans, and the consequences of these absurd reversals are soon revealed.

To introduce this theme, and its problems, one may turn to Ammianus Marcellinus. Ammianus, recent analysis has shown, was well aware of the genre of satire, and may occasionally have used Petronius as a model.[33] Certainly, his historical model, Tacitus, was an adept in satire and the use of the witty epigram.[34] In one story, Ammianus appears to exaggerate the barbarian's stereotypical ferocity, but if we look closer there is also a sense of irony and, possibly, incongruity. After the catastrophic battle of Adrianople, he tells us in one of the final chapters of the

---

[32] G. Larson, *The Far Side Gallery 2* (New York, 1986), p. 38.

[33] R. Rees, 'Ammianus satyricus', in *The Late Roman World and its Historian: Interpreting Ammianus Marcellinus*, ed. J. W. Drijvers and D. Hunt (London, 1999), pp. 141–55. See also Shanzer, above, pp. 33–4.

[34] P. Plass, *Wit and the Writing of History: The Rhetoric of Historiography in Imperial Rome* (Madison, WI, 1988).

Res Gestae, the Goths, with their Hunnic and Alanic allies, 'being extremely warlike and brave peoples, hardened to the difficulties of severe toils', were advancing upon Constantinople itself.[35] The Romans, in their hour of need, received reinforcements from Arabia. In a skirmish outside Constantinople, one of the Arab light cavalry, long-haired and naked except for a loincloth, killed a Goth, whereupon he fell upon the dying man and began to drink his blood.[36] At this, however 'warlike and brave' and 'hardened to the difficulties of severe toils' they may have been, the Goths were, perhaps unsurprisingly, somewhat shocked. Thereafter they did not act with their customary ferocity (*non ferocientes ex more*), but 'with cautious tread' (*ambiguis gressibus*). Irony is detectable here: the Goths may have been barbarous, may even have been amongst the most barbarous, but they were not *that* barbarous!

There is possibly even more to the story than this. The Arabs are fighting for the Romans. Thus the barbarians were shocked at the savagery of 'Roman' troops. This is possible, but here the problems of unravelling humour in inversion begin. Context, as usual, is everything. The sort of inversion of the norms discussed above can be seen very clearly in rhetorical pieces. Probably the best-known section of Salvian's *On the Governance of God*, that dealing with social struggles in northern Gaul,[37] repeatedly contrasts Roman tyranny with the liberty of the barbarians, freedom under the barbarians and slavery under Roman rule. This is a glaring and, to Salvian's audience, ridiculous, inversion of reality. Did Salvian intend it to be humorous? In the sense that he was trying to raise a laugh, this hardly seems likely. He may, however, have used this technique to mock his audience, to make them laugh at themselves and then realise their fault. Most likely, though, his message is simply that this ridiculous state of affairs, this whole case of a world turned upside-down, is their own fault. That is not funny.[38] On another occasion, Sidonius depicts the Gothic king, Theoderic, behaving in a way which is in all things appropriate for a Roman emperor. Again, the point is not to be humorous but to show that it is really not that bad to live under a Gothic king.[39] The contextual 'frame' for humorous statements is therefore vitally important.

---

[35] Amm. Marc. 31.16.3.   [36] Amm. Marc. 31.16.6.

[37] Salvian, *On the Governance of God* 5.4–7, in *MGH Auctores Antiquissimi* 1.1, ed. C. Halm (Berlin, 1877). See also Shanzer, above, p. 29.

[38] See Shanzer, above, pp. 28–9, for Christian treatments of humour, and Innes below, pp. 142–3, for the church's ideological difficulties with laughter. Haldon, above, pp. 62–3, gives a clearer instance of a churchman ridiculing his flock in order to make them change their ways.

[39] *Epistulae* 1.2. See Innes, below, pp. 138–40; Heather 'The barbarian in late antiquity', pp. 246–7.

Although there need be no doubt that the events took place as related in Ammianus' description of the Goths' repulse from the walls of
Constantinople, the passage may still be seen as written with intentional
humour. The passage has its cue both in Ammianus' reference to the
Goths and Huns being very warlike, ravaging far and wide, 'madly rushing on' and approaching the gates of Constantinople itself ('here they
come!'), but also, before the Arabs enter the fray, when Ammianus sets
up the scene by saying that the celestial power stopped the barbarian advance 'by this means'.[40] Ammianus continues to raise the readers' expectations when he invites them to remember what he has earlier said about
the Arabs' extreme barbarity.[41] Much humour, as many theorists have
argued, is about building up tensions, or particular expectations, and
then evaporating them. Here the warlike and fierce Goths and Huns
advance on Constantinople; the only defence is a *turma* of barbarous
Arabs who, says Ammianus, are more use in thieving than in open battle. They rush out to meet the Goths and Huns. One would expect the
Goths who, after all, have recently thrashed the eastern empire's field
army and killed the emperor Valens himself, to make a meal out of these
lightly armed Arabs. Yet the battle is hard fought, and the Arabs then
shock the barbarian Goths with their barbarism. It also has its punch
line, in the reference to the Goths acting with more circumspection afterwards. Here Ammianus shies away from pursuing the point of the story
too far. His punch line, as with the best jokes, is understated. Instead of
describing them fleeing in terror, Ammianus simply says that the Goths
were more careful afterwards (as we might put it, 'they didn't do that
again in a hurry'). Whether one can read into the story an extra level of
incongruity, regarding the irony of the fact that the most savage barbarians were fighting for the Romans, is less clear, and is not an argument
that should be stressed, but it is possible nevertheless.

MY DINNER WITH ATHAULF

Towards the end of the *Seven Books of History against the Pagans*,[42] Orosius
tells a story about Athaulf, the king of the Goths. Athaulf, says Orosius,
used to say that once upon a time he had thought of destroying the
Roman Empire and replacing Romania with Gothia. Later on, though,
realising that his Goths could never live according to the law, and that it is

---

[40] Amm. Marc. 31.16.4: *hoc casu caeleste reppulit numen.*   [41] Amm. Marc. 14.4.
[42] *Adversos Paganos* 7.43.4, *Orose: Histoires (Contre les Païens) Livre VII*, ed. and trans. M.-P. Arnaud-
Lindet (Paris, 1991).

not possible to have a state without law, he changed his mind and decided
to put his Goths at the service of the emperor and preserve the Roman
name. This is a story usually taken straight by historians. Ian Wood has
hinted that there is more to it than meets the eye, and Michael Wallace-
Hadrill called it 'a curious jest'.[43] Even Wallace-Hadrill, however, went
on to say that the solution is to take the tale at face value. Orosius
claims that he was told this by an eye-witness, a Narbonensian *vir inlustris*
(the highest senatorial rank) in the presence of Saint Jerome.[44] These
are fairly good credentials for taking this as reportage, one might think.
Most recently, John Matthews has interestingly discussed the passage in
the context of the post-Roman kings' use of Roman law.[45] Matthews
comments that previous treatments of the story as a rhetorical trope do
not do it justice: 'Nor, to me at least, do Athaulf's remarks have much
of the "curious jest" about them.'[46] Matthews believes that this was a
serious statement to a powerful audience and 'part of a plan': the use
of law as a deliberate strategy in the construction of Roman–Gothic
relations.

Let us look at the passage again. Leaving aside the fact that what
Athaulf says he had decided to do is not exactly what Gothic kings in
Gaul ended up doing, the joke is that even the barbarians know that they
cannot live according to the law, and thus that they can never replace the
Imperium Romanum. Even the barbarians are aware of their own supposed
limitations. One would expect a Roman, especially perhaps a former
praetorian prefect like the unnamed *vir inlustris*, to say that the barbarians
cannot live according to the law, but not the king of the barbarians. The
wrong person is speaking.

The whole story may be a wry little joke by Orosius, or perhaps his
informant. Certainly, given the stereotypes of the barbarian, which were
so well worn, so familiar and which dwelt so heavily upon the ideas
of law and freedom, it is very difficult to see beyond this heavy irony,
which would have been very apparent to Orosius' audience. After all,
in another passage of the *History against the Pagans*, Orosius comments,
with famous sarcasm, that people think it better to live in freedom under

---

[43] I. N. Wood, 'The barbarian invasions and first settlements', in *The Cambridge Ancient History*,
vol. XIII, *The Late Empire, A.D. 337–425*, ed. A. Cameron and P. Garnsey (Cambridge, 1998),
pp. 516–37, at p. 529; J. M. Wallace-Hadrill, 'Gothia and Romania', in his *The Long-haired Kings*
(London, 1962), pp. 25–48, at p. 25.

[44] J. Matthews, 'Gallic supporters of Theodosius', *Latomus* 30 (1971), pp. 1073–99, at pp. 1085–7,
for possible identification of the *vir inluster* as Marcellus.

[45] J. Matthews, 'Roman law and barbarian identity in the late Roman west', in *Ethnicity and Culture
in Late Antiquity*, ed. S. Mitchell and G. Greatrex (London, 2000), pp. 31–44, at pp. 31–4.

[46] Ibid., p. 32.

the barbarians than in slavery under the Romans.[47] Unlike that sarcasm (or Salvian's almost identical ironic comment, discussed above), this story seems to have the characteristics of a jest. It has features required by many theories of humour: absurdity, deviation from normal thought and representation, economy of thought and expression;[48] 'the orderly and the chaotic in incongruous juxtaposition'.[49] It has its cue: this was something which the senator had 'often' heard Athaulf say ('here comes a "bon mot"').[50] And it has its resolution: the topsy-turvy situation is resolved by Athaulf's decision to uphold the Roman Empire instead. In the generally up-beat context of the end of the *Adversos paganos*, it was entirely appropriate to underpin the eternity of Rome with a little twist, like this, on Roman attitudes to barbarians.

There may be yet more to it than that. Wallace-Hadrill is probably right that in some sense the story ought to be taken as reportage. As shown, Orosius goes to some lengths to authenticate the tale, associating it with none other than Saint Jerome.[51] If there is a joke here, it may well be that it is Athaulf's joke. Anyone spending any length of time within the empire, in contact with its more learned élite, would rapidly have picked up the Roman idea that what distinguished barbarians was their lack of law; Athaulf had spent most, if not all, of his life within the Roman Empire. A further level stems from the fact that the 'Goths' whom Athaulf ruled had, it seems, originated as a Roman army.[52] The joke thus possibly plays upon the fact that the 'barbarian' identity of the 'Goths' was one which had been consciously chosen, by people who were otherwise as Roman as anyone else. This may indeed be Athaulf's bon mot, trotted out with possibly tedious regularity when he was in learned company. The first time it was told, it may have been quite amusing... None of this materially affects the thrust of Matthews' argument about the fifth-century barbarian kings in Gaul and their use of Roman law. If it was Athaulf's joke, it may very well have been told in the context of his efforts to preserve and to promulgate imperial Roman law within his realms. The two aspects are not mutually exclusive. Politicians tell jokes (not always very well), and sometimes against themselves. More to the

---

[47] *Adversos Paganos* 7.41.7.

[48] Freud, *Jokes and their Relation to the Unconscious*, pp. 116–89.

[49] C. P. Wilson, *Jokes: Form, Content, Use and Function* (London, 1979), p. 20; see also J. K. Fiebleman, *In Praise of Comedy* (New York, 1939); L. Festinger, *Theory of Cognitive Dissonance* (New York, 1957).

[50] On the tradition of bons mots, see Shanzer, above, pp. 31–5.

[51] Jerome was no stranger to satire: D. S. Wiesen, *St Jerome as Satirist* (Ithaca, NY, 1964); Shanzer, above, pp. 39–40.

[52] T. S. Burns, *Barbarians within the Gates of Rome: A Study of Roman Military Policy and the Barbarians, ca. 375–425* (Bloomington, IN, 1994).

point, humour was an accepted part of Roman rhetoric.[53] The primary, 'overt' sense of the story is humorous.

There are many levels of interpretation of a text. One can simply take this passage as straight reportage that Athaulf used to say this, because it was true, and no more. However, given the obvious play upon one of the centrepieces of Graeco-Roman ethnographic writing about the difference between civilised man and the barbarians, it must really be deeply ironic. This is a more marked reading. However, a reading reconstructed from other sources about the realities behind the text, in this case the political and legal history of the Gothic realm in Gaul, is even more marked. This is not to discount the validity of those reconstructions, but it does move the reader further away from the sense of the passage itself. Whosesoever the joke was – Orosius', the Narbonensian *vir inlustris'* or Athaulf's – it was certainly not a tale to be taken, seriously, at face value. At face value, it is a joke.

GELIMER'S LAUGHTER: PROCOPIUS AND THE VANDALS

In spite of Averil Cameron's brilliant study,[54] Procopius is still a writer with secrets and complexities to reveal. There are, in particular, more jokes, and certainly a great deal more irony and satire, in Procopius' work than has, seemingly, been appreciated. Procopius had a keen sense of the absurd, and a cruel streak of humour, as the *Secret History* makes abundantly clear. In fact the *Secret History* may be read as a savage, extended parody of panegyric.[55] Here, I take Cameron's analysis as

---

[53] G. Kennedy, *The Art of Rhetoric in the Roman World, 300BC–AD300* (Princeton, 1972), p. 186, pp. 212–13; Cicero, *De oratore* 2.217–90. See also Humphries, above, p. 79, and Haldon, above, pp. 66–9.

[54] A. Cameron, *Procopius and the Sixth Century* (London, 1985). For Procopius' works, see *Procopius*, trans. H. B. Dewing (7 vols., London, 1914–40).

[55] Indeed, in the earliest reaction to the piece, the author of the tenth-century *Suda* described the *Secret History* as a *kômôdia*. Whilst not dismissing the similarities with satire, Cameron, *Procopius*, p. 60, sees Procopius in the *Secret History* as 'earnest', and feels that to see the *Secret History* as satire is too simplistic and fails to do justice to its complexity. Yet there is nothing necessarily 'simple' about satire. Though far and away the most persuasive analysis of this odd tract to date, Cameron's study still seems to fall short of doing it full justice. Procopius' views may have been 'earnest' but he expressed them in a satirical fashion. After all, many deeply sincere and earnest critics of governmental policies are comedians. Though there is not room here to develop the idea, it seems to me that in the *Secret History* Procopius is taking the elements of panegyric, inverting them and taking them to ludicrous extremes, to ridicule his targets. Sometimes the technique is more subtle. At *Secret History* 19.13–17, he takes, more or less unaltered, a commonplace of panegyric, the emperor's fame reaching to the ends of the earth and making barely known barbarian peoples come to seek his favour. With only the lightest of touches, he makes the entire concept ludicrous and, instead of praise, criticism of the emperor. For an analogy, see M. Humphries, 'Savage

a springboard to examine several episodes that play on the Roman–barbarian dichotomy. I shall, however, disagree to some extent with Cameron's contention that Procopius is 'earnest' and that to read aspects of Procopius' writing as irony and satire are 'easy ways out'[56] that do the texts' complexities no justice. Irony can be very complex. As an – at least possible – instance of irony in Procopius' work, take the latter part of Book 4 of the *Wars*, the second book dealing with the Vandal War and its aftermath. Here Procopius sprinkles his account with sometimes fairly lengthy comments on the utter faithlessness of the Moors;[57] here, again, one encounters that stereotypical barbarian trait. Yet the whole thrust of his narrative is about the treachery and labyrinthine – indeed, as we should say today, 'Byzantine' – plotting and counter-plotting of the Roman generals and their troops in North Africa.[58] Sometimes the very references about Moorish faithlessness come in the middle of accounts of Roman treachery and falsehood.

Earlier in Book 4, Procopius digresses on the decline of the Vandals, comparing Vandals and Moors. Gelimer, king of the Vandals, with his close relatives and other high aristocrats, has been driven to seek shelter with the Moors on Mount Papua. The mountain is then besieged by a Roman force, in fact composed of Heruls commanded by Pharas. At the beginning of his account of the siege, in a celebrated passage, Procopius says that of all the different peoples, the Vandals are the most luxurious and the Moors the hardiest:

For the Vandals, when they gained possession of Libya, used to indulge in baths, all of them, every day, and enjoyed a table abounding in all things, the sweetest and best that the earth could produce. And they wore gold very generally, and clothed themselves in the Medic garments which they now call 'seric', and passed their time, thus dressed, in theatres and hippodromes and in other pleasurable pursuits, and above all else in hunting. And they had dancers and mimes and

---

humour: Christian anti-panegyric in Hilary of Poitiers' *Against Constantius*', in *The Propaganda of Power: The Role of Panegyric in Late Antiquity*, ed. M. Whitby (Leiden, 1998), pp. 201–23.

56 Cameron, *Procopius*, p. 35. Cameron herself reads irony (e.g. ibid., p. 192) and 'mischief' (ibid., p. 212) into Procopius' writing, so any disagreement is only of degree.

57 *Wars* 4.13.37, 4.17.10 and 4.25.16. This does not, of course, mean that the general stereotype of the faithless Moor did not exist. Corippus also discussed this trait; see A. Cameron, 'Gelimer's laughter: the case of Byzantine Africa', in *Tradition and Innovation in Late Antiquity*, ed. M. Clover and R. S. Humphreys (Madison, WI, 1989), pp. 171–90, at p. 179. Without that stereotype, Procopius' deployment of it could not be read as ironic.

58 The difference between the modern view of 'Byzantine' intrigue and the sixth-century ideas that honesty and faithfulness were the Roman way, serves to underline the point that the codes which create humour are culturally specific, even if the general humorous strategies remain the same. A comment about treacherous Byzantines and upright barbarians would evince quite different responses today from those produced in the sixth century: see Haldon, above, p. 53.

all other things to hear and see which are of a musical nature or otherwise merit attention among men. And most of them dwelt in parks, which were well supplied with water and trees; and they had great numbers of banquets and all manner of sexual pleasures were in great vogue with them.[59]

This passage has, again, been taken straight far too often, and sometimes compared, with some puzzlement, with Salvian's statement that the Vandals were the most moral of all people.[60] Herwig Wolfram goes some way towards moving away from this view when he quite rightly says that what this amounts to is saying that the problem with the Vandals was that they enjoyed the lifestyle of any self-respecting Roman aristocrat.[61] Wolfram then, however, in some ways sidesteps the point by saying that this is just for purposes of contrast with the Moors, who are hardy and puritanical.

Procopius sets up the scene by saying that 'it came about that' the Vandals were suffering from the greatest of misery, which no one could possibly describe, no matter how eloquent. He builds up a set of expectations. Why should it be that the king of the Vandals and his highest aristocrats could not bear this siege on Mount Papua? Surely things must be bad if the savage barbarians could not stand it. Starvation or disease, the usual fate of the besieged? Or the stereotypical barbarian moodswings and tendency to become discouraged? No, it was because the Vandals are the most luxurious 'of all the nations which we know'. They were used to bathing, wearing nice clothes, eating well at licentious banquets and living in well-appointed country estates. To Procopius' learned eastern Roman aristocratic audience, the image presented would be immediately recognisable as their own lifestyle. That this was so obviously

---

[59] *Wars* 4.6.6–8.

[60] The passage is not much discussed in recent works, as explanations for the fall of the Vandal kingdom have become rather more sophisticated. Nevertheless, see M. McCormick, *Eternal Victory: Triumphal Rulership in Late Antiquity, Byzantium and the Early Medieval West* (Cambridge, 1986), p. 262; A. H. M. Jones' comment about the Vandal army losing its martial spirit, at *The Later Roman Empire, 284–602* (Oxford, 1964), p. 260, is presumably based at least partially upon this testimony. H. Wolfram, *The Roman Empire and its Germanic Peoples* (Berkeley, 1997), p. 181, discusses the nineteenth-century German historiography which took Procopius' comments as the basis for judgements on the Vandals' moral decline. See L. Schmidt, 'The Sueves, Alans and Vandals in Spain, 409–29: the Vandal dominion in Africa', in *Cambridge Medieval History*, vol. I, ed. H. M. Gwatkin and J. P. Whinney (2nd edn, Cambridge, 1924), pp. 304–22, at p. 321; for the French version of the same tradition, see C. Diehl, *L'Afrique Byzantine: Histoire de la Domination Byzantine en Afrique, 533–709* (2 vols., Paris, 1896), vol. I, p. 9; C. Courtois, *Les Vandales et l'Afrique* (Paris. 1955), p. 232; the English version can be traced in J. B. Bury, *History of the Later Roman Empire from the Death of Theodosius I to the Death of Justinian* (2 vols., New York, 1950), vol. II, pp. 127–8.

[61] Wolfram, *Roman Empire*, p. 181.

the way of life of the Roman aristocrat must give the passage the characteristics of satire. The point is driven home by the comparison with the Moors, which immediately follows it. This passage is the mirror of his account of the Vandals, but is also a patchwork of stereotypical barbarian features: their clothes are simple, they live in the basest of huts, their food and drink is barely different from that of animals, especially since they do not cook it. The Vandals' problems derived from the fact they were *not* barbarians.

The irony of this passage is only heightened by its sequel. Pharas writes to Gelimer saying that he, too, is a barbarian and likewise uncouth in matters of speech and writing (a rather pointed contrast with Procopius' account of the reasons for the Vandals' decline, and an even more pointed contrast with Gelimer's reply, as shall become clear). Pharas knows his place. His letter sets out why it is better to be a slave under the Romans than a king of the Moors; Gelimer's actions are making a mockery of the whole idea of liberty. Once again, Procopius is using that standard rhetorical device for distinguishing the barbarian from the civilised man: slavery versus freedom. Pharas says that even a noble barbarian should be pleased to serve an emperor. Gelimer was, however, unconvinced, and the passage returns to irony. At the end of his letter back to Pharas, Gelimer requested from him a loaf, a sponge and a lyre (*kithara*). Confused, as well he might have been, Pharas asked the messenger the reason for this request. The loaf was because Gelimer had not seen baked bread since the sicge began and the sponge was because one of his eyes was inflamed, but he had asked for the lyre so that he could perform the ode he had composed upon his current misfortune.[62] A barbarian plays the learned Roman.

The problem with the Vandals was that they had gone Roman and were thus unable to endure military hardships. This could be a dig by Procopius at the *rhomaioi* themselves; in this context, the point about sexual pleasures may be a critique of the Roman aristocracy. The most luxurious people (*ethne*) in the known world turn out to like all the things loved by Roman aristocratic culture. However, it seems more likely that this is simply a jibe at the Vandal barbarians. They would have been all right if only they had stayed barbarian. There was nothing worse, though, or indeed more disastrous for themselves, than barbarians who tried to be Romans. This is a point which Procopius makes in other

[62] *Wars* 4.6.30.

parts of the *Wars*. There is another clue to the ludicrous nature of the whole story. When he finally surrenders, Gelimer laughs out loud at his situation. This forced some people to suppose that he had gone mad, whilst others thought he was laughing at the caprices of fortune, and that the whole condition of man was worth no more than laughter.[63] Procopius says he will leave it for the reader to decide.[64]

THE PERILS OF GOTHIC EDUCATION

A slightly different spin on what happens when barbarians play at being Romans is found in Procopius' account of the education of Theoderic the Great's grandson, Athalaric.[65] Again, this is a story habitually taken as neutral reportage.[66] Athalaric's mother, Amalasuntha, had taken over the government of Italy on his behalf, reigning 'with the masculine temperament'. She harmed no Romans and did not give in to the Goths' 'mad desire to wrong them'. Amalasuntha wished to educate Athalaric to be like a Roman prince, and have him taught letters, and bade three elderly, refined Goths live with him. This in itself seems rather ironic. Why get the Goths to teach Athalaric how to behave like a Roman? If these three Goths were more refined than the others, this is faint praise indeed, coming after Procopius' comment about the Goths' 'mad desire' to harm Romans. In any case, the Goths were not happy about this, and wanted him to be educated so that he would rule 'after the barbarian fashion'.[67] This, says Procopius, would allow them to wrong their Roman subjects. After Athalaric fled in tears from a beating, 'the Goths' insisted that the queen send away the tutors and 'give to Athalaric some men of his own age to be his companions, who will pass through the period of youth with him and thus give him an impulse towards the excellence which is in keeping with the custom of the barbarians'.[68]

The upshot of this – the punch line of the story – was that these lads, enticing Athalaric to 'drunkenness and intercourse with women,

[63] *Wars* 4.7.14–16. This is a very Tacitean concept: cf. *Annals* 3.18.4.

[64] Cameron, *Procopius*, p. 175, points out that at this point Procopius adds a twist to his usual phrase, by adding 'whether enemy or friend'. In spite of the title, Cameron, 'Gelimer's laughter', does not, alas, elucidate this passage.

[65] *Wars* 5.2.6 ff.

[66] See, e.g., P. Heather, *The Goths* (London, 1996), p. 260; Jones, *The Later Roman Empire*, p. 274; Wolfram, *Roman Empire*, p. 226; P. Riché, *Éducation et culture dans l'Occident Barbare 6ᵉ–8ᵉ siècle* (Paris, 1962), p. 105, takes the story as an example of 'barbarian' military education. Cameron, *Procopius*, p. 199, comes closest by saying that the tale is a 'stereotyped display of "barbarian" as opposed to "Roman" manners'.

[67] *Wars* 5.2.8.   [68] *Wars* 5.2.17.

made him an exceptionally depraved youth, and of such stupid folly that he was disinclined to follow his mother's advice'.[69] This went on until, eventually, he plunged into 'a drunken revel which passed all bounds' and was seized by a wasting disease.[70] So much for the 'excellence which is in keeping with the custom of the barbarians'. The debauchery and untimely death of Athalaric may have been matters of record; the elaboration of the story, and especially the speech put in the mouths of 'the Goths', which is, of course, Procopius' own composition, are very deliberate ploys to ridicule the Goths. Twice Procopius stresses that they wished Athalaric to be raised in such a way that he ruled in the customary *barbarian* (not 'Gothic') way. The Goths do not want their king brought up with a Roman education and demand that he be trained as a proper barbarian. And what happens? He drinks himself into a stupor at an early age.

Before relating the upshot of Gothic education, however, Procopius is able to develop the ludicrously incongruous concept of barbarian education. If the idea of a barbarian education was a joke in itself, with a perhaps obvious punch line, then how much more ludicrous was the notion of a barbarian philosopher king? After Amalasuntha sends Athalaric to his 'training' Procopius introduces Theodahad, shortly to murder Amalasuntha and become king of the Goths. 'There was among the Goths one Theodahad [Procopius calls him Theodatos] by name, son of Amalafrida, the sister of Theoderic, a man already of mature years, versed in Latin literature and Platonic dogma, but without any experience whatever of war, and taking no active life.' Some barbarian, this! Yet, says Procopius, Theodahad was 'extraordinarily devoted to the pursuit of money'.[71] This statement is heavily ironic in itself, and, with its last phrase about Theodahad's *'philochrematia'*,[72] has some of the characteristics of a witty epigram. We surely are meant to expect to read that the reason for Theodahad's avoidance of public life was his extraordinary devotion to *philosophy*. What we actually read, however, is that he was 'well versed in the Latin literature and Platonic dogma, but without any experience whatever in war and taking no part in active life, yet extraordinarily devoted to philo—*chrematia*.' This is the technique called *para prosdokian* (violated expectation) discussed by Paul Plass in his analysis of Tacitus' wit,[73] and, since it was discussed by Aristotle, too,[74] it

---

[69] *Wars* 5.2.19.   [70] *Wars* 5.3.10.   [71] *Wars* 5.3.1.

[72] Theodahad's *philochrematia* is also mentioned at *Wars* 5.4.3.

[73] Plass, *Wit and the Writing of History*, esp. pp. 58–62.

[74] Aristotle, *Rhetoric* 1412a6, in *Aristotle: The 'Art' of Rhetoric*, ed. and trans. J. H. Freese (London, 1926). A relevant passage is quoted by Plass, *Wit and the Writing of History*, p. 58.

was doubtless familiar to Procopius. Needless to say, *philochrematia* is not a word used in any positive sense by Plato.[75] In the *Laws*, Plato declares that a law-maker who is found guilty of acting according to *philochrematia* should, if he is an alien, be expelled from the country and forbidden to return.[76] Most of Theodahad's role in the *Wars* is concerned with his attempts to leave Italy and acquire lands and a title in the east. This may be coincidence, but the glaring contradiction between saying that Theodahad was well versed in the teachings of Plato and that he was extraordinarily devoted to the love of *money* cannot be other than deeply and deliberately ironic.

The irony is developed in the next sentence, which describes how Theodahad had acquired most of the lands of Tuscany. There follows another epigrammatic comment: 'For to have a neighbour seemed to Theodahad a kind of misfortune.'[77] Coming so soon after the statement that Theodahad is well versed in the teachings of Plato this can only, at the very least, be heavy, deliberate irony, and is probably an outright joke. What Theodahad is up to is precisely what, according to Procopius, 'the Goths' wanted to do to their Roman subjects (and which, in turn, they thought they would be prevented from doing if Athalaric received a Roman education, such as Theodahad had allegedly acquired). This all adds to the incongruity. Yet Theodahad, who actually *was* despoiling the Romans, read Plato and Latin literature. Theodahad's subsequent behaviour as king, after his murder of Amalasuntha, throws this into further relief. His actions swing wildly back and forth between one extreme of emotion and another (characteristic of the barbarian), and are frequently described as folly.[78] Given the stress laid by Procopius upon Theodahad's pretence of being a philosopher (in various speeches and reported letters; again Procopius' compositions), the contrast with his actual, typically barbarian, 'folly' must surely be deliberate. Again, there can only be one outcome for the barbarian who plays the learned Roman.

---

[75] E.g. Plato, *Republic* 391c (Achilles overcome by the 'contradictory maladies' of arrogance towards men and Gods, and *philochrematia*); *Laws* 747b (arithmetic is the most valuable form of education for a law-maker, 'provided you can remove *philochrematia*'). See also *Republic* 391c, which is critical of a state that values wealth, and in which lovers of victory become *philochrematoi*. *Plato with an English Translation: The Laws*, ed. and trans. R. G. Bury (2 vols., London, 1926); *Plato: The Republic*, trans. P. Shorey (2 vols., London 1930, 1935).

[76] *Laws* 938b.   [77] *Wars* 5.3.2.

[78] *Wars* 5.4.31 (stupid folly); 5.6.1 (turns coward); 5.6.6 (seized with terror, so changes his mind); 5.6.10 ff. (pandered to by envoys, who play up to his Platonic pretences); 5.7.11 ff. (bold through terror, 'contrary to reason', so threatens imperial envoys, and then, outwitted, changes his mind); 5.9.1 ff. (terrified and consults a Jewish soothsayer).

BELISARIUS' LAUGHTER: THE SIEGE OF ROME

Procopius' account of the siege of Rome by Vittigis, king of the Goths, is well known as the focus of some of Procopius' most memorable writing; it is also the occasion for humour. Indeed, the image is presented of Belisarius on the battlements of Rome, laughing at the Goths' stupidity. Procopius' account seems to have numerous characteristics of deliberate incongruity, and suggests, at least on occasion, active deployment of irony or satire.[79] Once again, this is often taken simply as eyewitness description[80] (despite the fact that Procopius clearly wrote it up years after the event[81]). As Cameron has written, the account of the Italian wars is not to be taken as straightforward reportage, and is enmeshed in military historical and ethnographic rhetoric.[82]

The very scenario of the Gothic siege of Rome is a case of the world turned upside-down: the Romans, invading Italy, have captured Rome; the barbarians, the owners of Rome, want it back. This political situation is made clear in a speech at the start of the siege.[83] Vacis, a Gothic commander, admonishes the Romans for their faithlessness, accuses them of treason against their fatherland, and upbraids them for siding with Greek invaders. The speech is ironic and incongruous in that a barbarian is accusing the citizens of Rome of that stereotype of barbarism: unfaithfulness. The theme is taken up and elaborated in two speeches after the first military encounter of the siege, one by Vittigis' envoys, the other by Belisarius himself.[84] The envoys accuse Belisarius of rashness, a barbarian trait, rather than bravery in marching against Rome. They claim that he has imperilled the lives of the Romans, who lived a life of luxury and freedom under the rule of the Goths. The idea that a barbarian ruler could foster freedom in the population of Rome is a complete nonsense according to late antique ideas of civilisation and barbarism. That Procopius' word for the inhabitants of Rome is (like ours) exactly

---

[79] *Wars* 5.16–6.10.
[80] E.g. E. A. Thompson, *Romans and Barbarians: The Decline of the Western Empire* (Madison, WI, 1982), pp. 77–81 and 82–4.
[81] Books 1–7 of the *Wars* were published in 550, but were probably written during the 540s. It seems unlikely that any of the final text of the *Wars* was written before 540, when Procopius returned to Constantinople: Cameron, *Procopius*, p. 136. Though Procopius is assumed to have made notes during his involvement in Belisarius' campaigns, as a literary composition Procopius' account of the siege of Rome must have been written at least four years after the event. The cross-reference at *Wars* 5.24.32 to the events of Totila's siege of Rome in 546 suggests an even greater time-lapse between the events and Procopius' completion of his final account.
[82] Cameron, *Procopius*, pp. 188–206.   [83] *Wars* 5.18.40–1.   [84] *Wars* 5.20.8–18.

the same as that for inhabitants (or troops, like Belisarius' army) of the Roman Empire, *rhomaioi*, only heightens the irony. Belisarius' reply admits that the Romans have captured Rome but says that all that has happened is that the city has been relinquished, however unwillingly, to its original owners.

In the course of Procopius' lengthy narrative there is much play on the traditional barbarian inability to carry on siege warfare. The Goths build a siege tower, described in loving detail. Procopius says the Romans are terrified by this and other engines, saying that these were things with which the Romans 'were completely unfamiliar'. Procopius may have meant the inhabitants of Rome rather than the Roman army, but, unusually, he omits to specify this, creating possibly deliberate ambiguity and thus evoking at least a smile from a learned Byzantine audience: barbarian ineptitude at siege warfare was proverbial.[85] Belisarius' laughter, mentioned above, is provoked by the spectacle of the Goths drawing their siege tower towards the walls with oxen – which Belisarius promptly shoots. The Goths try other strategies but these are all outwitted by Belisarius.

Later, Procopius says that Belisarius repeatedly sent out small parties of his mounted bowmen, who lured large numbers of Goths into attacking them, only to be shot down from a distance.[86] The Romans then retreated, safe and sound, into the city. Increasing numbers of Goths are, in Procopius' narrative, slaughtered in this fashion. Seeing this, the Goths decide to copy the strategy, and send out small bodies of their own cavalry. However, because they are too stupid to have realised the reason for Belisarius' success, the Byzantine cavalry, sent out en masse, massacre them.[87] Afterwards, Belisarius is asked how he knew that his stratagems would work, whereupon he says that during the first battle during the siege, which he lost (Procopius, however, prepares the reader for this explanation by telling us after that battle that Belisarius had seen there and then how he would beat the Goths), he had noticed the key difference between the armies.[88] The Goths have no horse-archers,

[85] See above, p. 93. The episode is strangely reminiscent of the Batavians' similarly incompetent attempts to deploy siege towers in their attack on a Roman garrison: Tacitus, *Histories* 4.23. This is not the only instance of possible similarities between Procopius and Tacitus. The influence of Roman historiography on Procopius' writing could be greater than might at first be suspected. After all, the Greek world had been part of the Roman Empire for centuries and another easterner, Ammianus Marcellinus, 'a former soldier and a Greek' (Amm. Marc. 31.16.9), set out to be Tacitus' continuator.
[86] *Wars* 5.27.4–14.   [87] *Wars* 5.27.15–23.
[88] *Wars* 5.27.25–8. The earlier cue, which leaves the reader in suspense, wondering what Belisarius had noticed, and is only now resolved, is at *Wars* 5.18.42.

whereas the Roman army was full of them. This is a passage that has attracted curiosity; how could Belisarius only just have noticed this, after fighting the Goths for a year?[89] Cameron says that Procopius deploys this speech so that he can include a military historical set-piece about fighting techniques.[90] Were the Goths *really* that stupid? Or is this also a case where Procopius is making an extended joke on the theme of barbarian stupidity, rashness and incompetence?

It is worth repeating the point[91] that late antique Greek historians were expected to write not in the spoken language of the day but in the, by then artificial, language of Attic Greek. In the historical genres, this meant using the phrases and vocabulary of the great Greek narrative historians – Herodotus, Thucydides and Polybius – so that words unknown in these sources had to be introduced with fairly tortuous circumlocutions: 'the *excubatores* (for such the Romans call their guards)'; 'men who are very exact in their practice of religion, whom we have always been accustomed to call "monks"'.[92] Peoples such as the Huns, unknown to Herodotus and the other models for the genre, are usually referred to by Procopius as *Massagetae*,[93] and so on. Here one encounters the next level of the late antique code about barbarians. Words were chosen, one presumes, because of their rough appropriateness, and the audience can be assumed to have been equally attuned to the images they would conjure up from the classics. This, however, means that one may be able, equally, to see *inappropriate* uses of classical terms. The very rigidity of Greek historiographical traditions aids such study. A learned writer knew how terms should be used, and knew that his audience was equally aware of that correct usage. Thus, if one can locate instances where terminology seems inappropriate, there is a strong likelihood that this incongruity was deliberate. Such deliberate incongruity, in turn, could surely have been humorous.

One such instance comes in the middle of Procopius' discussion of the reasons for Belisarius' success against the Gothic cavalry. He says that the Goths have no mounted bowmen; their archers advance on foot, protected by their heavy infantry.[94] The word he uses for heavy infantry is *'oplitoi* – hoplites – derived from the large round shield (*'oplon*) that they carried. All of Procopius' educated audience would be well aware that in Attic Greek this term was used for the infantry of ancient

---

[89] E.g. Thompson, *Romans and Barbarians*, p. 79.
[90] Cameron, *Procopius*, p. 202.   [91] Haldon, above, p. 51.
[92] *Excubatores*: *Wars* 4.12.17; monks: *Wars* 4.26.17.
[93] E.g. *Wars* 3.11.9: 'the Massagetae whom they now call Huns'.   [94] *Wars* 5.27.27.

Greece. Descriptively, it is fairly adequate; early medieval warriors were also armed with spears and large round shields, though Procopius does not use the word in this context elsewhere; his usual word for foot-soldiers is *pezoi* and his word for a large Gothic shield is *thureos* rather than *'oplon*. In implication, however, it is entirely inappropriate. There was more than a merely military association with ancient Greece in the word 'hoplites'. Hoplites were not merely heavy infantry, they were *citizen* soldiers. Indeed, Aristotle uses the term to denote those with full involvement in the state, in contrast to other groups.[95] In the thought-world of the great models of Attic Greek narrative history, the hoplite was the mainstay of civilisation. At the very least, Procopius' use of the term in relation to Goths besieging Rome is heavily ironic, backing up the world-turned-upside-down nature of the situation, a clever word-play within the rules of Atticism, which would certainly have evinced a smile from his audience.

There is possibly yet more to this irony, however. In the next chapter of the *Wars* there is a lengthy treatment of how the Roman infantry is fairly useless in battle.[96] Some of them have acquired horses and become cavalry; the rest run away at the first sight of the enemy because their officers are all mounted, do not share their perils and flee on horseback at the start of every battle.[97] One speech put into the mouth of one of Belisarius' *doryphoroi* explicitly says that this is not how things were in the days of Rome's greatness. The passage also perhaps draws attention to the very opening of Procopius' *Wars*, where he compares the fighting techniques of the present with those of the past, to defend them against critics who condemn the sixth-century army for including too many archers. In the days of the ancients, says Procopius,[98] archers had to hide behind tombstones, mounds or the shields (though he uses *aspis* rather than *'oplon*) of their comrades. The resonance with the passage during the siege of Rome becomes evident. Rome has been captured by the Romans; the barbarians wish to restore it to 'freedom'. In the ensuing siege, the barbarians try to play the civilised man by deploying scientific siege engines. Moreover, the barbarian infantry fights as though it is a heroic ancient Greek army; the Roman infantry has no military value.

---

[95] Aristotle, *Politics* 1326a23, in *Aristotle: Politics*, ed. and trans. H. Rackham (London, 1932).

[96] *Wars* 5.28.21–2 and 24–6.

[97] See G. Halsall, *Warfare and Society in the Barbarian West, c.450–c.900* (London, 2002) for how these features make the east Roman army remarkably similar to its western European counterparts.

[98] *Wars* 1.1.8–15. Here, as has often been pointed out, he is taking his cue from Thucydides and the opening to his *History*, where he, too, compares current military and political affairs with those of Homer's day.

The world, indeed, is topsy-turvy. However, this incongruity is possibly turned into wry humour by its resolution: the repeated and, indeed, literally laughable failures of the Gothic army.

Procopius thus uses inversion to ridicule the barbarians, and especially makes fun of those barbarians who try to emulate the Romans. This is important. As is well known, by the end of the *Wars*, Procopius makes clear his respect for the Gothic king, Totila, as a noble barbarian. Yet Totila never plays the Roman; he is a barbarian through and through, who behaves as a barbarian ought. If there is nobility in his actions it does not stem from any claimed *Romanitas*. In a sense, therefore, Totila could be incorporated in Procopius' view of how things should be in the world. The same could not be said of barbarians who tried to emulate Roman culture and manners, and lay claim to be 'heirs of Rome'.[99] This sheds an interesting light on contemporary Constantinopolitan reactions to the *Romanitas* of post-Roman rulers, so vaunted in recent scholarship.

CONCLUSION

These selected passages were probably never intended to evince guffaws of laughter. They do, however, represent very pointed irony and satire through strategies of playing with accepted stereotypes of, and attitudes towards, barbarians, and were intended to be humorous to an audience heavily attuned to the usual employment of these stereotypes. Usually the butt of the joke is the barbarian, sometimes it may be the Roman, but these inversions, these strategies of incongruity and inappropriateness, did not undermine or blur that binary distinction between the civilised and the barbarian; rather, this humour tended to reinforce it. In the changing world of the late fourth to sixth centuries, it may be that one literary response to these changes was to emphasise this division, however much it was becoming divorced from reality. The rhetorical figure of the barbarian was therefore not merely 'good to laugh at' but 'good to laugh with'.[100]

---

99 I do not, therefore, agree with Cameron's statement ('Gelimer's laughter', p. 171) that Procopius *admired* Gelimer.
100 I would like to thank the audience at Leeds in 1998 for their comments on the original, considerably more flippant and superficial, version of this paper. The fellow contributors to this volume provided much encouragement. Mark Humphries and Danuta Shanzer, in particular, have been very helpful. I am, as ever, grateful to my colleague at Birkbeck, Dr Emma Dench, for helpful leads and advice about classical ethnography and wit in the ancient historians.

CHAPTER 5

Liutprand of Cremona's sense of humour

Ross Balzaretti

The relationship between humour, history and gender is still neglected by historians despite a recent fashion for books about humour as an historical phenomenon.[1] This chapter illustrates the degree to which these three issues were linked together by Liutprand of Cremona (c.920/5–72) in his various writings.[2] Liutprand's *Antapodosis* (or 'Book of Revenge', written 958–62), *Liber de Ottone rege* (965) and *Relatio de legatione Constantinopolitana* (969–70),[3] each contain humorous passages, which are a fundamental feature of his unique literary style.[4] The most developed of

---

[1] *Humour and History*, ed. K. Cameron (Oxford, 1993); *A Cultural History of Humour*, ed. J. Bremmer and H. Roodenberg (London, 1997), with bibliography at pp. 242–52. There is an important discussion of medieval evidence in A. Gurevich, *Medieval Popular Culture: Problems of Belief and Perception* (Cambridge, 1988), pp. 176–210. However, gender issues are underplayed in each of these books.

[2] A useful introduction to Liutprand's work is provided by Brian Scott in his edition and translation of Liutprand's *Relatio de legatione Constantinopolitana* (Bristol, 1993), pp. vii–xxvii. The standard biography is J. N. Sutherland, *Liudprand of Cremona* (Spoleto, 1988). In addition to his own works, Liutprand also appears in eight Cremonese charters between 962 and 970 (*Codex diplomaticus Langobardiae*, ed. G. Porro Lambertenghi (Turin, 1873), nos. 651, 689, 695, 697, 699, 710, 717 and 718), five *diplomata* of Otto I (*MGH Diplomata Regum et Imperatorum Germaniae* I, ed. T. Von Sickel (Hanover, 1879–84), nos. 340, 341, 374a, 380a, 531) and one Italian court case (*I Placiti del 'Regnum Italiae'*, ed. C. Manaresi (3 vols., Rome, 1955–60), vol. II, no. 164).

[3] Joseph Becker's old edition (*Liutprandi Opera, MGH SRG* (Hanover, 1915)) is still useful for *Antapodosis*. Essential editorial discussions are F. Köhler, 'Beiträge zur Textkritik Liutprands von Cremona', *Neues Archiv* 8 (1883), pp. 49–89; J. Becker, *Textsgeschichte Liudprands von Cremona* (Munich, 1908); also his 'Zur handschriftlichen überlieferung Liudprands von Cremona', *Neues Archiv* 36 (1910/11), pp. 209–11; P. Chiesa, 'Un *descriptus* smascherato. Sulla posizione stemmatica della "vulgata" di Liutprando', *Filologia Mediolatina* 1 (1994), pp. 81–110; also his *Liutprando di Cremona e il codice di Frisinga Clm 6388* (Autographia Medii Aevi 1) (Turnhout, 1994). The most important examinations of Liutprand's historical style in addition to Leyser's articles are: G. Arnaldi, 'Liutprando e la storiografia contemporanea nell'Italia centro-settentrionale', *Settimane di Spoleto* 17(2) (1970), pp. 497–519 and 719–22; H. Hofman, 'Profil der lateinischen Historiographie im zehnten Jahrhundert', *Settimane di Spoleto* 38 (1991), pp. 837–905; and N. Staubach, 'Historia oder satira? Zur literarischen Stellung der Antapodosis Liudprands von Cremona', in *Lateinische Kultur im X Jahrhundert*, ed. W. Berschin (Stuttgart, 1991), pp. 461–87.

[4] These passages are (with 'keywords' in brackets): *Antapodosis* 1.1 (*faceti Tullii; utili comoediarum risu*); 1.11 (*memoria risuque dignas egit; subridens igitur imperator*); 1.12 (*egit ludum; pro hoc ludo; sed hilarem reddidit; magno est imperator cachinno inflatus; gaudio*); 1.22 (*redit hilarior*); 1.33 (*cantus ludicres*); 1.41 (*temolenti post*

all Liutprand's jokes (or *ludibrium*,[5] as he has it) is a tale that appears in *Antapodosis* 4.10, inserted into an otherwise anodyne report of a battle, which took place in the late 920s, between Tedbald, a relative of King Hugh of Italy, Liutprand's sometime patron, and some Greeks. I quote this in full in Frederic Wright's translation:[6]

Let me here insert the story of a witty (*ludibrium*), or rather a clever (*sapientiam*), trick which a certain woman played on this occasion. [1] One day some Greeks in company with the men of the countryside went out from a fortress to fight against the aforesaid Tedbald,[7] and a certain number of them were taken prisoners by him. [2] As he was taking them off to be castrated (*eunuchizaret*), a certain woman, fired by love (*amore*) for her husband and very disturbed for the safety of his members (*membris*), rushed out in a frenzy from the fortress with her hair all flying loose.[8] Tearing her cheeks with her nails until the blood came, she took her stand before Tedbald's tent and began to cry out and wail aloud. [3] At last Tedbald appeared and said to her: 'What is the matter with you, woman, that you are making such a loud and lamentable din?' [4] To that – a pretence of folly is at the proper time the height of wisdom[9] – [5] she replied: 'These

nonnulla inutilia tragodimata id est cantiones); 2.59 (*hyronica hac responsione*); 2.63 (*riso omnes emoririer*); 3.35 (*risum facile; risum; comoedia; ridiculus*); 3.41 (*fabulae vero ludum*); 3.52 (*urbanitate*); 4.10 (*ludibrium; cachinno commoti; risum*); 4.12 (*hilarior redditus; ha! ha! he!*); 4.15 (*facetia; Tullium facetia*); 5.31 (*cachynno*); 6.9 (*magno inflatus cachinno*); and 6.10 (*subridens itaque imperator*). Liber de Ottone rege 14 (a linguistic play on a double negative). Relatio 3 (description of Nicephorus); 10 (another description of Nicephorus); 21 (*ut de vobis ludum haberet*); 23 (*ad risum me non parum illexit*); 28 (description of Nicephorus' father); and 63 (wordplay on *capones* and *caupones*). Facetia, of course, became an important genre for joke-telling in Renaissance Italy; see C. Speroni, *Wit and Wisdom of the Italian Renaissance* (Berkeley and Los Angeles, 1964).

5 In light of the subject matter of this passage it is worth noting that *ludibrium* (standard classical Latin for 'joke') is etymologically related to *ludus*, which can have a sexual meaning in Latin, as 'play' can in English: J. N. Adams, *The Latin Sexual Vocabulary* (London, 1982), p. 162.

6 For reasons of space I have quoted throughout the English translation by Frederic A. Wright, *The Works of Liutprand of Cremona* (London, 1930; reprinted in 1993 as *The Embassy to Constantinople and Other Writings* with an introduction by John Julius Norwich). Wright brilliantly reproduces Liutprand's vivid style, although his vocabulary is often quaint. Where Wright's interpretation is open to question I have included the Latin in parentheses. I am preparing a new English translation of *Antapodosis* for Manchester University Press. I have added some pointers (numbers 1–8 in the text) to the narrative structure of the passage. The chapter falls into eight sections: 1. Announcement of joke; 2. Statement of the situation; 3. Action; 4. Dialogue; 5. Moral comment; 6. Resumed dialogue (the longest section in the woman's voice); 7. End of the story; 8. Final moral comment about laughter.

7 Tedbald was related to King Hugh of Provence, who later became king of Italy, by marriage (*Antapodosis* 4.9), and became marquis of Camerino and Spoleto. Liutprand notes that he was dead in *Antapodosis* 5.4.

8 'Frenzy' refers to Virgil, *Aeneid* 4.646 (the death of Dido: *interiora domus inrumpit limina et altos conscendit furibunda rogos ensemque recludit Dardanium* . . .); 'loose hair' to *Aeneid* 1.480 (*interea ad templum non aequae Palladis ibant crinibus Iliades passis peplumque ferebant suppliciter*. . .) and 2.404 (*ecce trahebatur passis Priameia virgo crinibus a templo Cassandra* . . .), where the phrasing is very similar; in *Virgil: Aeneid* I–VI, ed. R. D. Williams (London, 1972), pp. 94, 16 and 37 respectively.

9 This moral is taken from *Disticha Catonis* 2.8, a text used in Carolingian education (*Texts and Transmission: A Survey of the Latin Classics*, ed. L. D. Reynolds (Oxford, 1983)).

are strange and unheard-of doings, heroes to make war against women who cannot attack you back. None of our daughters are descended from the stock of the Amazons. We devote our lives to Minerva's work and are quite ignorant of weapons.'[10] Tedbald then said to her: 'What hero in his right mind ever made war upon women, except in the days of the Amazons?' 'What more cruel war', she answered, 'can you make on women, or what more grievous loss can you inflict upon them, than to seek to deprive their husbands of that member on which the warmth of our bodies depends and in which, most important of all, our hopes of children in the future are centred (*quam ut earum viris certetis orchidia amputare, in quibus nostri refocilatio corporis et, quod omnium potissimum est, nasciturae spes extat prolis?*). By castrating (*eunuchizatis*) our men you rob them of something which is not theirs but ours. I ask you, did the flocks of sheep and herds of cattle that you took from me last week bring me as a suppliant to your camp? I willingly agree to give up the animals, but this other loss, so serious, so cruel and so irreparable, I shudder at, I shrink from, I refuse. May all the Gods above protect me from such a calamity! (*Sancti dei omnes talem a mea avertite pestem!*)'[11] [6] At this the whole army burst into a guffaw (*cachinno commoti*), and her arguments were received with such favour that they earned for her not only the return of her husband intact (*virum suum integrum*) but also of the beasts that had been driven away. As she was going off with her belongings Tedbald sent a page after her to ask what part of her husband he should remove if he came out again from the fortress to fight against him. 'My husband', she said, 'has a nose, eyes, hands and feet. If he comes out again, let your master remove those parts that belong to him; but let him leave me, his humble servant, what is mine.' [7] Such was the answer she sent back by the messenger, for she realised, by the laughter (*risum*) that her first speech had evoked and by the return of her husband, that she had the favour of the army on her side.[12] [8].

This brilliant passage, which is surely distinctive enough to be called Liutprandian, raises three issues that face every historian of humour: its recognition, intention and narration.

RECOGNITION

How can historians be sure something is meant to be funny in their sources? Jokes obviously come in and out of fashion and humour varies so widely now that recapturing past humour is bound to be difficult and frequently impossible. This problem is widely seen as common to the historical analysis of humour at all periods, but it tends to be worse the

---

[10] *Aeneid* 5.284 (not literally the same but clearly alluding to this passage).

[11] *Aeneid* 3.620 (where the phrase is spoken by a man, Achaemenides: *di talem terris avertite pestem!*).

[12] The best edition is *Liutprandi Cremonensis opera omnia, Corpus Christianorum*, Continuatio Mediaevalis, CLVI, ed. P. Chiesa (Turnhout, 1998), pp. 101–3.

further back one goes, mainly because we have an imperfect understanding of the social context in which the humour appears.[13] In Liutprand's case the matter is relatively straightforward because his text alerts the reader to funny stories with certain key words and phrases: what Amy Richlin, in her investigation of Roman humour, has termed 'cueing'.[14] In *Antapodosis* 4.10 these words are *ludibrium*, *cachinnum* and *risus*. In the work as a whole the most common 'funny words' are *cachinnum*, *facetus*, *risus*, *hilarior* and *ludus*.[15] Liutprand's self-conscious indication of humour in this way, although it is typical of Roman comedic and satirical texts, singles him out in the early medieval context as one of very few authors who dare to tell jokes.[16] What is more, he does so in a manner which leaves us in no doubt that he, and one presumes his contemporary readers if he had any, had a sense of humour, which is still recognisable to us over a thousand years later.

INTENTION

Why does an author use humour? This issue is particularly important in analysing Liutprand because so many of his modern readers have used these apparently frivolous passages to attack his worth as an historian.[17] Liutprand himself is quite clear about humour in the first preface to *Antapodosis* (1.1), which he addressed to Recemund, bishop of Elvira in Spain, whom he had probably encountered at Otto I's court:[18]

Lovers of learning are like men sick of the dropsy: as these thirst the more ardently the more water they drink, so students, the more they read, the more

---

[13] The importance of this aspect is brought out by M. Douglas, 'Jokes', in her *Implicit Meanings: Essays in Anthropology* (London, 1975), pp. 90–114.

[14] A. Richlin, *The Garden of Priapus: Sexuality and Aggression in Roman Humour* (rev. edn, New York, 1992), pp. 64–5; also Halsall, above, pp. 90–1.

[15] See n. 4, above. Some of these words had long been associated with laughter in monastic writing, a fact of which Liutprand was probably aware, although not himself a monk: see J. Le Goff, 'Le Rire dans les règles monastiques du haut moyen âge', in *Haut Moyen Age: culture, education et société. Etudes offerts à P. Riché*, ed. M. Sot (Nantes, 1990), pp. 93–103; also his 'Laughter in the Middle Ages', in *A Cultural History of Humour*, ed. Bremmer and Roodenberg, pp. 40–53; and I. M. Resnick, '"*Risus monasticus*": laughter and medieval monastic culture', *Revue Bénédictine* 97 (1987), pp. 90–100.

[16] For instance Notker and Hrotswitha: D. Ganz, 'Humour as history in Notker's *Gesta Karoli Magni*', in *Monks, Nuns and Friars in Medieval Society* (Sewanee Medieval Studies 4), ed. E. B. King, J. T. Schaefer and W. B. Wadley (Sewanee, TN, 1989), pp. 171–83; P. Dronke, *Women Writers of the Middle Ages* (Cambridge, 1984), pp. 54–83.

[17] Most obviously those nineteenth-century German critics listed in n. 3, above. John Julius Norwich, in his introduction to the reprint of Wright's translation (p. xv), singles out Liutprand's wit as a distinctive and positive quality for modern readers.

[18] The so-called 'Second Preface' (*Antapodosis* 3.1) is also addressed to this person (Sutherland, *Liutprand*, pp. 52–4 and Leyser 'Ends and means', pp. 131–5).

eagerly they seek after new knowledge [*quia phylosophi ydropicorum?, qui quo amplius bibunt, eo ardentius sitiunt*].[19] Let students then, when they are wearied by the difficult perusal [*perplexa lectione*] of Cicero's wit [*faceti Tullii*],[20] find recreation in these outpourings of mine. For, if I am not mistaken, just as the eyes are dazzled and blinded by the sun's rays, unless some substance intervenes to cloud their pure brilliancy, so in the case of our academic, peripatetic and stoic philosophers [*achademicorum, peripatheticorum, stoicorumque*] the mind is weakened by the constant study of their doctrines unless it finds refreshment in the useful humours of a comedy [*utili comoediarum risu*] or in the delectable histories of heroic men [*heroum delectibili historia*].

This explicit statement about the function of humour at the outset of *Antapodosis* is essential to an understanding of the entire text. Liutprand seems to be suggesting that his writing will combine the traditionally unrelated genres of comedy (*comoedia*) and history (*historia*). He is clear that he intends to employ what we call humour to make his book, to which he never gives the name 'history', more readable and, indeed, entertaining. In particular, this section provides further evidence that Liutprand is one of the very few early medieval writers to employ humour quite deliberately. In the books that followed he certainly carried out this aim, self-consciously inserting humorous incidents: he uses the word '*inserere*'.[21] These passages prove that Liutprand used humour deliberately as a rhetorical device, as Cicero had suggested.[22]

NARRATION

How does Liutprand tell his humorous stories? Let us return to the complex joke in book 4.10. The tale itself owes most to the classical practice of *inventio*, the deliberate invention of material, intended to persuade the reader of a greater truth and much used by classical historians.[23] It is

---

[19] Augustine, *Sermones* 177 (*PL* 38, col. 956): *Volendo ergo dives esse, desiderat, aestat, sitit; et tanquam hydropsis morbo, plus bibendo, plus sitit.*

[20] Book 4.30 has *Tulliana facetia* in a story about Henry I. Cicero was famed for his wit and discussed humour at length in *De oratore* and *De officiis*: see M. L. Clarke, *Rhetoric at Rome: A Historical Survey* (London, 1953), pp. 59–60 and 77–8 and F. Graf, 'Cicero, Plautus and Roman laughter', in *A Cultural History of Humour*, ed. Bremmer and Roodenburg , pp. 29–39. Liutprand's knowledge of Cicero was considerable but did not, apparently, include either of these texts (*Liutprandi opera omnia*, pp. 226–7).

[21] Book 1.11, 1.22, 3.41, 4.10. Book 4.12 is similar in effect but does not actually use *inserere*.

[22] Graf, 'Cicero', p. 31. Other ancient theories of humour are usefully examined by G. E. Duckworth, *The Nature of Roman Comedy* (2nd edn, London, 1994; 1st edn 1952), pp. 305–14.

[23] R. Ray, 'The triumph of Greco-Roman rhetorical assumptions in pre-Carolingian historiography', in *The Inheritance of Historiography*, ed. C. Holdsworth and T. P. Wiseman (Exeter, 1986); P. Ricoeur, 'History and rhetoric', in *The Social Responsibility of the Historian*, ed. F. Bédarida (Providence, RI, 1994), pp. 7–24.

impossible to tell if the event as Liutprand recounts it actually happened as it is not recorded elsewhere, but this fact alone suggests that Liutprand did indeed invent it, despite his protestations elsewhere that he was an eyewitness.[24] Such invention had to be realistic and one of the ways to achieve this was with dialogue, which is precisely what Liutprand does.[25] The situation is not of itself funny but it is certainly realistic and vivid. A man has been captured by his enemy and is about to be castrated. His wife pleads for mercy, which is granted by the generous hero. This is surely the main moral point of telling the story: mercy is an important quality in a just and heroic ruler. How Liutprand turns this seemingly poor material into a joke is the crux of my argument concerning his sense of humour. He does this by adding gender, by adding a speaking woman to what is otherwise an all-male event.

At one level, the crudity of Liutprand's gendering is intriguingly like that of a modern stand-up comedian: both depend on stereotypical and ostensibly universal gender figures.[26] In Liutprand's joke the unnamed woman and her unnamed husband are apparently intended to represent married couples in general rather than an actual couple, in contrast to the rest of the characters in the tale who are named and really lived. Liutprand stresses that the woman's active need for sex lies behind her concern for her passive husband, which is quite surprising given that married life, for Liutprand and most other contemporary clerics, represented either the dominance of the man over his wife or equality between them, but never the dominance of the woman.[27] Perhaps Liutprand's blatant transgression of these norms in book 4.10 was the funniest aspect for contemporary readers? Such transgression is, after all, what makes many a joke a joke in the first place. Yet this is not a simple tale of improper womanly behaviour, for she is certainly properly passive in the face of Tedbald, the main male authority figure. In other respects, too, this woman behaves in what Liutprand would have one believe is a typically female way. Her physicality is evident in all her actions. Her hair is long but loose, as a wife's hair could be in times of

---

[24] *Antapodosis* 4.1, a commonplace statement in medieval historical writing; E. Van Houts, *Memory and Gender in Medieval Europe 900–1200* (London, 1999), pp. 20–6.

[25] Ray, 'Triumph', p. 73. For the use of dialogues in tenth-century education, see H. Fichtenau, *Living in the Tenth Century* (English trans., Chicago, 1991; German original, Stuttgart, 1984), pp. 290–2.

[26] M. Mulkay, *On Humour: Its Nature and Its Place in Modern Society* (Cambridge, 1988), pp. 134–51.

[27] R. Balzaretti, 'Men and sex in tenth-century Italy', in *Masculinity in Medieval Europe*, ed. D. M. Hadley (London, 1999), pp. 143–59, at p. 147; J. A. Brundage, *Law, Sex, and Christian Society in Medieval Europe* (Chicago, 1987), pp. 174–5.

crisis,[28] and the blood runs from her torn cheeks. She wails and is both unpredictable (she *might* be an Amazon) and devious. But above all she desires the man's penis (where have we heard that before?). At the start of the story this woman's love (*amor*) for her husband is set alongside her need for his penis but her love is not taken up later on, when only desire is important. We are left in no doubt that her relationship to her husband is primarily a sexual one, in which what we may care to see as her Freudian desire for his penis, although couched in terms of procreation rather than pleasure, is presented as something she needs and, indeed, has rights over. Her situation is also typically female: she is in the fortress ('at home'), where she works and does not fight.

Stereotyping women was hardly new, as Liutprand's pointed allusions to Minerva and the Amazons make clear. Men's mocking of women was commonplace in Roman comedy and Liutprand's presentation of a woman as a diversion for men, as something at which a male collectivity can laugh, duly adds another element to his joke about women's sexual desires. By the end, if we laugh at all it is *because* the story has been gendered. It might be objected that the woman gets what she wants as her husband is not castrated and is released. While true, this does not mean that Liutprand had an enlightened view of women but rather that he did not have a fully worked out, consistent view of gender in which all parts added up to a coherent whole. Instead, he employed some tired and very ancient gender stereotypes about the differences between men and women to add humour to his already scurrilous polemic. This point is only reinforced when one considers some of the jokes he makes about real, rather than imaginary, people.

Two chapters on (*Antapodosis* 4.12), Liutprand tells a joke about Queen Willa, wife of Boso and mother of Willa the wife of Berengar II, one of Liutprand's main political targets.[29] According to Liutprand, King Hugh wanted a valuable jewelled belt, which belonged to his brother Boso. Hugh expelled Boso's wife Willa from Italy because she was responsible for their plot against him. As Willa was leaving:

---

[28] Loose hair in women was often associated with mourning: R. Bartlett, 'Symbolic meanings of hair in the Middle Ages', *Transactions of the Royal Historical Society*, 6th ser., 4 (1994), pp. 43–60, at pp. 53–5. The subject of *Aeneid* 1.480, to which Liutprand alludes, is a funeral.

[29] P. Buc, 'Italian hussies and German matrons: Liutprand of Cremona on dynastic legitimacy', *Frühmittelalterliche Studien* 29 (1995), pp. 207–25, esp. pp. 210 and 215. I thank Philippe Buc for kindly allowing me to read this important article before publication. P. Stafford, *Queens, Concubines and Dowagers* (Leicester, 1998; 1st edn 1983), pp. 20 and 24 (where the two Willas are confused!); and E. Colonna, 'Figure femminili in Liutprando di Cremona', *Quaderni medievali* 14 (1982), pp. 29–60.

they stripped the queen completely naked. All the honest soldiers turned their eyes away rather than behold such a shameful and unprecedented sight; but one of the servants ventured to look keenly at her and saw a piece of string hanging close by the round and rosy hemispheres of her buttocks. This string the shameless rascal caught and pulled: and lo and behold, the belt made its appearance from the very intimate retreat where it had been hidden. The man, so far from blushing at his disgusting act, burst into a laugh [*hilarior redditus*]. 'Ha, ha, ha!' he cried, 'we soldiers know something of midwifery. Here is a ruddy youngster for the mistress. I hope he will get on well . . .'³⁰ This finished the business: the belt was taken to the king, and the lady was packed off to Burgundy. Whether it was the hider or the searcher who showed the greater lack of decency is a very ticklish question. But it is obvious that both Hugh and Willa were inspired by an excessive love of jewels and gold.³¹

This is perhaps Liutprand's most vulgar anecdote, as he himself duly notes (*uno turpissimo descripto*, 4.11), and it may well have been intended to titillate his male readership with its explicit treatment of Willa's body. Nevertheless, Liutprand is reluctant to push the joke to quite the obscene lengths that were common in Roman writing.³² This is a very different joke to *Antapodosis* 4.10: it is far more vicious in its mockery of Willa and relies on humiliation and ridicule for its effect. Liutprand, as he said at the start of book 3, was indeed getting his own back (*antapodosis, hoc est retributio*).

Not all of Liutprand's jokes were centred on women. Following again in the traditions of Roman satire Liutprand has the male genitals ranking high amongst funny objects.³³ The *size* of a man's penis, in particular, gave rise to obvious 'nudge, nudge, wink, wink' jokes. In *Antapodosis* 5.32 Liutprand reports the adulterous liaison (*crimen incesti*) of Willa, Berengar's wife, with her chaplain Dominic who, when they were discovered, was castrated. Liutprand adds a jokey aside that her attraction to him was explained by his large penis: 'Those who turned the priest into a eunuch declared that there was good reason for the love his mistress bore him: his weapon, they discovered, was worthy of Priapus himself.'³⁴ Although the difference in status between the queen and her servant is an important part of the joke, the discovery of Dominic's large

---

³⁰ Terence, *Andria* 486–487: '. . . *deos queso ut sit superstes*' (P. Terenti Afri, *Andria*, ed. G. P. Shipp (Melbourne, 1960), p. 87), which Liutprand quotes exactly.

³¹ *Antapodosis* 4.12. *Liutprandi omnia opera*, pp. 103–4.

³² As is clear from Richlin, *Garden of Priapus*, particularly ch. 3, which includes another helpful discussion of theories of humour.

³³ Adams, *Latin Sexual Vocabulary*, pp. 9–79.

³⁴ *Dixerunt autem, qui eum eunuchizaverunt, quod merito illum domina amaret, quem priapeia portare arma constaret.*

penis constitutes the punch line. *Arma*, the word used here for penis, was the normal word in classical Latin literature for Priapus' penis, used by Martial and Ovid (and later Augustine).[35] In this way Liutprand could show off his knowledge of pagan literature while simultaneously telling sexual jokes with a most contemporary resonance. Despite this apparent frivolity, a more serious point about desire may underlie this type of joke. Surely it is possible that Liutprand is here taking a swipe at Willa's husband Berengar by implying that his penis could not satisfy Willa because it was too small? Perhaps Liutprand is telling us that he and his aristocratic male contemporaries regarded the large penis, representing a really masculine man, as an understandable object of desire for women? It is with some irony, then, that cutting off the penis, whether castration as a punishment or the creation of eunuchs as servants, was apparently funnier still.[36] As seen above, it is the subject of an elaborate joke in *Antapodosis* 4.10, this one about Dominic and various others in Liutprand's *Relatio*.[37]

Liutprand jokes elsewhere about men. In the course of narrating the fight for the Italian throne between Berengar II and Adalbert in *Antapodosis* 2.63 Liutprand recorded the following incident:

Giselbert (count of Bergamo) for his part was recognised, and after being whipped and put in chains was dragged before Berengar half naked [*seminudus*].[38] He had no drawers on and only a short tunic, so that when he fell down hastily on his face at the king's feet the whole company almost died with laughter to see his genitals [or testicles, perhaps?] plainly revealed [*in genitalium ostensione membrorum riso omnes emoririer*].[39] King Berengar, however, loving piety as always, listened again to the voice of mercy, although Giselbert did not deserve it, and instead of gratifying the people's wish by returning evil for evil, he had him taken to a bath at once and supplied with rich raiment . . .

---

[35] Adams, *Latin Sexual Vocabulary*, pp. 16 and 21.

[36] For the Greek context, with which Liutprand was to become so familiar, see S. F. Tougher, 'Byzantine eunuchs: an overview, with special reference to their creation and origin', in *Women, Men and Eunuchs: Gender in Byzantium*, ed. L. James (London, 1997), pp. 168–184; also his 'Images of effeminate men: the case of Byzantine eunuchs', in *Masculinity in Medieval Europe*, ed. Hadley, pp. 89–100. Of course, Greek and Roman writers provided Liutprand with material on this subject, notably Terence's *Eunuchus*, which is cited eighteen times in *Antapodosis*, five times in *Legatio* and twice in *Liber Ottonis*.

[37] For example, *Relatio* 63 where Liutprand makes fun of eunuch-bishops.

[38] Suetonius, *De vita Caesarum, Vitellius* 17: '*donec religatis post terga manibus ineicto cervicibus laqueo, veste discussa seminudus in forum tractatus est inter magna rerum verborumque ludibria per totum viae sacrae spatium*', in *Galba, Otho, Vitellius*, ed. C. L. Murison (London, 1992), p. 22. Liutprand must have known this passage in some form. Liutprand also uses *cachinnus*, a Suetonian favourite, in the same way as Suetonius, namely when soldiers are laughing (Adams, *Latin Sexual Vocabulary*, p. 4).

[39] *Terence: Eunuchus*, ed. J. Barsby (Cambridge, 1999), 432: *risu omnes qui aderant emoriri* ('all the company died of laughter straight off'). Barsby points out (p. 164) that '"to die of laughter" goes back to Homer, though it does not otherwise appear in surviving Latin literature', strongly suggesting that Liutprand did indeed know precisely this passage.

Once more, the moral point of this story – that Berengar was a pious king as demonstrated by the clemency he showed Giselbert – is not what makes it funny. It is not certain why the exposure of Giselbert's testicles to the soldiers should be so funny but this was probably seen as something particularly humiliating, which other men should not see. The joke is once again gendered by inversion because Giselbert's passivity meant that he was not behaving as a proper man: he had been symbolically, rather than literally, emasculated. Liutprand's male characters spend a great deal of their time actively fighting battles, something which seems to have been an important component of their masculine identity and which women, generally speaking, did not do.[40] A comparison with the castration story in *Antapodosis* 4.10 is again apt: Liutprand again connects sex and politics, in this case the sexual humiliation of a man with his political humiliation, and has his soldiers once more laughing together at the joke.

LIUTPRAND'S SENSE OF HUMOUR

Surely an Ottonian audience, given its strong sense of its own ethnic identity, would have enjoyed these jokes about its numerous enemies? Cultural superiority explains Liutprand's more obvious racial humour, too. Like most educated westerners in the tenth century he found Greek habits especially funny and rarely lost an opportunity to mock them.[41] The unnamed husband and wife in *Antapodosis* 4.10 were, of course, Greeks and this ethnic difference adds yet another dimension to this joke. He makes further 'Greek jokes' in *Antapodosis* 1.11, 1.12, 3.35, 3.41, 6.9 and 6.10, and throughout the *Relatio*, particularly taking the rise out of eunuchs and the *basileus*. Much more surprising in view of the commonly held assumption that Liutprand's intended audience encompassed both

---

[40] I do not have space here to explore the extent to which Liutprand had absorbed contemporary 'heroic' values and might be undermining these in a passage such as this. For some interesting suggestions regarding *Waltharius*, see D. Townsend, 'Ironic intertextuality and the reader's resistance to heroic masculinity in the *Waltharius*', in *Becoming Male in the Middle Ages*, ed. J. J. Cohen and B. Wheeler (New York, 1997), pp. 67–86. However, it should not be assumed that fighting was an unproblematic activity for all members of the aristocracy: J. L. Nelson, 'Monks, secular men and masculinity, c.900', in *Masculinity in Medieval Europe*, ed. Hadley, pp. 121–42. On *Waltharius*, see also Innes, below, p. 152, n. 60.

[41] K. J. Leyser 'The tenth century in Byzantine–western relationships', in *Relations between East and West in the Middle Ages*, ed. D. Baker (Edinburgh, 1973). H. Mayr-Harting, 'Liudprand of Cremona's account of his legation to Constantinople (968) and Ottonian imperial strategy', *English Historical Review* 116 (2001), pp. 539–56. See also Kershaw, below, pp. 194–5. For the other side of the coin, see Haldon, above, pp. 58–9.

a Spanish bishop and the severe Otto himself,[42] is the striking fact that in
Antapodosis Liutprand's humour is preoccupied with men's genitals. Why
should penises raise so many laughs in an ostensibly serious work?[43] It
may be thought that he was simply copying Roman practice, quoting
as he does various passages from Virgil, Terence and Suetonius in his
own humorous tales.[44] But, as these quotations are only rarely humorous
in themselves, there must be rather more to it than mere imitation of
Roman humour. To understand what Liutprand was doing one must
turn to his relationship with his own society and to think further about
gender.

Genitals are unavoidably sexed male and female. For this reason
Liutprand could signal all sorts of gendered relationships to his readers
simply by making jokes about penises.[45] He could, for example, laugh off
contemporary taboos about nakedness by having soldiers laugh equally
at the unexpected exposure of men's and women's genitalia.[46] Difference
between men and women, exemplified by the penis, was an essential part
of what one might call Liutprand's 'world view' of his own society. It is
abundantly clear from almost every page of *Antapodosis* that he did not
regard women and men as equals, least of all in the political arena, his
main concern after all. Philippe Buc has recently tried to argue away
Liutprand's obvious misogyny by suggesting that his outlook was determined by considerations of dynastic legitimacy rather than concepts
of gender.[47] Although he argues convincingly that Liutprand's literary
venom was directed at particular rather than all women, namely those
associated with the Italian branches of the Carolingian family, and that
Liutprand's praise for Ottonian women was unfettered, nevertheless
Buc's view of the motivations behind *Antapodosis* results in a binary
interpretation, which is too simplistic. A writer as clever as Liutprand

[42] Leyser, *Communications and Power*, pp. 131–5 (Recemund of Elvira); K. J. Leyser, *Rule and Conflict in an Early Medieval Society: Ottonian Saxony* (London, 1979), pp. 35–6 (contemporaries' views of Otto I).
[43] Karl Leyser has proved the most convincing advocate of the serious, 'homiletic': K. J. Leyser, 'Liudprand of Cremona: preacher and homilist' and 'Ends and means in Liudprand of Cremona', in *Communications and Power in Medieval Europe: The Carolingian and Ottoman Centuries*, ed. T. Reuter (London, 1994), pp. 109–24 and 125–42.
[44] Liutprand's knowledge of classical writers was much wider than these three: *Liutprandi opera omnia*, pp. 223–34 and Sutherland, *Liudprand*, pp. 21–4.
[45] The relevant bibliography on gender is far too large to list here. It can be accessed in J. M. H. Smith, 'Gender and ideology in the early Middle Ages', *Studies in Church History* 34 (1998), pp. 51–73. I have found Nancy Partner's formulations particularly useful: 'No sex, no gender', *Speculum* 68 (1993), pp. 419–44.
[46] Richlin, *Garden of Priapus*, pp. 57 and 64 for Roman precedent.
[47] Buc, 'Italian hussies', esp. pp. 210 and 215.

could easily adopt many literary strategies: he could certainly blacken the reputations of Carolingian women while moralising about the place of women in society at large. Moreover, even if Liutprand does present Ottonian women in 'an unfailingly positive light',[48] Buc is unjustified in claiming 'no misogyny there' because at the root of misogyny is not simple hatred of women but rather a refusal to portray women as they really are. Adelaide and Matilda could surely not have been as docile as Liutprand would have his readers think. The point is reinforced if one considers the representation of men in *Antapodosis* with gender in mind, which Buc ignores. Women may be funny when active or passive but men could only be funny when passive, as far as can be seen. Men who do not behave as Liutprand *expects* men to behave get laughed at as though they were women. Indeed, Liutprand tellingly saw them as *principum effeminatorum*, which really does mean 'effeminate princes' (Wright's translation) and not Buc's bizarre 'female-addicted princes'.[49]

Few other tenth-century writers dealt with gender as explicitly and as humorously as Liutprand. Indeed, if Peter Dronke is right to see a 'precious world' at the centre of Otto I's court, Liutprand, with his rather crude sense of humour, may well have felt ill at ease there.[50] Ratherius of Verona, eccentric as ever, admits to having a sense of humour, only at once to censure himself for it.[51] Hrotswitha's humour, as displayed in her plays and other verse,[52] was at times so 'supersubtle' that some readers might question its very existence.[53] Yet her *Gesta Ottonis*, written c.963/73 and perhaps the most interesting contemporary comparison with

---

[48] Ibid., p. 211.   [49] *Antapodosis* 1.1; Buc 'Italian hussies', p. 215.

[50] Dronke, *Women Writers*, p. 59. The nature of Otto's court, and even its existence, continues to be controversial: see T. Reuter, *Germany in the Early Middle Ages* (London, 1991), pp. 246–52; K. Wilson, *Hrotsvitha of Gandersheim: The Ethics of Authorial Stance* (Leiden, 1988), pp. 145–56; C. J. Jaeger, *The Envy of Angels: Cathedral Schools and Social Ideals in Medieval Europe, 950–1250* (Philadelphia, 1994), pp. 37–52; and especially J. Fleckenstein, 'Königshof und Bischofsschule unter Otto dem Grossen', *Archiv für Kulturgeschichte* 38 (1956), pp. 38–62.

[51] *The Complete Works of Ratherius of Verona*, trans. P. L. D. Reid (Binghampton, NY, 1991), pp. 12 and 434. Ratherius' humour, recognised by Liutprand as *urbanitas* (*Antapodosis* 3.52), awaits its historian. Another monastic author in whom some have detected a sense of humour is Letaldus of Micy: see C. E. Lutz, 'Letaldus, a wit of the tenth century', *Viator* 1 (1970), pp. 97–106 and *Letaldo di Micy: Within Piscator*, ed. F. Bertini (Florence, 1995). For the development of the attitudes that informed Ratherius' self-censure, see Innes, below, pp. 142–3.

[52] *The Plays of Hrotsvit of Gandersheim*, trans. K. Wilson (New York and London, 1989), p. xii. The most famous example is the much-discussed comic scene in *Dulcitius*, where Dulcitius is observed by a group of hidden virgins kissing pots and pans thinking he is kissing them (*Hrotsvithae Opera, MGH SRG* 34, ed. P. de Winterfeld (Berlin, 1967), pp. 128–9; *Plays of Hrotsvit*, trans. Wilson, pp. 41–2); discussed by Lutz, 'Letaldus', pp. 97–8 and S. Sticca, 'Hrotswitha's "Dulcitius" and Christian symbolism', *Mediaeval Studies* 32 (1970), pp. 108–27, at p. 126, who argues that Hrotswitha's humour is designed only to tell truths about Christianity).

[53] Dronke, *Women Writers*, pp. 59, 70, 74 and 83.

Antapodosis, appears to have little space for humour.[54] Importantly, Hrotswitha's understanding of contemporary gender relations was very different to Liutprand's for she did not find powerful women odd and did not use humour to ridicule Ottonian enemies. Similar conclusions emerge from reading the works of the other Ottonian historians, Widukind of Corvey and Adalberg of Magdeburg.[55] There is a remarkable absence of humour in their resolutely serious histories.[56]

This contrast between the historiographical seriousness of most tenth-century writers and Liutprand may lead one to wonder if his deliberate use of humour to enliven his historical work was something of his own invention. Roman historians, such as Livy or Sallust, whose works Liutprand may have known, did not generally use humour in *historia*. The only real exception was Suetonius, who Liutprand only cites directly twice. Liutprand certainly knew what *historia* was and one can be fairly sure that he was not writing it in the sense in which he and his contemporaries normally understood it.[57] His *libellulus* (*Antapodosis*, 1.1 and 3.1) was, as he explicitly says, a mix of *historia* and *comedia*. Today it might best be called historical satire.[58]

Jacques Le Goff has suggested that the history of early medieval humour falls into two distinct phases: repressed and stifled monastic laughter between the fourth and tenth centuries; and the liberation and control

---

[54] *Hrotsvithae Opera*, ed. De Winterfeld, pp. 201–28. English translation: B. Hill, *Medieval Monarchy in Action* (London, 1967), pp. 118–37. Important discussions of Hrotswitha: Dronke, *Women Writers*, pp. 55–83; P. Corbet, *Les Saintes ottoniens* (Sigmaringen, 1986), pp. 111–20; J. L. Nelson, 'Gender and genre in women historians of the early Middle Ages', in her *The Frankish World* (London, 1995); Wilson, *Hrotswitha of Gandersheim*, esp. pp. 111–42 on her epics; E. M. Van Houts, 'Women and the writing of history in the early Middle Ages: the case of Abbess Matilda of Essen and Aethelweard', *Early Medieval Europe* 1(1) (1992), pp. 53–68.

[55] *Widukindi monachi Corbeiensis rerum gestarum Saxonicarum libri tres*, ed. H.-E. Lohmann and P. Hirsch, *MGH SRG* 60 (Hanover, 1935); H. Beumann, *Widukind von Corvei* (Weimar, 1950); *Reginonis Abbatis Prumiensis chronicon cum continuatione Treverensi*, *MGH SRG* 50, ed. F. Kurze (Hanover, 1890). Tim Reuter (*Germany in the Early Middle Ages*, p. 249) argues that 'Ottonian house historiography' did not exist as such. Be that as it may, the seriousness with which these two writers regarded the events of their own times is certainly evident in Leyser, *Rule and Conflict*, whose opening sentence is: 'The world of the tenth century is, or ought to be, strange to us, much stranger than that of the twelfth with its lyrical, individualistic, witty and rationalising traits.' Here Liutprand is very much the exception that proves the rule.

[56] Karl Leyser's high opinion of Widukind as a historian is clear from remarks in *Communications and Power*, pp. 27 (a brief sketch of Widukind) and 229 (where Widukind, and Liutprand, are praised for their vividness and timelessness).

[57] E. Van Houts, *Local and Regional Chronicles* (Turnhout, 1995), pp. 13–16 is a convenient summary of the various genres which should, however, be read in conjunction with F. Lifshitz, 'Beyond positivism and genre: "hagiographical" texts as historical narrative', *Viator* 25 (1994), pp. 95–113, and Hofman, 'Profil'. It is worth stressing here that Liutprand's knowledge of important early historians such as Gregory of Tours and Bede requires further research.

[58] Staubach, 'Historia oder satira?'

of laughter in satire and parody in the eleventh and twelfth centuries.[59] Liutprand surely fits into the second phase and may, indeed, herald it. How did this come about? Perhaps his attachment to humour was something he had learnt before he was exposed to Otto's court culture, namely at the court of King Hugh in Pavia where he stayed in 931 and 932.[60] Liutprand claims that King Hugh was particularly taken with his singing and other references to Pavia suggest some fondness for the place, epitomised in his devotion to the town's patron, Syrus, and his opening acknowledgement of 'the wise Boethius' (on whose *De consolatione* he modelled much of the *Antapodosis*).[61] But it is hard to pin down the nature of Liutprand's educational experience in the town as, although other sources make clear that Pavia was one of the most important places in Europe for legal learning at this time, one cannot know as much as one would like about its monastic scriptoria nor its schools in the first half of the tenth century.[62] Ratherius may have lamented his lack of books while imprisoned in Pavia by Hugh between February 934 and August 936 but one may fairly presume that the great display of erudition found in his *Praeloquia* does not reflect the availability of texts in the town.[63] Therefore, the most interesting question of all – how Liutprand became so attached to literary humour – has, for the moment, to be left open.

In conclusion, Liutprand is a very important author in the history of humorous writing in the west because it is possible to recognise when he means to be funny; to follow how he is being funny; and to understand why he is being funny. These three things, together with the fact that he is funny at all, make him an unusual early medieval writer (although, as is clear from other essays in this volume, there were others). But, in my view, it is how history, humour and gender come together in Liutprand's writing that is so interesting. Having discussed *Antapodosis* 4.10 in numerous seminars I can report that it never fails to raise a laugh with modern audiences, in my experience rare with early medieval jokes, which are usually of the most basic sort. If people still laugh at Liutprand's crudely gendered jokes today, what does this mean? There can be little doubt

[59] Le Goff, 'Laughter in the Middle Ages', p. 50.

[60] Sutherland, *Liudprand*, p. 5.　　[61] *Antapodosis* 4.1, 3.5–6 and 1.1.

[62] The best treatment of the schools remains D. A. Bullough, 'Le scuole cattedrali e la cultura dell'Italia settentrionale prima dei communi', in *Vescovi e diocesi in Italia nel medioevo (Atti del Secondo Convegno di Storia della Chiesa in Italia)* (Italia Sacra 5) (Padua, 1964), pp. 111–43; also Sutherland, *Liutprand*, pp. 3–5, 12 and 22.

[63] *Praeloquia* 6.26, in *Rather of Verona*, trans. Reid, p. 206. Fichtenau, *Living in the Tenth Century*, p. 293, bizarrely attributes Ratherius' 'success' in Pavia to the extent of his classical knowledge!

that Liutprand's sense of humour, which I would characterise as male and heterosexual, was, and is, a type of abstract humour well suited to all patriarchal societies, even though it arose in a very concrete political context. Finally, I believe that Liutprand really did have a *sense* of humour. He was self-consciously making jokes that amused him. Self-awareness may have been characteristic of many tenth-century writers, notably Ratherius and Hrotswitha, but their humour was different to Liutprand's, which was characteristically all his own.[64]

---

[64] Freud noted a long time ago that humour is fundamentally egotistical ('Humour', in *The Standard Edition of the Complete Psychological Works of Sigmund Freud*, ed. J. Strachey *et al.* (24 vols., London, 1961), vol. XXI, pp. 160–6). I thank audiences in Leeds, London, Nottingham and Southampton who have heard me talk about Liutprand over the years for some lively discussions. I am indebted to Janet Nelson, Susan Reynolds, Patricia Skinner and Jocelyn Wogan-Browne for comments on earlier written drafts, and most especially to Paolo Chiesa who sent me his splendid new edition of Liutprand just in time for me to use it here.

PART III

Humour, history and politics in the Carolingian world

CHAPTER 6

'He never even allowed his white teeth to be bared in laughter': the politics of humour in the Carolingian renaissance

Matthew Innes

Humour is scarcely a topic that looms large in Carolingian history. The overriding seriousness of a dynasty that saw its mission as the creation of a Christian society dominated not only contemporary discourse, but also that of modern interpreters. In a political culture wherein argument was prosecuted whenever possible with pen rather than sword, written texts were used to elevate personal and factional interests to the moral high ground.[1] In this cultural context – or at least in recent work upon it – there has often seemed little space for humour: a good vehicle for ridiculing rivals but a poor one for appropriating rectitude in past, present and future.

The period's modern students may have accentuated the humourlessness of Carolingian political discourse. Pamphlet wars make for plentiful sources, and allow modern historians to apply, consciously and unconsciously, criteria for the evaluation and selection of those sources. Given a – by early medieval standards – superabundance of material, writers who used humour to drive home their point have tended to suffer at the hands of modern critics and find themselves largely excluded from the approved canon of 'reliable' sources. Thus Notker of St-Gall, condemned as a worthless gossip earlier in the twentieth century, has only slowly been rehabilitated, and then primarily as a source for socio-cultural history.[2]

---

[1] See J. L. Nelson, 'Public histories and private history in the work of Nithard', *Speculum* 60 (1985), pp. 251–93; also her 'History-writing at the courts of Louis the Pious and Charles the Bald', in *Historiographie im frühen Mittelalter* (Veröffentlichungen des Instituts für Österreichische Geschichtsforschung 32), ed. A. Scharer and G. Scheibelreiter (Vienna, 1994), pp. 435–42; M. Innes and R. McKitterick, 'The writing of history', in *Carolingian Culture: Emulation and Innovation*, ed. R. McKitterick (Cambridge, 1994), pp. 193–220.

[2] The highpoint in denigration of Notker as useless in positivistic terms came with L. Halphen, 'Etudes critiques sur l'histoire de Charlemagne IV: le moine de St. Gall', *Revue Historique* 128 (1918), pp. 26–98, reprinted in L. Halphen, *Etudes critiques sur l'histoire de Charlemagne* (Paris, 1921); rehabilitation came first through the study of Notker's political ideas, by scholars such as T. Siegrist, *Herrscher und Weltsicht bei Notker Balbulus: Untersuchungen zu den Gesta Karoli* (Zurich, 1963), and of his social and cultural world, by Hans-Werner Goetz, *Strukturen der spätkarolingischen Epoche*

Were Carolingianists in a position more like that of historians of sixth-century Gaul or tenth-century Italy, with no choice but to rely heavily upon humorous interlocutors such as Gregory of Tours and Liutprand of Cremona[3] respectively, our picture of the ninth century might be radically different. Notwithstanding the filtering effects of the distaste for humour evident in much nineteenth- and twentieth-century source-criticism, the paucity of humour in the sources seems real. Whilst Notker could square amusement at the futility of human action and the vanity of human ambition with a sense of the immanence of divine will,[4] for most authors humour was not useful in delineating the fate of the Franks and their rulers; after all, the overriding imperative of Carolingian historiography in its various guises was the demonstration of God's backing for, and active intervention on behalf of, their side. But is this lack of humour primarily a feature of the written registers of Carolingian political discourse and their concern with polemical claims for the moral high ground? In the face-to-face world of personal political conversation and negotiation between kings and their aristocrats, might not humour have had a larger role to play than the written sources would suggest? It is difficult to imagine the hunts and feasts which were among the pre-eminent rituals of consensus in the Carolingian world not being occasions shot through with laughter, whilst political rituals such as the *harmscara*, a public humiliation in which the victim was saddled like a horse, worked through ridicule.[5] Thinking about the role of humour in Carolingian political culture thus involves grasping thorny historiographical problems about the relationship between the primary sources' contemporary function, their modern critics' interpretative agenda, and the image of past society that historical scholarship produces.[6]

---

im Spiegel der Vorstellungen eines zeitgenössischen Mönchs: Eine Interpretation der Gesta Karoli Notkers von Sankt Gallen (Bonn, 1981); only most recently has his political relevance been reassessed by S. MacLean, 'The reign of Charles the Fat (876–888)' (unpublished Ph.D. dissertation, University of London, 2000), drawing on the insights of H. Löwe, 'Das Karlsbuch Notkers von St-Gallen und sein zeitgeschichtlicher Hintergrund', *Schweizerische Zeitschrift für Geschichte* 20 (1970), pp. 269–302.

3 See Balzaretti, above, pp. 114–28.

4 D. Ganz, 'Humour as history in Notker's *Gesta Karoli Magni*', in *Monks, Nuns and Friars in Medieval Society* (Sewanee Medieval Studies 4), ed. E. B. King, J. T. Schaefer and W. B. Wadley (Sewanee, TN, 1989); see also Kershaw, below, pp. 191–9.

5 On *harmscara* see M. De Jong, 'Power and humility in Carolingian society: the public penance of Louis the Pious', *EME* 1 (1992), pp. 29–52, at pp. 43–7; for the centrality of 'low-level' ritual focussing on hunting and feasting in Carolingian politics, see J. L. Nelson, 'The Lord's Anointed and the people's choice: Carolingian royal ritual', in *Rituals of Royalty*, ed. D. Cannadine and S. Price (London, 1987), pp. 137–80. On humiliation and ridicule, see also Haldon, above, pp. 65–7.

6 See R. McKitterick, 'Introduction: sources and interpretation', in *New Cambridge Medieval History*, vol. II, *700–900*, ed. R. McKitterick (Cambridge, 1995), pp. 1–17, and M. Innes, 'Introduction:

With these concerns in mind, this chapter examines an image of Carolingian rulership characterised by its denial of humour. It focuses on the description of a Carolingian king who, in the ultimately consensual setting of a feast, refused to join in the mirth of those around him and 'never even allowed his white teeth to be bared in laughter'. Our straight-faced Carolingian is Emperor Louis the Pious (814–40) – or, rather, Louis as represented in a fascinating, but neglected, account written by Thegan, a suffragan bishop of Trier, in 836.[7] A carefully contextualised reading of Thegan's description of Louis allows one to trace a debate about the moral value of humour, and thus to discuss the politics of humour in the Carolingian renaissance. Reconstructing this debate involves considering the potential uses of humour, and its denial, as strategies of power, and thus analysing the political sociology of humour. It will also entail confronting some of the problems facing the would-be historian of the emotions: the epistemological difficulties involved in interpreting sources that are literary representations rather than transparent reports, and the ontological challenge of moving from reading those sources to analysing past human emotion.

THEGAN AND LOUIS THE PIOUS

Thegan's is a short book, written whilst Louis still lived, and in the aftermath of the greatest crisis of his reign. A detailed political narrative, seeking to lay bare what Thegan saw as the reasons for the revolts of 830–5, makes up the bulk of the work – one reader called it 'a little book, written in the manner of annals'.[8] At only one point does Thegan eschew chronological narrative and give sustained description or comment. Significantly, this comes in two chapters placed immediately after the description of the pope's coronation of Louis at Rheims in 816, a crucial event for Thegan, and the point within the narrative immediately before the beginnings of Louis' troubles. Thegan first offers a vivid account of Louis' court and his conduct, before going on to launch, in the next chapter, a scathing condemnation of the bad and disloyal advisors, most notably Ebbo of Rheims, on whose shoulders Thegan laid the

---

using the past, interpreting the present, influencing the future', in *The Uses of the Past in the Early Middle Ages*, ed. Y. Hen and M. Innes (Cambridge, 2000), pp. 1–9.

[7] Thegan, *Gesta Hludovici imperatoris*, in *Thegan: Täten Kaiser Ludwigs, MGH SRG* 64, ed. E. Tremp (Hanover, 1995); for an English translation of the old (1829) *MGH* edition, see P. Dutton, *Carolingian Civilisation* (Peterborough, Ontario, 1994), pp. 141–55, on which my translations are based. On Thegan and his book, E. Tremp, *Studien zu den Gesta Hludovici imperatoris des Trierer Chorbischofs Thegan* (Schriften der MGH 32) (Hanover, 1988), is fundamental.

[8] Walahfrid Strabo, 'Introduction' to *Thegan*, ed. Tremp.

blame for the political crisis of the early 830s. The first chapter of this section is of concern here. Thegan begins by describing Louis' appearance, his linguistic skills as manifested in his virtuosity at biblical interpretation and his distaste for the 'gentile poems and songs' which he had learned in his youth; his humility and frequent tears in his daily prayer; and his generosity, surpassing that of his ancestors, and particularly his habit of making outright grants of royal villas to faithful followers. This catalogue of virtues climaxes in a description of Louis' appearance on the great feast days. Like his father, Thegan tells us, Louis wore splendid golden vestments only on such occasions. Louis' golden appearance, decked out in dazzling regalia, is then minutely detailed. At these feasts:

> He never raised his voice in laughter, not even at the height of the festivities when, to the joy [*laetitia*] of the people, actors, jesters and mimes with flutes and cithars appeared before him, not even as the people [*populus*] in his presence laughed in measure; he never even allowed his white teeth to be bared in laughter.

Thegan completes his account of Louis by noting his care for the poor and his love of hunting.[9]

The impact of this striking vignette, and particularly of Louis' refusal to enjoy the festivities of the feast, has been profound. It has been read by a succession of modern commentators as a window onto Louis' character and conduct. This uncritical evaluation of Thegan's work underpins a deeply embedded view of Louis' reign; in spite of some important recent advances, the sense that Louis was 'the greater father's lesser son' has proved hard to shake off.[10] It will not do, however, to cite Thegan as evidence for alleged 'depressive inner anxieties', and then to use such a construct as the key to unlocking political and cultural developments.[11]

---

[9] Thegan 19 (my translation): *Nunquam in risum exaltavit vocem suam, nec quando in summis festivitatibus ad laeticiam populi procedebant themilici, scurri et mimi cum coraulis et citharistis ad mensam coram eo, tunc ad mensuram ridebat populus coram eo, ille numquam nec dentes candidos suos in risum ostendit.* Note that the translation reproduced by Dutton translates the final clause as 'never bared his white teeth in a smile', to avoid repetition with the first clause 'he never raised his voice in laughter'; in fact, as this first clause is an echo of Ecclesiasticus 2.23 this repetition is intentional, patterning the whole passage as Louis' exposition of a biblical injunction. Mayke De Jong has kindly pointed out to me that, although in their translation of this passage both Dutton and Tremp suggest uncontrolled laughter around Louis, Thegan is explicit that the *populus* laughed *ad mensuram*: measured, dignified laughter in keeping with the injunctions of Carolingian tracts of moral advice for the laity. See further below, pp. 144–6.

[10] On Louis, *Charlemagne's Heir: New Perspectives on the Reign of Louis the Pious (814–40)*, ed. P. Godman and R. Collins (Oxford, 1990); a negative comparison between Louis and Charlemagne still lurks in E. Boshof, *Ludwig der Fromme* (Darmstadt, 1996) and in R. Collins, *Charlemagne* (London, 1998).

[11] For 'depressive inner anxieties', see K. Hauck, 'Versuch eine Gesamtdeutung des Einhard-Kreuzes', in *Das Einhardskreuz. Vörträge und Studien der Münsteraner Diskussion zur arcus Einhardi*, (Abhandlungen der Gesellschaft der Wissenschaften im Göttingen phil.-hist. Kl. 87), ed.

Such a reading treats Thegan's work as naïve reportage, when it is clearly a polemical representation of the recent past written for immediate political purposes.[12]

In any case, Thegan's description does not attempt to sketch the character, personality or psychology of an inner self radically separated from Louis' public role. Such a sense of a private self is a modern invention, and for Thegan and his contemporaries ruling involved taking up a divinely ordained ministry (*ministerium*), which incorporated the personal and the political. For Thegan, Louis' appearance and deportment illustrated the moral qualities of his fulfilment of the imperial mission, for which he would ultimately be held to account before God.[13] In a world in which ritual was a central means of political communication, and external appearances reflected internal realities, Thegan's was an analysis of Louis' conduct as emperor. In decoding this, modern valuations of particular human actions cannot be uncritically applied to wholly different cultural contexts: Thegan's picture of Louis' behaviour can only be properly understood by reference to contemporary cultural codes.[14] Even if humour is a universal aspect of human behaviour, we cannot understand its appearance in any specific historical context without knowledge of the possible interpretations and valuations placed on it in that particular context.[15]

As with any other piece of early medieval historical writing, Thegan's work must be read in context. Writing in the immediate aftermath of

K. Hauck (Göttingen, 1974), pp. 143–230, at p. 170. Louis' personality remains central to revisionist interpretations of his reign, e.g. T. F. X. Noble, 'Louis the Pious and his piety reconsidered', *Revue Belge de Philologie et d'Histoire* 58 (1980), pp. 297–316.

[12] Thegan's historiographical and narrative skill is in need of reassessment. W. Berschin, *Biographie und Epochenstil* (3 vols., Stuttgart, 1991), vol. III, pp. 220–7, gives the best overview; see also E. Tremp, 'Thegan und Astronomus, die beiden Geschichtsschreibern Ludwigs des Frommen', in *Charlemagne's Heir*, ed. Godman and Collins, pp. 691–700. Literary depictions of Louis produced in the crisis of his reign are discussed by H. Sièmes, 'Beiträge zum literarischen Bild Ludwigs des Frommen in der Karolingerzeit' (unpublished dissertation, Freiburg-im-Briesgau, 1966).

[13] S. Airlie, 'Private bodies and the body politic in the divorce of Lothar II', *Past and Present* 161 (1999), pp. 3–38; A. Borst, 'The invention and fissure of the public persona', in his *Medieval Worlds: Barbarians, Heretics and Artists in the Middle Ages* (Cambridge, 1991), pp. 123–60; M. Innes, *State and Society in the Early Middle Ages: The Middle Rhine Valley, 400–1000* (Cambridge, 2000), pp. 254–63; J. L. Nelson, 'The problematic in the private', *Social History* 15 (1990), pp. 355–65; T. Zotz, 'In Amt und Würden. Zur Eigenart "offizieller" Positionen im früheren Mittelalter', *Tel Aviver Jahrbuch für deutsche Geschichte* 22 (1993), pp. 1–23.

[14] See G. Althoff, 'Empörung, Tränen, Zerknirschung. Emotionen in der öffentliche Kommunikation des Mittelalters', *Frühmittelalterliche Studien* 30 (1996), pp. 60–79, reprinted in his *Spielregeln der Politik im Mittelalter: Kommunikation im Frieden und Fehden* (Darmstadt, 1997), pp. 258–81.

[15] For the possibilities of such 'thick description', see H. Fichtenau, *Living in the Tenth Century: Mentalities and Social Orders*, trans. P. Geary (Chicago, 1991). See also Haldon, above, pp. 54–5; Introduction, above, pp. 7–9.

Louis' deposition and subsequent reinstallation in 834–5, Thegan presented a rationale for the emperor's reconstructed régime, identifying the fall guys responsible for the recent problems and praising his patrons, members of the winning aristocratic faction in the newly created consensus.[16] Thegan not only squarely fingered Ebbo of Rheims and Hugh of Tours as the villains of the piece, but in casting them as the good prince's bad advisors he dissociated Louis himself from the problems his régime had recently experienced; indeed, according to Thegan, the main criticism that could be levelled at Louis was that he had listened too much to their counsel, and suffered from their self-interested advice. The criticism which had been made of Louis in the earlier 830s – like so much Carolingian political debate – had concentrated on the court's morality as a microcosm of disorder in the kingdom, with the empress accused of adultery and the palace allegedly given up to games and pleasure. Thegan had to respond to these accusations, and his description of Louis refusing the join in court festivities might be read as another attempt to distance the emperor from supposed moral laxity at court, and place the real responsibility for earlier scandals on those now-discredited advisors who had previously dominated the court.

Thegan's portrait of the emperor who never bared his teeth in laughter thus needs decoding very carefully, and in this very particular political context. The value of the activities Thegan details – laughter, feasting, the performances of actors, jesters and mimes – were all matters of intense cultural debate in the Carolingian renaissance. Decoding Thegan's description of Louis thus involves reconstructing a broader cultural context as well as locating the author politically. As Thegan drew on a literary tradition that laid down certain expectations as to how rulers were to be described, his work must be placed in its literary context if its argument is to be fully understood. Thus the historiographical topos that 'texts should be read in context' should not encourage a narrow and ultimately political understanding of context which tacitly makes a political interpretation the only legitimate goal of historical enquiry; rather, context should be understood in its totality, as a broad canvas of contemporary information which can be used to understand a multiplicity of historical phenomena embedded in a given text.

---

[16] Innes, *State and Society*, p. 202, drawing on Tremp, *Studien*, pp. 26–44.

DESCRIBING KINGS: EINHARD, THEGAN AND SIDONIUS

The literary context within which Thegan was working was itself marked by controversy. Thegan was the first of a series of ninth-century authors who responded to Einhard's essay in royal biography, the *Life of Charles*, which had defined itself by reference to classical literary traditions, in opposition to the hagiographical norms of biography exemplified by Sulpicius Severus' *Life of Martin*.[17] Thegan indubitably knew Einhard's work; he makes frequent and direct citations.[18] But his engagement with Einhard went beyond mere borrowing. Ernst Tremp has recently shown how Einhard and Thegan present the death of Charlemagne in strikingly different terms, Einhard's version a secular and classicising account of the death of a hero, whilst Thegan's presented Charlemagne as a model Christian reconciling himself to his death, correcting the Bible and hence piously devoted to the royal mission to reform to the very end.[19] Thegan was clearly responding to Einhard's models of biography and kingship. Thegan's literary relationship with Einhard is the key to understanding the passage describing Louis' refusal to laugh. This comes in the middle of the only passage in the biography that abandons chronological narrative (very consciously avoided by Einhard) and instead offers personal description designed to highlight moral and personal qualities (such as Einhard had practised in his *Life of Charles*). Thegan's description of Louis is literally Einhardian, in that it is replete with verbal echoes of the *Life of Charles*; Thegan, indeed, makes his debt clear by explicitly comparing his account of Louis' dress on feast days to Einhard's account of Charlemagne. The image of Louis Thegan creates in this passage is, in fact, a complex reaction to the literary and political model provided by Einhard's Charlemagne. And rather than simply dressing his Louis in the clothes of Einhard's Charlemagne, Thegan goes out of his way to alter – on occasion to invert – his model. Whereas Einhard's Charlemagne had been distinguished by his height, Thegan began with Louis' 'mediocre

---

[17] Einhard, *Vita karoli*, in *MGH SRG* 25, ed. O. Holder-Egger (Hanover and Leipzig, 1911); Sulpicius Severus, *Vita S. Martini*, in *Sulpice Sévère: Vie de St Martin* (Sources Chrétiennes 133), ed. J. Fontaine (Paris, 1967). See S. Hellmann, 'Einhards literarische Stellung', in his *Ausgewählte Abhandlungen zur Historiographie und Geistesgeschichte des Mittelalters* (Darmstadt, 1961), pp. 159–229; H. Beumann, 'Topos und Gedenkgefüge bei Einhard', *Archiv für Kulturgeschichte* 33 (1951), pp. 339–50; M. Kempshall, 'Some Ciceronian aspects of Einhard's *Life of Charlemagne*', *Viator* 26 (1995), pp. 11–38; M. Innes, 'The classical tradition in the Carolingian renaissance: ninth-century encounters with Suetonius', *International Journal for the Classical Tradition* 3 (1997), pp. 265–82.

[18] Tremp, *Studien*, pp. 55–62.

[19] See E. Tremp, 'Die letzten Wort des frommen Kaisers Ludwig. Von Sinn und Unsinn heutiger Textedition', *Deutsches Archiv für die Erforschung des Mittelalters* 48 (1992), pp. 17–36, esp. pp. 29–36.

stature'; whereas, for Einhard, Charlemagne's eyes had been 'noticeably large and full of life', to Thegan, Louis' are 'great and clear'; and so on.[20]

Intertextuality here served to suggest comparison – pointed comparison – in that Thegan was reacting to that section of Einhard's life which was constructed largely from borrowings from Suetonius' *Lives of the Caesars*. In focussing on these passages, Thegan contested Einhard's classicising and humanistic tendencies, and his reliance on a pagan antique model. Whilst Einhard was aware of the model for all early medieval descriptions of kings – Sidonius Apollinaris' fifth-century panegyric of the Visigothic king, Theodoric II – he cited it just once and chose to ignore the well-proportioned, virile and martial image it supplied, turning instead to Suetonius, and attempting to avoid the stereotypical. Hence the hero of the *Life of Charles* can appear uncomfortably human for one used to the conventional royal descriptions that are the standard fare of early medieval writers: 'his voice was distinct, but not as strong as might have been expected for his size', whilst 'his neck seemed short and thick and his stomach seemed to stick out'. Thegan's Louis, on the other hand, is a clear restatement of the conventional image of the Christian king.[21]

The complex intertextuality involved becomes clear from a comparison of the treatment of Charles' and Louis' habits at table in Einhard's and Thegan's works. Both Carolingian authors clearly engaged with Sidonius' model description.[22] Sidonius claimed that Theodoric II's dinner table was 'on all but festival days just like that of a private household', with drunkenness avoided and silence considered the only alternative to serious conversation. Einhard told how Charlemagne was normally moderate in food and drink and hated drunkenness – four courses and three drinks was his habit – although he did complain about fasting, particularly when doctors prescribed it. Thegan struck no such humanistic note: his Louis was simply (perhaps stereotypically) sober in drinking and moderate in eating. Sidonius had stressed Theodoric II's moderation to suggest that the Gothic ruler did not fit the traditional Roman image of the barbarian, unable to control his emotions and so a slave

---

[20] See Einhard, *Vita Karoli* 22–7; in *MGH SRG* 25, ed. O. Holder-Egger, with Thegan, *Gesta Hludovici* 19. Tremp, *Studien*, pp. 57–63, catalogues the borrowing. See now W. Bershin, 'Personenbeschreibung in der Biographie des frühen Mittelalters', in *Historiographie im frühen Mittelalter*, ed. Scharer and Scheibelreiter, pp. 186–93.

[21] For the single citation of Sidonius and its significance, see R. Morse, *Truth and Convention in the Middle Ages* (Cambridge, 1991), p. 145 and Bershin, 'Personenbeschreibung', p. 189 or his *Biographie und Epochenstil*, vol. III, p. 211, but note the influence of Sidonius on both Einhard's and Thegan's treatment of conduct at table.

[22] Einhard, *Vita Karoli* 24; Thegan, *Gesta Hludovici* 19; and Sidonius Apollinaris, *Epistulae* 1.2, in *Sidonius: Poems and Letters*, ed. and trans. W. B. Anderson (2 vols., London, 1936 and 1965).

to his passions: at this barbarian court 'you can find Greek elegance, Gallic plenty, Italian briskness; the dignity of state, the attentiveness of a private home, the ordered discipline of royalty'.[23] For the connoisseurs of Carolingian royalty, on the other hand, such sobriety signified the application of practices of ultimately monastic origin to the household of the king, who saw his mission in explicitly Christian terms and thus shaped his court as a Christian community; Thegan even described how the monastic practice of feeding the poor each day was adopted at Louis' court. Carolingian royal wariness about the dangers of the feast may explain the prominence of the hunt as the primary institution of consensus in the ninth century.

In Sidonius' model, only feast days were the exception to the general rule of moderation: 'as to the luxury of the festival days I had better hold my tongue, for even the lowest person cannot fail to notice it'. Einhard and Thegan reacted rather differently to the cue afforded by this rather cautious admission. Einhard made no direct comment on feasts at Charlemagne's court, other than stating that they were rare, but generally implied that they were exceptions to the normal order of things; hence Charlemagne usually wore normal Frankish clothes, indistinguishable from that of the people, except on feast days. Thegan explicitly referred back to this passage in Einhard when he wrote that Louis, like his father, only wore regalia on feast days, but he then took the opportunity to describe the magnificence of Louis' garb on these occasions, with an incantation-like application of the adjective 'golden' to each item. Thus whilst Einhard and Thegan actually agree on the basics of Carolingian royal dress, the differing emphases in their differing accounts lead to radically different representations of their respective subjects, the reader left with a mental image of Charlemagne dressed in everyday Frankish clothes, but Louis wreathed in golden robes and regalia.

Thegan's conscious playing off of Einhard and Sidonius climaxes in the image of Louis' distaste for the frivolous entertainment associated with dining. According to Sidonius, Theodoric II had turned his back on classical secular entertainment at table, preferring simple music that was beneficial for his soul, and, moreover, only rarely admitting 'the banter of low comedians', and then ensuring that 'they are not allowed to assail any guest with the gall of a biting tongue'. Charlemagne, claimed Einhard, liked to listen to 'histories and the deeds of the ancients', although Augustine's *City of God* was his real favourite; such readings were

<hr />

[23] See also Halsall, above, p. 98.

the everyday fare at his table. When Thegan described Louis' refusal to enjoy the performances of the actors, jesters, mimes and musicians even on the greatest feast days, he was thus drawing on a long-established tradition of royal high-mindedness at table, and stressing Louis' distaste for secular entertainment even on those occasions when it was the norm.

In refusing to join in the general mirth at the performers, Thegan's Louis distanced himself from the people (*populus*) present. Einhard, throughout his description of Charlemagne's clothing and habits, had stressed the horizontal bonds uniting the ruler and the Franks, most memorably in the famous image of Charlemagne bathing, surrounded by a hundred or more Franks. Thegan, on the other hand, was far more concerned with the vertical distance between an emperor and his subjects, hence his choice to portray Louis in imperial garb on a feast day, and as not participating in the joy of the *populus* 'even at the height of festivities'. The shared laughter of those present reinforced the horizontal bonds between them, also expressed in their commensality and shared enjoyment of the feast. But in refusing to laugh, Thegan's Louis consciously placed himself above those bonds.[24]

Thegan's depiction of Louis' refusal to participate in the secular entertainment offered to the populace on the great feast days went beyond a denial of laughter: there is a careful focus on Louis' facial demeanour, and his refusal even to bare his teeth. This image again needs understanding in the context of the expectations and models derived from established literary traditions. Sidonius Apollinaris' Theodoric II and Einhard's Charlemagne had shared a 'joyful and cheerful expression' (*vultu laeti et hilari*), probably borrowed from Sulpicius Severus' Saint Martin, who had 'a kind of joy [*laetitia*] shining in his face'.[25] Thegan, in his initial description of Louis' appearance, had already signalled a distance from these templates, whilst also stressing straightforward openness, in describing Louis' facial expression as 'lucid'. In going on to contrast Louis' refusal to bare his white teeth in laughter with the *laetitia* of the *populus*, Thegan chose his words carefully: *laetitia* (joy) was one of the

---

[24] On commensality see G. Althoff, *Verwandte, Freunde und Getreue: Zum politische Stellenwert der Gruppenbindung im früheren Mittelalter* (Darmstadt, 1990), pp. 203–11; H. Magennis, *Images of Community in Anglo-Saxon Literature* (Cambridge, 1996). For shared laughter, see also Aaron Gurevich's work, whose framework is inspired by the oeuvre of Mikhail Bakhtin: for example, Gurevich's *Historical Anthropology of the Middle Ages* (Cambridge, 1992), pp. 122–76.

[25] Saint Martin: Sulpicius Severus, *Vita S. Martini* 27, in *Sulpice Sévère: Vie de St Martin*, ed. Fontaine; T. Head and T. Noble, *Soldiers of Christ* (London, 1996), pp. 1–29. This is directly copied by Einhard: Bershin, *Biographie und Epochenstil*, vol. III, pp. 214–15; also his 'Personenbeschreibung'. See Humphries, above, p. 83, for Roman ideas about the imperial smile.

key words which came up time and again in describing the royal visage. The insistence that kings kept on smiling is so consistent over such a wide range of sources of different types – it even found its way into coronation rites – that this one tradition was clearly not only operative on the level of literary depiction, but also informed actual royal behaviour.[26] So Louis' refusal to participate in the joy of the people was a shocking transgression of the norms of royal deportment and the expectations of his public about the proper demeanour of the king.

The key to this very conscious transgression may lie in an alternative tradition that had long lain dormant in the west. Louis' distant sobriety recalled the public persona both of the Roman emperors of late antiquity and of Louis' Byzantine contemporaries. In the course of the fourth century, emperors had adopted a statuesque, static persona, demonstrating an unruffled self-control, which marked a radical departure from earlier patterns of spontaneous accessibility.[27] This new 'verticality' was expressed in panegyric, official art and imperial ritual, perhaps described most memorably in Ammianus Marcellinus' account of the ceremonial entry of Constantius II to Rome in 357, when the iconic figure of the emperor remained unmoved with an unchanging, sober, expression.[28] With the advent of the Theodosian dynasty, imperial deportment became something for which emperors-to-be could be trained from their earliest youth: thus Theodosius II and Arcadius were trained in the non-expression of emotion and the maintenance of a static visage.[29] Such imperial practices influenced the representation of late antique barbarian rulers: in the fifth century, Priscus of Pannium describes a banquet at Attila's court, the highlight of which was the performance of the jester Zercon the Moor, who 'put all in a good humour and caused all to burst into uncontrollable laughter, except Attila [who] remained unmoved with no change of expression, and neither said nor did anything that hinted at laughter'. Priscus may here, as elsewhere, have been using Attila's court to offer a critique of the empire, and hence chose to portray Attila demonstrating the archetypal imperial virtue of self-control;

---

[26] Royal deportment (which deserves a full study): Fichtenau, *Living in the Tenth Century*, pp. 58–64, useful material also in Bershin, 'Personenbeschreibung' and H. Grundmann, *Der Cappenberger Barbarossakopf* (Cologne and Graz, 1959).

[27] S. MacCormack, *Art and Ceremony in Late Antiquity* (Berkeley, 1981). Note, too, the significance of popular *laetitia* at the imperial presence.

[28] Amm. Marc. 16.10, on which see MacCormack, *Art and Ceremony*, pp. 39–45. Ammianus' work was rarely known in the Carolingian period, and not used by Thegan.

[29] K. Holum, *Theodosian Empresses: Women and Imperial Dominion in Late Antiquity* (London, 1982), p. 92.

be that as it may, Attila's refusal to change expression bears remarkable testimony to the impact of norms about imperial deportment.[30] These norms were developed and elaborated in early medieval Byzantium, where the ritualised public persona of a stationary emperor reached its apogee.[31] The image of a statuesque, expressionless emperor may thus be directly inspired by contemporary reports of Byzantine court ritual, rather than from late Roman practices preserved in literary tradition or official art. Whatever the mechanism of transmission, Thegan's Louis was departing from the norms of western kingship to behave in a distinctly imperial manner.[32]

MONASTIC KINSHIP AND THE DANGERS OF SECULARITY

Ultimately, self-control allowed Thegan's Louis to place himself above the people. Mastery of the self lay at the heart of the late antique traditions of asceticism that were so influential in early medieval culture; laughter posed a real threat to the possibility of controlling the body. Horror of the ultimate inability of human discipline to triumph over bodily urges led to particular condemnation of the dangers of immoderate and un-controlled laughter: thus Gregory the Great admitted that there would be joyful laughter in heaven, but insisted that it would be laughter of the soul, not lascivious, corporeal, laughter.[33] When Alcuin grappled with the story of Sarah and Abraham rejoicing at the news they would have a son, deciding to name their child Isaac, literally 'laughter', he betrayed a similar unease. Picking up on the contrast between the Bible's condemnation of Sarah but praise of Abraham, Alcuin argued that there was a qualitative difference between their laughter: Abraham's had reverently expressed his pious joy at God's goodness, but Sarah's had been fuelled

---

[30] Priscus fragment 13.1–2, in *The Fragmentary Classicising Historians of the Later Roman Empire*, vol. II, ed. and trans. R. C. Blockley (2 vols., Liverpool, 1983), pp. 286–9. For criticism of Rome, see the story of the merchant who preferred life under Attila to its Roman alternative: fragment 11/12, ed. and trans. Blockley, pp. 266–73. There is no evidence or likelihood of Priscus' direct influence on Thegan.

[31] For Byzantine imperial ritual and representation, see O. Treitinger, *Die oströmische Kaiser- und Reichsidee* (Darmstadt, 1956). I am grateful to John Haldon and Jonathan Shepard for discussion of the Byzantine elements. There is evidence for 'Byzantinising' tendencies in Louis' court ritual: subjects kissing the emperor's feet, proskynesis used in both prayer and politics.

[32] Michael Richter has already suggested the possibility of a Roman model for Louis' behaviour: *The Formation of the Medieval West: Studies in the Oral Culture of the Barbarians* (Dublin, 1994), p. 132, n. 3.

[33] I. M. Resnick, ' "Risus monasticus": laughter and medieval monastic culture', *Revue Bénédictine* 97 (1987), pp. 90–100, at p. 92, discussing Gregory the Great, *Moralia in Job* 8:52:88, in *PL* 75, cols. 855–6.

by doubt at the possibility that God had granted her a son.[34] Laughter was permissible so long as it remained controlled and had a pious object, but there was always the danger of its escaping physical and moral control. Hence the Carolingian moralist Paulinus of Aquileia could advise his friend Count Heiric to avoid the dangerous excesses of undignified laughter, just as Alcuin warned Count Wido against scurrilous humour. Such injunctions had real force: Thegan, depicting the mirth of the feast from which Louis was distant, stressed that the courtiers around the emperor 'laughed in measure [*ad mensuram*]'.[35]

These traditions were particularly strong in early medieval monasticism, rooted as it was in late antique ascetic traditions of self-control. The late antique holy man, Saint Martin, who according to Sulpicius Severus had avoided all extremes of emotion – 'no one ever saw him angered, no one saw him excited, none saw him grieving, none saw him laughing; he was always just the same' – was a powerful exemplar.[36] Monastic legislation, including the *Rule of Benedict*, condemned laughter as idle and pointless, incompatible with prayer and proper reverence for the suffering of Christ, indicative of a lack of moderation and loss of self-control, and likely to lead to argument and dissension within the community; even where laughter was not condemned outright, it was graded, with cultivated and controlled laughter with an appropriate subject allowed whilst uncontrolled and ill-directed laughter was forbidden. In the Carolingian period, the reforms of Louis' reign, inspired by Benedict of Aniane, took a hard line against laughter of any kind, and entrenched this line in the version of the monastic rule that became the basis for a unified monastic observance across the Carolingian Empire. For Benedict, laughter exemplified the sin of pride; for his contemporary ally, Smaragdus of St-Mihiel, it demonstrated levity.[37]

---

34 Alcuin, *Questions and Answers on Genesis*, in *PL* 100, col. 540, discussion by Resnick, ' "Risus monasticus" ', pp. 90–1.

35 Alcuin, *On Virtues and Vices* 28, in *PL* 101, col. 633. Paulinus, *Book of Exhortation* 16, in *PL* 99, col. 209, significantly also warning against excessive feasting and enjoyment of the performances of *histriones*. On this genre of advice for the laity, see now J. M. H. Smith, 'Gender and ideology in the early Middle Ages', *Studies in Church History* 34 (1998), pp. 51–73.

36 Sulpicius Severus, *Vita S. Martini* 27.

37 On monastic attitudes towards laughter, see Resnick, ' "Risus monasticus" '; J. Le Goff, 'Le Rire dans les règles monastiques du haut moyen âge', in *Haut Moyen Age: culture, education et société. Etudes offerts à P. Riché*, ed. M. Sot (Nantes, 1990), pp. 93–103; G. Schmitz, '. . . quod rident homo, plurandum est. Der Unwert des Lachen im monastische geprägten Vorstellungen der spätantike und des frühen Mittelalters', in *Stadtverfassung, Verfassungstaat, Pressepolitik. Festschrift E. Naujoks*, ed. F. Quarthal and W. Setzler (Sigmaringen, 1980), pp. 3–15. U. Eco, *The Name of the Rose* (London, 1983), inspired interest in these issues; see Shanzer, above, pp. 28–9. Benedict, *Concordia Regularum* 20, in *PL* 103, cols. 861–2; Smaragdus, *Commentarium in Regulam S. Benedicti*, in *PL* 102, col. 825.

Thegan, whose circle of patrons included such prominent reforming abbots as Marcward of Prüm and Grimald of St-Gall, would doubtless have been aware of these injunctions. His insistence that Louis had demonstrated the self-control to conquer laughter thus paralleled the imperial office with the vocation of the monk, and suggested that Louis as emperor acted like a perfect monk, following the prescriptions set down by Benedict of Aniane. The application of monastic ideals to the office of kingship was very much current at the time at which Thegan wrote. Louis' régime had adopted the monastic ideal as a model for empire, with unity embodied in the church and in the common monastic observance implanted across the empire, and Louis was presented in terms borrowed from monastic thought. The king had first to rule himself to demonstrate his worthiness to take on the sacred burden of Christian kingship.[38]

Thegan's placing of Louis' refusal to laugh in the very specific setting of the secular entertainment offered by actors, mimes, musicians and jesters during a banquet ties his portrait into another area of contemporary debate and legislation. One recurrent worry in the minds of contemporary churchmen concerned clerical and monastic participation in practices associated with feasting, particularly the performance of secular songs and lays. Alcuin, Benedict of Aniane's teacher and a key influence from beyond the grave on the court of Louis, had berated several of his correspondents for their enjoyment of the secular performances of actors and mimes, all too often in a context of drunken feasting, which he saw as inappropriate pastimes for members of a religious community. These concerns eventually fed into ecclesiastical and royal legislation, which urged priests and monks who attended secular feasts to behave in a controlled and sober manner, as befitted their office, and to avoid participation, or even presence at, the performances of singers and mimes on these occasions; Carolingian legislation was concerned about clerical participation in these secular rites, not with the elimination of the rites themselves. These performances, intimately associated with communal eating, became the emblematic rites of secular community in the minds of Carolingian legislators, hence the insistence that monks and priests desist from them and avoid compromising their sacred status; in Benedict

---

[38] T. F. X. Noble, 'The monastic ideal as a model for empire: the case of Louis the Pious', *Revue Bénédictine* 86 (1976), pp. 235–50; De Jong, 'Power and humility'; Nikolaus Staubach's work also contains important insights on Louis' reign; esp. Staubach, *Das Herrscherbild Karls des Kahlen: Formen und Funktionen monarchischer Repräsentation im frühen Mittelalter* (Münster, 1982) and his *Rex christianus: Hofkultur und Herrschaftspropaganda im Reich Karls des Kahlen* (Cologne, 1993). For monastic practice directly influencing kingship, see Smaragdus, *Via regia*, in *PL* 102 cols. 951–70. For Roman roots of this thinking, see Humphries, above, pp. 75–9.

of Aniane's monastic reforms typical Carolingian concerns about the interaction between the cloister and the world manifested themselves in the regulation of contact between monks and secular guests, particularly at table.[39]

The behaviour of Thegan's Louis is clearly influenced by these injunctions aimed at bishops, priests and monks. Yet lavish entertainment on feast days and the performance of jesters, mimes and actors were long-established and cohesive practices that defined the political community. Einhard had famously claimed that Charlemagne had 'the ancient and most barbarous songs, in which the deeds of the kings of old were told', recorded in writing for the first time. This was a consciously imperial action, part of Charlemagne's care for a distinctively Frankish cultural heritage, and thus of a piece with Einhard's stress on the horizontal bonds uniting Charlemagne and the Frankish people. Einhard thus suggests that, within the secular world, the performance of traditions about 'the kings of old' was socially and politically central, although he also approvingly noted Charlemagne's moderation at table and rare feasts.[40]

Thegan distanced Louis from the totality of these cultural traditions, stressing Louis' distaste for orally transmitted songs about 'the kings of old', so prized in Einhard's account. Claiming that Louis 'would not read, or listen to, those gentile lays and songs which he had learned in his youth', Thegan instead emphasised Louis' virtuosity in biblical interpretation, and his mastery of all four senses of Scripture. As Mayke De Jong shows, Thegan portrays Louis undergoing a *conversio*, renouncing the secular traditions of his youth in favour of the pursuit of the sacred wisdom befitting a Christian emperor; Louis' refusal to participate in the feast days' secular entertainment demonstrates the sincerity of this *conversio*.[41] The portrayal of *conversio* is directly based on an important

---

[39] The Carolingian legislation, and evidence from the narrative sources, is assembled by Richter, *Formation of the Medieval West*, esp. pp. 125–45; also his *The Oral Tradition in the Middle Ages* (Typologie des sources du moyen âge occidental 71) (Turnhout, 1995). Richter sympathetically reconstructs these secular cultural traditions, demonstrating the importance of gesture and music in their performance, which suggests that they also need to be discussed in the context of the late antique dramatic tradition, and the church's opposition to *histriones*. For monastic reform and secularity, see M. De Jong, 'Carolingian monasticism: the power of prayer', in *New Cambridge Medieval History*, vol. II, ed. McKitterick, pp. 622–53. For Alcuin see *Epistolae* 124, 175, 237, 271, in *MGH Epistolae* 4, ed. E. Dümmler (Berlin, 1895); as Richter shows, such exhortations eventually fed into legislation, culminating in the condemnation of priestly participation in these cultural traditions at the great reform councils of 813. For Byzantine parallels, see Haldon, above, pp. 60–2.

[40] Einhard, *Vita Karoli* 29; see M. Innes, 'Teutons or Trojans? The Carolingians and the Germanic past', in *Uses of the Past*, ed. Hen and Innes, pp. 227–49, at pp. 237–46.

[41] Thegan, *Gesta Hludovici* 19; see now M. De Jong, 'The empire as *ecclesia*: Hrabanus Maurus and biblical *historia* for kings', in *Uses of the Past*, ed. Hen and Innes, pp. 191–226, at pp. 196–7.

passage of the anonymous *Life of Alcuin* written in the 820s, as Thegan's most recent editor has noted: it tells of Alcuin's rejection of the classical pagan texts he had loved in his youth, his refusal to allow them to be read or listened to in his presence, and his chiding of pupils who secretly read those works he had rejected. That these classical texts lay outside the canon of Christian knowledge underpinned Alcuin's rejection: they were not active carriers of classical paganism, but distractions from contemplation of Christian wisdom.[42] Alcuin himself had condemned the performances of secular epics in almost identical terms; Thegan uses the same adjective as Alcuin, 'gentile', in his denunciation of this material. 'Gentile' here denotes that which is outside the *ecclesia* and the canon of Christian learning, and should not be read as indicating a residual active element of pre-Christian religion in these traditions; Alcuin's and Thegan's dislike of secular heroic poetry is at one with the *Life of Alcuin*'s unease about Virgil. At issue here are attempts, via a redrawing of boundaries between sacred and secular, to label some cultural activities as inappropriate for those devoted to Christian wisdom, not a head-on clash between the church and a sealed, separate and unchanging secular counter-culture.[43]

Thegan's Louis thus once again followed the recommendations of contemporary reformers who aimed at correcting the behaviour of the religious caste charged with the direction of Frankish society. Carolingian legislation did not aim at the wholesale elimination of oral traditions performed in a context of drinking and feasting, but urged monks and priests to avoid contamination by these rites, which articulated a sense of secular community. Indeed, Carolingian reformers, in trying to create a firmer division between sacred and secular than had previously existed, particularly in dividing priests and monks from secular men, were redefining traditional rituals of community, embracing layman, monk and priest alike, as something appropriate only for the laity.[44] Thegan's

---

[42] *Vita Alcuini* 16, in *MGH Scriptores* 15.1, ed. W. Arndt (Hanover, 1887), pp. 182–97.

[43] For 'gentile' see De Jong, 'Empire as *ecclesia*', pp. 196–7. See Alcuin, *Ep.* 124: *Verbum Dei legantur in sacerdotali convivio. Ibi decet lectorem audiri, non citharistam; sermones patrum, non carmina gentilium. Quod Hieneldus cum Christo?* This is a passage rich in biblical and patristic echoes: Richter, *Formation of the Medieval West*, p. 130, n. 27, and for the specific context, D. Bullough, 'What has Ingeld to do with Lindisfarne', *Anglo-Saxon England* 22 (1993), pp. 93–125. Innes, 'Teutons or Trojans?', critiques the established interpretation that this material constituted a self-contained and sealed counter-culture more or less untouched by Christianity.

[44] Carolingian legislation emphatically does not denounce these rites per se, but is concerned with priestly and monastic participation in them; Thegan's Louis does not aim to stop these practices (*pace* Richter, *Formation of the Medieval West*, p. 138, talking of Louis' 'failure' in the face of entrenched cultural traditions) and moralists writing for the laity warn against excess rather than participation (see, e.g., Paulinus and Alcuin, n. 35, above, or Jonas of Orléans, *De institutione Laicali*, in *PL* 106, col. 164).

Louis, therefore, was once more employing norms initially applied to monks and priests to the imperial office, not attempting to outlaw the rites of secular community.[45]

For Thegan in his depiction of Louis, as for reformers in their exhortations, the closely linked phenomena of laughter, feasting, drinking and the performance of songs were becoming central images of secularity, exemplifying lack of control as opposed to self-control, the transient pleasures of this world rather than the eternal truths of the next, pride in human action as opposed to humility before divine wisdom. On the level of ideological categorisation, the concern is with the creation of a binary opposition which defined the priestly caste against a secular Other. Carolingian society, however, was too complex, and sacred and secular too interweaved, to allow this bipolar model to map easily onto social action, even if it informed the basic cultural categories which contemporaries used to cope with the tensions arising from attempts to build a Christian society divided between clergy and laity. Both laymen and clerics struggled to produce a model of secular behaviour that incorporated significant elements of monastic codes, notably of self-control and piety, whilst acknowledging that the procreation and weapon-carrying of the lay order were necessary for the continuation of Christian society: hence Louis' courtiers only laughed 'in measure'.[46] In a literary context such as Thegan's description of Louis, the world of the feast served as a rhetorical trope, emphasising Louis' perfection. By avoiding potentially polluting contact with the uncontrolled hilarity and contaminating lewdness of secular rites, the emperor projected a sacred persona.

CHRIST AND THE EMPEROR IN THEGAN AND NOTKER

Thegan's image of Louis was not merely monastic and imperial. Arguments about the value of laughter went back to an apocryphal Greek tradition, repeated by John Chrysostom and transmitted to the Latin world through Rufinus and Salvian, which held that Christ had never laughed in all the time he spent on Earth. According to Sulpicius

---

[45] There is actually little support in the historical evidence, or the patterns of survival of vernacular literature, for the deeply embedded interpretation which sees the contrast between Einhard's depiction of Charlemagne's sympathy for the 'most barbarous and ancient songs' and Louis' distaste for 'gentile songs and lays' as indicating a change in royal policy towards secular epic and the vernacular languages: D. Geuenich, 'Die volkssprachige Überlieferung der Karolingerzeit aus der Sicht des Historikers', *Deutsches Archiv für die Erforschung des Mittelalters* 39 (1983), pp. 113–35.

[46] See, e.g., S. Airlie, 'The anxiety of sanctity: St Gerald of Aurillac and his maker', *Journal of Ecclesiastical History* 42 (1992), pp. 372–95; J. L. Nelson, 'Monks, secular men and masculinity, c.900', in *Masculinity in Medieval Europe*, ed. D. M. Hadley (London, 1999), pp. 121–42.

Severus, in Saint Martin's refusal to exhibit any emotion 'he seemed more than human; there was never anything on his lips but Christ'. Significantly, Louis' advisor Benedict of Aniane drew on these late antique authorities, basing his definitive stance against monastic laughter on the contention that Christ had never laughed, and that the monastic life should be lived in imitation of Christ.[47]

Thegan had stressed Louis' personal relationship to Christ from the beginning of his work, which opened with an extravagant incarnation dating, placing Louis' reign 'in the reign of our Lord Jesus Christ which will endure forever', before giving genealogies of Louis' paternal and maternal ancestors, which also stressed the links between Christ and Louis: Louis' paternal ancestry was traced back to his peculiar heavenly patron, Arnulf of Metz, whom Thegan styled 'pontiff of Christ' and ended with Charlemagne's imperial coronation 'on the birthday of Christ'.[48] Thegan's stress on Louis' humble demeanour and tears in prayer, for example, were a daily remainder of Christ's own suffering, and one of the earliest examples of a ninth-century trend for Christomimetic royal prayer.[49] Thegan's Louis – dressed in gold like Christ in majesty, standing above and apart from the population, focussing on the sacred and thus detached from the secular world, and refusing to laugh – could thus be seen as acting in direct imitation of Christ.

At least one reader of Thegan made such a connection. In his *Deeds of Charlemagne*, written in 885–6, Notker of St-Gall included a number of stories about Louis the Pious, which take the bare bones of Thegan's biography as their starting point, just as many of Notker's stories about Charlemagne are expositions of points made by Einhard.[50] In particular, what survives of Notker's work ends with a long account, of great value for the historian of royal ritual, of Louis' procession to church 'on the day when Christ left his earthly body and assumed his heavenly one'. As he progressed through the palace complex at Aachen, Louis distributed

---

[47] For the tradition, see Le Goff, 'Le Rire'; Resnick, ' "Risus monasticus" '; Schmitz, '. . . quod rident homines . . .'. Sulpicius Severus, *Vita S. Martini* 27. Benedict of Anian, *Concordia regularum* 20, in *PL* 103, col. 863.

[48] Thegan, *Gesta Hludovici* 1.

[49] See, e.g., R. Deshman, '*Christus rex et magi reges*: kingship and Christology in Ottonian and Anglo-Saxon art', *Frühmittelalterliche Studien* 10 (1976), pp. 375–405; also his 'The exalted servant: the ruler theology of the prayer book of Charles the Bald', *Viator* 11 (1980), pp. 385–417. Thegan's depiction of Louis' prayer is based again on the *Vita Alcuini*, which claimed that Alcuin instructed Louis in piety.

[50] Notker, *Gesta Karoli*, in *MGH SRG* n.s. 12, ed. H. Haefele (Berlin, 1959); *Two Lives of Charlemagne*, trans. L. Thorpe (London, 1969). On Notker's *modus operandi*, see Ganz, 'Humour as history', and M. Innes, 'Memory, orality and literacy in an early medieval society', *Past and Present* 158 (1998), pp. 3–36.

gifts of clothing to the people who flocked around him, 'each according to their rank'. These Easter gifts of clothing from the emperor parallel the gift of baptismal robes to those undergoing their formal inauguration into the Christian faith in a ritual which similarly took place, in the Carolingian world, at Easter, and which was seen as constituting a rebirth in Christ, staged on the anniversary of his resurrection.[51] The grateful recipients of Louis' Easter gifts acclaimed Louis in terms reminiscent of Christ: 'Kyrie Eleison to the blessed Louis!' Notker, who frequently used humour to drive home a moral message hidden in an anecdote, went on to tell a story about an unusual event that took place one particular Easter:

On one of these occasions, a jester said facetiously: 'Happy art thou, O Louis, who has clothed so many men on one day. By Christ, no one in the whole length and breadth of the empire has clad more men than you – except, of course, Hatto.' Louis asked the fool how Hatto had managed to clothe even more people but he, delighted at having secured the emperor's attention, merely replied with a bellow of laughter: 'Hatto has given away more clothes today.' Louis, with a most kindly expression still on his face, took this for the silly joke that it was, and proceeded humbly and devoutly into church. Once inside he acted with reverence as if the Lord Jesus Christ himself had appeared before him.[52]

It is fair to say that this is probably one of the least funny of Notker's stories, and certainly the only one that requires explication in the august pages of *Deutsches Archiv für die Erforschung des Mittelalters*![53] The jester's 'silly joke' turns on the parallels between Louis and Christ that run through the passage (hence his exclamation 'By Christ!'), and above all on the Easter setting and its baptismal overtones. As Louis progressed giving out clothes, he was echoing baptismal rituals, and the joking jester was drawing attention to the Christ-like nature of Louis' behaviour. The humour in Notker's story disappears in translation from its original cultural context to that of the early twenty-first century, and the loss of the whole set of associations between Christ, Easter, baptism and the giving away of clothes on which it turns. Moreover, the punch line turns on the person of the unidentified Hatto, and relies on the presence of an informed audience with circumstantial knowledge about him – a reminder of how

---

[51] Royal involvement in baptismal ritual, and parallels between royal ritual and baptismal ritual, are interestingly a central theme in several of Notker's stories about Louis: *Gesta Karoli* 2.19 and 2.22.

[52] Notker, *Gesta Karoli* 2.21.

[53] H. Haefele, 'Studien zu Notkers *Gesta Karoli*', *Deutsches Archiv für die Erforschung des Mittelalters* 15 (1959), pp. 358–92, at pp. 379–85.

much humour is implicated in local knowledge and specific expectations about particular individuals and circumstances.

If our ignorance of Hatto means that even today Notker's story cannot be fully decoded, and its original humour is lost, it is none the less an intriguing anecdote, which turns on Louis' refusal to laugh on a great feast day, and draws recurrent and explicit parallels between the emperor and Christ. There is, in fact, every reason to read this passage as Notker's exposition on Thegan's description of Louis. Not only was Notker's *Deeds of Charlemagne* structured as a series of anecdotal variations on themes set down by earlier Carolingian royal biographers (notably Einhard), but Thegan acted as Notker's primary textual point of departure in his stories about Louis. The location and language of Notker's story likewise draw on Thegan: the careful setting at Aachen on a great feast day, with Louis surrounded by the *populus*, and with entertainers (Notker's term, *scurrus*, had been used by Thegan) present; the contrast drawn between popular rejoicing and royal self-control, between the jester's uncontrolled 'bellow of laughter' and Louis' humility. Notker plays the Christomimetic card as a trump, not only highlighting a series of associations between Christ and emperor in the course of his story, but also ending with the emperor's prayer as if Christ were physically present, an invocation of a direct and personal relationship between Louis, ruler on this earth, and Christ, the king of heaven.

Notker's little vignette makes for a striking demonstration of self-control, and of humour and its denial, as strategies of power. The jester, in Notker's account, used humour as a safe means of disrupting the stately progress of a ritual designed to accentuate the identification of the emperor and Christ. Humour here was a strategy of transgression and inversion, which allowed the suspension of normal rules of behaviour and thus permitted contestation of the accepted meaning of a ritual. Moreover, just as Sidonius had been aware of the possibility that 'the gall of a biting tongue' could be used to direct humour as a weapon against an individual, so Louis' jester attempted to canalise the general Easter rejoicing into laughter against the unidentified Hatto who was the butt of his joke. None the less, it is striking that Notker's Louis is able to ride out the contestation of this particular ritual through a demonstration of royal self-control of the approved form. Thus Louis both imitates Christ and maintains the appropriate humility before Christ. By ending his story with Louis' invocation of Christ in prayer, Notker affirms the intended, hegemonic, meaning of the imperial Easter visit to church, and, like Louis, dismisses its contestation. In other words, even for Notker with his keen awareness of the value of humour, here the demonstration of self-control through the denial of humour was an effective strategy of power.[54]

Notker's willingness to expand on Thegan's image of a Louis who exercised power through the denial of humour is a telling reminder of the potential ambivalence of laughter for even the ninth century's best-known champion of the value of humour. Notker was not only one of the few Carolingian authors who used humour; he also revived a tradition, reaching back to Aristotle through Boethius and Martianus Capella, which held that the ability to laugh defined the human condition.[55] Yet he is clear that the jester's joke is 'silly' and contrasts his uncontrolled 'bellow of laughter' with Louis' Christ-like humility on this most sacred of days. Indeed, Notker's lack of sympathy for the jester is reminiscent of his judgement on another similar figure: the cleric whose eloquence and voice made him a star in both the performance of the liturgy and the recitation of secular poems, but whose pride led to his downfall, a reminder that his powers were granted by God.[56] Thus, even Notker did not see humour as something to be admired in all its manifestations. In fact, Notker's valuation of humour is intimately related to its relationship to the sacred–secular divide. The jester who challenged Louis is 'silly' because he pollutes a sacred occasion with an inappropriate attempt at humour, behaving without humility and self-control and placing himself in the proper place of Christ's representative, the emperor. Compare another of Notker's stories, in which a jester who interrupts Charlemagne in a resolutely secular setting – the hunt – to make a political jest, actually succeeds in making his point and changing Charlemagne's mind.[57] Humour in an appropriate context could be legitimately and successfully deployed, but the sacred aura of imperial prayer at Easter was neither the right time nor place. The cleric who doubled as a secular performer similarly inappropriately confused the sacred performance of liturgy with the world of secular songs, exhibiting a vain pride in his innate abilities that might have been acceptable in a jester but certainly was not in a priest.

---

[54] For wider attempts to impose meaning on ritual, see P. Buc, 'Ritual and interpretation: the early medieval case', *EME* 9(2) (2000), pp. 183–210.

[55] See Ganz, 'Humour as history', p. 172.

[56] Notker, *Gesta Karoli* 1.32; see Kershaw, below, p. 193. Clause 12 of the 747 Council of Clofesho (A. Haddan and W. Stubbs, *Councils and Ecclesiastical Documents* (Oxford, 1871), p. 366), influenced by the Roman synod of 679 (ibid., p. 133), banned the recitation of the liturgy in the manner of vernacular poetry; Carolingian reform of chant (a favourite topic of Notker's) may have aimed at a firmer separation between liturgy and secular performance.

[57] Notker, *Gesta Karoli* 1.13.

Where Notker differed from Thegan was in his positive assessment of the possibility of using humour as a means of furthering human understanding of God's plan, and indeed as a means of casting down the proud who neglected God and trusted too much in themselves. As David Ganz has brilliantly shown, in the *Deeds of Charlemagne*, as in his monastic classroom, Notker used humour as a means of illustrating divine truths, and of mocking those who were blind to them.[58] Frequently Notker's humour is not only edificatory, but essentially monastic, in that it involves laughing at the meaninglessness and vanity of the lives of people who lack the direction of a monastic vocation, notably the powerful who were all too likely to get puffed up. In this moralising and monastic perspective, Notker is typical of ninth-century texts that use humour.[59] Even the genre whose hilarity the sources insist on, secular lays, can only be accessed via fragments of monastic provenance, which, in their surviving form, bear the imprint of that origin: the surviving version of the lay of Walter of Aquitaine, *Waltharius*, is suffused with an earthy and violent humour, but a humour directed at the stereotype of the hard-drinking, hard-fighting nobleman and thus affirming the monastic identity of the redactor of the surviving Latin text.[60] It is both striking and alarming to realise that those specimens of ninth-century humour, which are accessible today because they made it into a written form that survived, are so overwhelmingly examples of monks laughing at stereotypes of secular pride.

The divide between sacred and secular was central to the attitudes to humour of both Notker and Thegan. Thus, in spite of the obvious contrast between Notker's comic genius and Thegan's lack of laughs, much unites them in their awareness of the complexity of the relationship between humour and power, and of the value of self-control as a strategy of power. Like Notker's, Thegan's Louis uses the denial of humour to order a potentially uncontrolled situation; Notker's Charlemagne, on the other hand, uses humour, like anger, as a means of asserting control. In

[58] Ganz, 'Humour as history'.   [59] See Kershaw, below, pp. 191–9.
[60] *Waltharius*: *MGH PLAC* 4, ed. K. Strecker (Berlin, 1909), pp. 1–93; I follow D. Kratz, *Mocking Epic: Waltharius, the Alexanderreis and the Problem of Christian Response* (Madrid, 1980). However, recent research on the Old High German *Hildebrandslied* (a tragic rather than a comic text) likewise stresses its monastic provenance and role as commentary on secular pride, whilst the Old High German *Ludwigslied* has been read as a monastic send-up of secular literature. It may be necessary to turn, with all necessary care, to later, cognate Anglo-Saxon or Icelandic vernacular traditions if we are to gain unmediated access to the type of secular hilarity associated by Thegan with the performances of *scurri*. Even then, care about the context of the surviving written texts is required: see *Humour in Anglo-Saxon Literature*, ed. J. Wilcox (Cambridge, 2000), esp. Wilcox's introduction, pp. 1–10.

all of these images, the king is quite literally central, the figure around whom everyone else revolves, and royal regulation of humour ensures that centrality. Thegan himself underlines the paramount importance of control in the implicit contrast between his portrayal of Louis, and its counterpoint in one of the few other extended discussions he gives of any other individual, his comments on Count Hugh. Alongside Ebbo of Rheims, Hugh is Thegan's *bête noire*, a bad and unfaithful counsellor to be blamed for the problems which Louis' régime had experienced. Thegan, drawing attention to the abortive Spanish campaign that had led to Hugh's political downfall, nicknames Hugh 'the timid'; Thegan ridicules Hugh, retelling with glee how members of his own household mocked their lord for this cowardice, chanting at him 'He daren't come out of his own doorway.'[61] Not only does Thegan's humour here effectively serve to blacken Hugh's reputation, but Hugh's powerlessness in the face of the ridicule of his own household stands in telling contrast to Louis' behaviour. Where Louis exerts his authority through superior self-control, and is able to tame potentially subversive humour at his table, Hugh can control neither his emotions nor his household, and so becomes the butt of their humour. The intimate relationship between self-control and political power was a commonplace in the mirrors for princes that ninth-century thinkers wrote for the likes of Louis and Hugh. Thegan encapsulates and illustrates their teaching in a striking contrast between the hero and one of the villains of his work. Self-control, the ability to rule oneself, is vital if one is to exercise rule over others.[62]

THE POLITICS OF HUMOUR IN THE CAROLINGIAN RENAISSANCE

Humour, like any other emotion, is a challenging subject for the historian. This chapter has attempted to meet this challenge by focussing on debate about the meaning and value of humour within the surviving sources. This has proved far from straightforward: understanding the description of an unlaughing emperor involves reconstructing the complex literary and cultural traditions which Thegan consciously manipulated to give a many-layered meaning to what on an initial reading looks like a relatively candid image.

But how does Thegan's representation relate to the 'real Louis'? The layering of references to a series of literary models and the complex

---

[61] Thegan, *Gesta Hludovici* 28, and see also 55.   [62] See Humphries, above, pp. 76–9.

intertextuality with them prevent us from reading Thegan as a disinterested reflection of developments at Louis' court. We can only move
beyond the discourses that constitute our primary sources if we admit
that these discourses were written to be decoded by a contemporary audience, and that the representations within them were therefore subject
to a form of preventative censure; that is, authorial freedom was subject
to limits of plausibility. In that Thegan draws on ideas current at Louis'
court, and wrote as the mouthpiece of a faction at that court, we can read
him as an interested representation of the public image of the régime.[63]

This methodology may leave us shy of a daring ontological leap from
literary sources to past human emotions, but it is not necessarily a counsel of despair. After all, it ought to be possible to reconstruct the history
of an emotion such as humour by focussing on the ways in which authors
evaluated and represented that emotion by drawing on and reshaping
available cultural models and stereotypes. Such an approach might, indeed, encourage a move beyond the crude bipolar division between
'essentialists', who see emotions as universal across time and space, and
'constructivists', who stress the role of cultural models and social experience in shaping emotions.[64] Examining the ways in which the authors
of the source material worked within and so subtly transformed the cultural systems they inherited, might aid research into the ways in which
human action is structured through cultural systems, which are in their
turn restructured through their use by human actors.[65]

This methodology does, however, leave us facing one key problem:
our total reliance on surviving sources that offer a far from disinterested
or neutral representation of their authors' society. Even admitting that
we are effectively restricted to the upper echelons of that society, there
is still a world of conversation and gestures that is unlikely to find any
place in the written record. Our only response can be to be painfully
aware of the particular perspective of the sources, and to attempt to
integrate an explanation of that perspective and its peculiarity into our
analysis. After all, in the context of the current study, the reluctance of
most Carolingian sources to represent humour clearly is significant, and

---

[63] See G. Althoff, 'Quedlinburg and Gandersheim: Ottonische Frauenkloster als Herrschafts- und
Uberlieferungszentren', *Frühmittelalterliche Studien* 25 (1991), pp. 125–44.

[64] For the debate, see *Anger's Past: The Social Construction of an Emotion in the Middle Ages*, ed. B. H.
Rosenwein (Ithaca, NY, 1997), with references.

[65] My model is, of course, heavily influenced by works such as A. Giddens, *The Constitution of Society:
Outline of the Theory of Structuration* (London, 1984) and P. Bourdieu, *Outline of a Theory of Practice*,
trans. R. Nice (Cambridge, 1977), which seem to me to suggest a way of combining structure
and agency. See also Haldon, above, pp. 53–5.

owes much to the dominance of monastic ideals in the Carolingian world, and the centrality of self-control to codes of conduct even amongst the secular élite.[66]

This moral ambivalence was encouraged by the sociology of humour. Humour is not easily fixed, forced or reproduced at will, though nor is it inherently spontaneous and in the gift of the audience. With skill and experience, laughter can be solicited, but it cannot easily be institutionalised or tapped simply on demand. It is implicated in a two-way, if unequal, exchange, and hence attempts to institutionalise in order to reinforce a power relationship tend, ultimately, to succeed in form only, losing the actual humorous content. Because of this resistance to institutionalisation, humour always has the potential for ambivalence in relation to extant power relations.[67] Whilst the powerful may well be able to use their control over the options open to others to make them objects of mockery or ridicule, it is always possible to work humour against a power gradient, as a strategy of contestation and resistance. Even undirected humour, laughter with one's fellows as a celebration of community, may gain some of its force from the suspension of normal hierarchies.[68] It is always possible to turn undirected humour into directed humour, to move from laughing with to laughing at, in a process that the powerful can never wholly control.

For rulers, then, humour may be most useful as a strategy reinforcing dominance in a context of interpersonal relationships, with mockery and ridicule effective in imposing means of controlling patriarchal space. In a politics based on the royal family and the royal household, humour may have been of most value in furthering royal domination of the court, the heart of the Carolingian political system; certainly this is its primary function in Notker's account of Charlemagne and his heirs. In the definition and institutionalisation of political relationships that could not be wholly subsumed within the familial sphere nor wholly located within the royal household, the value of humour may have been much more

---

[66] For courtly codes of conduct, see M. Innes, '"A place of discipline": aristocratic youths and Carolingian courts', in *Court Culture in the Early Middle Ages*, ed. C. Cubitt (forthcoming).

[67] Sociologically, humour has a close affinity to those forms of power which Max Weber identified as 'charismatic', and my comments on the sociology of humour owe a clear debt to Weber's comments on charisma and its institutionalisation: see *Weber: Selections*, ed. W. G. Runciman (Cambridge, 1978), pp. 225–50.

[68] For this Bakhtinian notion of laughter applied to the early Middle Ages, see Gurevich, *Historical Anthropology*. On 'undirected' versus 'directed' humour, see also M. I. Steblin-Kamenskij, 'On the history of laughter', *Medieval Scandinavia* 11 (1978–9), pp. 154–61, although I would see attempts to direct humour as a recurrent social process (similar to that which Weber posited for charisma), not as part of some metahistorical teleology leading towards modernity.

limited. So much in the Carolingian project centred on the definition and institutionalisation of political relationships, through the application of Christian norms of behaviour to all orders of society, through the swearing of oaths defining the obligations of all free men to God and king, through the interpretation of power according to an ideology of divinely ordained power descending from above. The Carolingians, whose initial success had been dependent on personal loyalties within an emergent élite, attempted, once established, to accentuate the vertical distance separating them from their followers, and de-emphasise the horizontal bonds on which they ultimately relied. Whilst horizontal rituals of face-to-face consensus and personal loyalty were as central as ever to the successful functioning of the political system, in the public domain of written comment on politics they fell under the shadow of the claims of a monastically inspired Christomimetic kingship.[69]

[69] Thanks are due to my audience at Leeds, and to Guy Halsall for suggesting that I talk on this subject, to Stuart Airlie for showing me work in progress on royal deportment, to Paul Kershaw for discussing his own work on Carolingian humour, and to Mayke De Jong for sharing her forthcoming work on Carolingian kingship, and her understanding of Carolingian monasticism, with me; I should also acknowledge the influence of Paul Dutton's *The Politics of Dreaming in the Carolingian Empire* (Lincon, NB, 1994), which inspired my subtitle. My long-standing interest in Thegan has benefited from many discussions of his work, notably with Rosamond McKitterick; I think it safe to say that I never imagined that it would first find written form in a paper on Carolingian humour!

CHAPTER 7

Alcuin's Disputatio Pippini *and the early medieval riddle tradition*

Martha Bayless

The early medieval period saw a flowering of riddles and riddle collections, both religious and secular, both earnest and light-hearted. To date the greater part of scholarly attention has been focussed on the Old English riddles of the *Exeter Book*, on the grounds both of literary merit and of mystery – the text does not include the answers, an omission that has provided happy occupation for decades of scholars. These two features – literary merit and mystery – also appear in what is perhaps a yet more remarkable riddle collection, the *Disputatio regalis et nobilissimi iuvenis Pippini cum Albino scholastico* of Alcuin.[1] The *Disputatio* is unusual in that it intermingles prose riddles with wisdom literature; that, unlike all other examples of the form, it puts the dialogue in the mouths of contemporary interlocutors (one Alcuin, the other Pippin, the son of Charlemagne), and represents itself as conversation between them; and that, to a degree rarely seen in dialogues, it is playful, teasing and genuinely witty. For the most part, however, scholarship has ignored the *Disputatio*, and the text has yet to claim its rightful place as a remarkable reflection of the strength a dialogue could obtain in the hands of a master craftsman such as Alcuin.

The early medieval tradition of literary riddling was inspired by Symphosius (or Symposius), a Late Latin poet whose exact identity is uncertain.[2] Symphosius' hundred riddles, each consisting of three verse lines, circulated widely in the medieval period; later riddle collections frequently rephrased those of Symphosius or simply borrowed riddles from him wholesale. The earliest surviving medieval collection is the *Bern Riddles*, apparently written in the seventh century by one Tullius,

---

[1] The *Disputatio* is edited by W. Suchier in L. W. Daly and W. Suchier, *Altercatio Hadriani Augusti et Epicteti Philosophi* (Illinois Studies in Language & Literature 24) (Urbana, IL, 1939), pp. 137–43. It is reprinted below. For bibliography on the text see M.-H. Jullien and F. Perelman, *Clavis des auteurs latins du Moyen Age: territoire français 735–987*, vol. II, *Alcuin* (Turnhout, 1999), pp. 164–5.

[2] For Symphosius' riddles, see *Variae Collectiones Aenigmatum Merovingicae Aetatis*, *CCSL* 133A, ed. F. Glorie (Turnhout, 1968), pp. 611–721.

whose origins and provenance are not yet fully understood.[3] Tullius, like Symphosius, wrote in verse; each riddle is six lines long. This period also saw a proliferation of riddle collections by Anglo-Latin writers. Latin riddle sequences were composed by the Anglo-Saxons Aldhelm (d. 709 or 710), Boniface (c.675–754), Tatwine (d.734) and Eusebius. Aldhelm's collection consisted of 100 verse riddles, varying in length, with an underlying theme of the wonders of creation, and culminating in an eighty-three-line riddle on 'Creation' itself.[4] Boniface, missionary to Germany and author of a number of works, was the author of a strictly edificatory set of twenty riddles, ten on virtues and ten on vices.[5] Tatwine, archbishop of Canterbury and the author of a Latin grammar, composed forty verse riddles, more didactic than descriptive, treating not only concrete objects but also abstractions such as 'the four senses of Scripture'.[6] These were rounded out to 100 by one Eusebius, perhaps to be identified with Hwætberht, abbot of Wearmouth-Jarrow in the early eighth century.[7] Eusebius' sixty verse riddles are a hotchpotch of lofty topics ('heaven'), opposites ('land and sea') and marvellous creatures ('ship-retaining fish').

These riddles all appeared as a part of formal collections, but there is also evidence that Latin riddles circulated independently and without the imprimatur of a named author. A number of riddles occur, *inter alia*, in the pseudo-Bede *Collectanea*, a compilation of materials assembled on the continent by an eighth-century cleric who had access to both Irish and English material.[8] The assemblage includes five riddles of Symphosius and five of Aldhelm, as well as eleven anonymous prose riddles. Of the prose riddles, only two seem to have no extant analogues: the others are

---

[3] *MGH PLAC* 4.2, ed. K. Strecker (Berlin, 1923), pp. 737–59, and *Variae Collectiones Aenigmatum, CCSL* 133A, ed. Glorie, pp. 541–610. On the collection and the varying contents of the manuscripts, see C. E. Finch, 'The Bern Riddles in Codex Vat. Reg. Lat. 1553', *Transactions and Proceedings of the American Philological Association* 92 (1961), pp. 145–55.

[4] Aldhelm's *enigmata* are edited by R. Ehwald, *Aldhelmi Opera, MGH Auctores Antiquissimi* 15 (Berlin, 1919), and reprinted in *Variae*, ed. Glorie, pp. 359–540. They are also reprinted and translated by J. Hall Pitman, *The Riddles of Aldhelm* (New Haven and London, 1925). On the riddles see M. Lapidge, 'Introduction to the *Enigmata*', in *Aldhelm: The Poetic Works*, ed. M. Lapidge and J. L. Rosier (Cambridge, 1985), pp. 61–9.

[5] *MGH PLAC* 1, ed. E. Dümmler (Berlin, 1881), pp. 3–15, and *Variae*, ed. Glorie, pp. 273–343.

[6] Tatwine's riddles may be found in *Variae*, ed. Glorie, pp. 165–208. See also F. H. Whitman, 'Aenigmata Tatwini', *Neuphilologische Mitteilungen* 88 (1987), pp. 8–17.

[7] *Variae*, ed. Glorie, pp. 209–71.

[8] *Collectanea Pseudo-Bedae* (Scriptores Latini Hiberniae 14), ed. M. Bayless and M. Lapidge (Dublin, 1998). On the riddles specifically, see the chapter by Bayless, 'The *Collectanea* and medieval dialogues and riddles', pp. 13–24.

paralleled in Aldhelm, Eusebius and riddle collections of later centuries (the Lorsch collection, St-Gall, Stiftsbibliothek 196 and the *Exeter Book*). This may serve as a useful reminder that, despite the seeming monumentality of riddle collections, riddles at heart were a more informal genre, and must have circulated singly, orally and in prose, as much as in verse and in manuscript. No prose riddle collections are found in manuscript, however, until the late eighth century, with the appearance of two contemporary assemblages: the pseudo-Bede *Collectanea* and Alcuin's *Disputatio Pippini*.

Later centuries reflect a greater variety of registers and forms. The twelve riddles in the ninth- or tenth-century Lorsch collection appear in verse, but are only supplied with answers by the modern editor.[9] Both formal and informal groups appear in the 'Cambridge Songs' manuscript, Cambridge, UL Gg.5.35, an eleventh-century classbook from Canterbury containing copies of the riddle collections of Symphosius, Aldhelm, Boniface, Tatwine and Eusebius. The manuscript also includes two other collections: a group of verse riddles on school subjects and nineteen prose Latin logographic riddles, riddles that encode the name of the object in the body of the riddle.[10] The scribe who first wrote or copied out the logographic riddles provided no solutions, but a second hand of the same period both supplied and explained the answers. As the riddles' modern editor remarks, 'his solutions, unlike so many of those fastened by modern scholarship upon early riddles, have the not small merit of really solving the problems to which they are attached'.[11]

Prose Latin riddles have also survived in other manuscripts of the period, such as St-Gall, Stiftsbibliothek 196, a manuscript of the tenth century that appends three prose riddles to those of Symphosius and a biblical curiosity dialogue.[12] Verse riddles also occur singly, such as the Leiden riddle[13] and the Latin verse riddle on 'Æthelwold's bowl' found

---

[9] *MGH PLAC* 1, ed. Dümmler, pp. 20–3, and *Variae*, ed. Glorie, pp. 345–58.

[10] On the Cambridge Songs manuscript, see A. G. Rigg and G. R. Wieland, 'A Canterbury classbook of the mid-eleventh century (the "Cambridge Songs" manuscript)', *Anglo-Saxon England* 4 (1975), pp. 113–30 (esp. pp. 120–30). For the verse riddles, see *Anecdota Bedae, Lanfranci et Aliorum*, ed. J. A. Giles (London, 1851, repr. New York, 1967), pp. 50–3; for the logographic riddles, see F. Tupper, Jr, 'Riddles of the Bede tradition', *Modern Philology* 2 (1904–5), pp. 1–12 (at pp. 8–11).

[11] Tupper, 'Riddles', p. 7.

[12] The three riddles are printed in Daly and Suchier, *Altercatio Hadriani* p. 144, n. 91.

[13] For the Leiden riddle, see *The Anglo-Saxon Minor Poems* (Anglo-Saxon Poetic Records 6), ed. E. v. K. Dobbie (New York, 1942), p. 109. It and the *Exeter Book* version are translations of Aldhelm's 'Lorica' riddle; all three are printed by C. Williamson, *The Old English Riddles of the Exeter Book* (Chapel Hill, NC, 1977), pp. 88–9 and 243–4.

in an eleventh-century manuscript.[14] Finally, the vernacular tradition of riddles surfaces in the ninety-one or so Old English verse riddles of the *Exeter Book*, copied around the year 1000.[15]

Alcuin's dialogue thus forms a very early example of a more informal and conversational framework for riddles, although it is one that reflects their origins – as questions and answers, a guessing game between two people – more clearly than the monumental and often unguessable riddles of the verse collections. Uniquely among riddle collections, however, Alcuin's *Disputatio* also partakes of a second tradition, that of wisdom and curiosity dialogues.

Wisdom dialogues were question-and-answer texts that defined common objects or concepts in terms of metaphors.[16] Typical examples included, for instance, '*Quid est epistola? Tacitus nuntius*' and '*Quid est somnus? Imago mortis*': 'What is a letter? A silent messenger' and 'What is sleep? The image of death.' In a sense, these were embryonic riddles, the building blocks of poetry. Curiosity dialogues, by contrast, were catechisms of biblical riddles, chiefly concerned with paradox: 'Who died and was never born? Adam', and so forth.[17] Curiosity dialogues often incorporated items from wisdom dialogues, and paradox riddles were sometimes intermingled.[18] These three forms – riddle collections, wisdom dialogues and curiosity dialogues – served similar functions: to evoke wonder at the glory of God and the everyday marvels of his world, which included his ability to unite opposites in paradox, and to provide pleasure while doing so.

Alcuin's *Disputatio* is confected from these three components: wisdom dialogues, curiosity dialogues and riddle collections. The framework of

---

[14] See D. W. Porter. 'A double solution to the Latin riddle in MS Antwerp, Plantin-Moretus Museum M16.2.', *ANQ (American Notes & Queries)* 9 (1996), pp. 3–9, and 'Æthelwold's bowl and *The Chronicle of Abingdon*', *Neuphilologische Mitteilungen* 97 (1996), pp. 163–7. On other early medieval riddles, see G. Polara, 'Aenigmata', in *Lo spazio letterario del medioevo*, series 1: *Il medioevo latino*, vol. I, *La produzione del testo*, ed. G. Cavallo et al. (2 vols., Rome, 1993), vol. II, pp. 197–216.

[15] *The Exeter Book* (Anglo-Saxon Poetic Records 3), ed. G. P. Krapp and E. v. K. Dobbie (New York, 1936), pp. 180–210, 224–5 and 229–43; Williamson, *Old English Riddles*.

[16] For the history of wisdom dialogues and many examples of the form, see Daly & Suchier, *Altercatio Hadriani*. Other wisdom questions are found in the dialogues printed by W. Suchier, *Das mittellateinische Gespräch Adrian und Epictitus nebst verwandten Texten (Joca Monachorum)* (Tübingen, 1955).

[17] The *locus classicus* for items of this type is the set of dialogues known as the *Ioca monachorum*, although they also appear in dialogues such as *Adrianus et Epictitus*. Both types are printed in Suchier, *Gespräch*. In other studies I have also referred to curiosity dialogues as trivia dialogues; they are the same form. See also Shanzer, above, pp. 26–7.

[18] These are of the briefest type, not the more complex paradoxes favoured by Alcuin and other named authors. For instance, *Adrianus et Epictitus* version AE_2 asks '*Quid tangitur et non videtur? – Anima. Quid videtur et non tangitur? – Celum*' (Suchier, *Gespräch*, p. 33, nos. 49–50).

the text is adopted from a version of a widely circulating wisdom dialogue, the *Altercatio Hadriani Augusti et Epicteti philosophi*.[19] Where the *Altercatio Hadriani* remains sober and straightforward, however, Alcuin's dialogue goes wildly astray: the questioner and the respondent exchange roles, sombre metaphors are abandoned for spirited riddles, and the clarity of answers is cast aside for teasing, hinting and impish evasiveness.

Both the milieu – the high-spirited erudition of Charlemagne's court – and Alcuin's own character set the stage for the playfulness of the *Disputatio*. As master of Charlemagne's court school, Alcuin seems to have had a flair for imaginative and playful teaching. He is credited with introducing into circulation important texts that had been abandoned for centuries, among them Priscian's grammatical work the *Institutiones grammaticae*, and the treatise on logic *De decem categoriis*. Where texts did not exist, or where the available authorities were too dry or unsuitable, Alcuin composed his own texts.

Typical of these is the *Dialogus Franconis et Saxonis de octo partibus orationis*, a grammar in the form of a dialogue between a Frankish pupil and his Saxon comrade, with interventions from Alcuin himself.[20] The dialogue recasts the information in Priscian's *Institutiones grammaticae* into more easily digestible form, and occasionally comments on the differences in the taxonomies set forth by Priscian and those of the other great grammatical authority, Donatus, in the way that such queries might be raised in lessons. The details of the students' ages suggest that the boys were actual pupils at the court school, and that the text served as a way of enlivening otherwise dull grammatical instruction, as well as giving the boys a vehicle for rehearsing the material among themselves. *De rhetorica et virtutibus* was another teaching dialogue, this one framed as a conversation between Alcuin and Charlemagne.[21] Alcuin is also the likely author of a collection of story problems, the *Propositiones ad acuendos*

---

[19] The *Altercatio* is edited by Daly and Suchier, *Altercatio Hadriani*, pp. 104–7, along with a number of related texts. Alcuin's *Disputatio* borrows a number of elements from a lost recension of the text printed as the *Altercatio*, but other parts of Alcuin's text are more closely related to other wisdom dialogues, notably the *Vita Secundi* (ed. Daly and Suchier, pp. 152–9, esp. pp. 158–9) and an addition to *Adrianus et Epictitus* found in manuscript C (ed. Suchier, *Gespräch*, p. 37). It is also worth noting that some of these versions are retailed under the title *Disputatio*, so that Alcuin's title sets the text in the tradition of wisdom dialogues.

[20] The text is may be found in *PL* 101, cols. 854–902.

[21] For the *De rhetorica*, see *PL* 101, cols. 919–46 and *Rhetores Latini minores*, ed. C. Halm (Leipzig, 1863), pp. 523–50. Halm's edition is reprinted with a few changes, and a translation, by W. S. Howell, *The Rhetoric of Alcuin and Charlemagne* (Princeton, 1941). On Alcuin's dialogues, see also E. Ann Matter, 'Alcuin's question-and-answer texts', *Rivista di storia della filosofia* 4 (1990), pp. 645–56.

iuvenes.[22] Many of these are number problems, but among them is the famous 'About the wolf and the goat and the bundle of cabbages', in which a man has to take a goat, a wolf and a bundle of cabbages across a river in a boat too small to carry more than one item at once.[23] All of these teaching texts share Alcuin's stamp: a concern with engaging his pupils, with personalising his materials, and with expressing human warmth as he did so.

Alcuin's imaginative teaching style seems to have been part and parcel of Carolingian court life, which valued wit and play as well as learning.[24] A poem by Theodulf, a member of the royal entourage, depicts the lively tenor of the court:

> Ludicris haec mixta iocis per ludicra currat,
> Saepeque tangatur qualibet illa manu.
> Laude iocoque simul hunc illita carta revisat,
> Quem tribuente celer ipse videbo deo.[25]

> Let this poem romp amidst the mirth and amusements,
> And may it often be held by every hand.
> And, covered with praise and delight, may it return to him
> Whom, God granting, I will see soon.

The poem portrays the court on an ideal day, with all its members present in their accustomed roles. Alcuin is depicted in what is presumably his typical occupation: in the midst of the court, setting problems on a variety of subjects for others to work out. As the poem is in praise of Charlemagne, Theodulf expresses his wishes that Charlemagne will be the one to solve the conundrums Alcuin sets:

> Sit praesto et Flaccus, nostrorum gloria vatum . . .
> Quique sophista potens est, quique poeta melodus,
> Quique potens sensu, quique potens opere est.

---

[22] The text is edited by M. Folkerts and H. Gericke, *Die Alkuin zugeschriebenen Propositiones ad acuendos iuvenes* (Aufgaben zur Schärfung des Geistes der Jugend)', in *Science in Western and Eastern Civilization in Carolingian Times*, ed. P. L. Butzer and D. Lohrmann (Basel, 1993), pp. 283–362. On the text and transmission, see also M. Folkerts, 'Die Alkuin zugeschriebenen "Propositiones ad acuendos iuvenes"', in *Science in Western and Eastern Civilization*, ed. Butzer and Lohrmann, pp. 273–81.

[23] Folkerts and Gericke, *Propositiones*, pp. 316–17 (no. 18).

[24] For further discussion of Carolingian courts and humour, see Innes, above, pp. 142–56.

[25] *MGH PLAC* 1, ed. Dümmler, p. 483, no. 25, lines 9–12; also repr. and trans. P. Godman, *Poetry of the Carolingian Renaissance* (Norman, OK, 1985), no. 15, pp. 150–63; this passage is at pp. 150–1. The translations above are my own.

Et pia de sanctis scripturis dogmata promat,
    Et solvat numeri vincla favente ioco.
Et modo sit facilis, modo scrupea quaestio Flacci,
    Nunc mundanam artem, nunc redibens superam:
Solvere de multis rex ipse volentibus unus
    Sit bene qui possit solvere Flaccidica.[26]

Let Flaccus [i.e. Alcuin] be present as well, the glory of our poets . . .
He is a powerful scholar and a melodious poet,
Great in perception and great in his works.
May he propound the pious teachings of holy Scripture,
And loosen the chains of numbers with an encouraging jest.
Though sometimes Flaccus' questions may be easy, sometimes difficult,
Now on a worldly topic, now on higher things,
Among the many who want to solve the Flaccidities,
May the king himself be the one who can solve them well.

There is plentiful evidence of Alcuin's love of such puzzles and games. In addition to the *Disputatio*, he wrote at least seven surviving verse riddles, all of them apparently original: one on a comb, one on a furnace, and five logogriphic enigmata.[27] He was so fond of the comb riddle that it appears again, paraphrased, in a letter.[28] In addition to these examples of literary play, Alcuin composed acrostic verses and, indeed, appears to have introduced the form to the Carolingian court, starting a trend which resulted in the presentation of a set of such verses to Charlemagne.[29] His letters also testify to the extent to which encoding was, for Alcuin, a sign of affection or familiarity.[30] Even his habit of bestowing by-names on the members of the court is an expression of his delight in encoding and transforming things by the use of language.[31]

[26] *MGH PLAC* 1, ed. Dümmler, p. 486, lines 131 and 133–40; repr. and trans. Godman, *Poetry*, pp. 156–7.
[27] For these riddles, see *MGH PLAC* 1, ed. Dümmler, pp. 223 (no. 5, the comb riddle) and 281–3.
[28] *MGH Epistolae* 4, ed. E. Dümmler (Berlin, 1895) no. 26, p. 67. The riddle is discussed by P. Sorrell, 'Alcuin's "comb" riddle', *Neophilologus* 80 (1996), pp. 311–18.
[29] See M. Garrison, 'The emergence of Carolingian Latin literature and the court of Charlemagne (780–814)', in *Carolingian Culture: Emulation and Innovation*, ed. R. McKitterick (Cambridge, 1994), pp. 111–40, at pp. 121–2.
[30] See, for example, *MGH Epistolae* 4, ed. Dümmler, no. 176, p. 291, and the commentary by M. Garrison, 'The social world of Alcuin: nicknames at York and at the Carolingian court', in *Alcuin of York: Scholar at the Carolingian Court* (Germania Latina 3), ed. L. A. J. R. Houwen and A. A. MacDonald (Groningen, 1998), pp. 59–79, at pp. 74–5, n. 54. This encoding of words was not unique to Alcuin: another example from the Carolingian court is discussed by Keith Sidwell, 'Theodulf of Orléans, Cadac-Andreas and Old Irish phonology: a conundrum', *Journal of Medieval Latin* 2 (1992), pp. 55–62.
[31] On this see Garrison, 'Social world of Alcuin'.

The court welcomed such diversions and entertainments, and riddling in particular became almost an heroic pastime among contending poets. Between 782 and 786 Charlemagne, Peter of Pisa and Paul the Deacon exchanged a series of riddle poems and challenges. One poem depicts Charlemagne challenging Paul the Deacon to solve a riddle overnight, and Paul trying to distract Charlemagne from the challenge by sending him a competing set of riddles.[32]

The *Disputatio*, then, is only one text in a lively tradition that combined learning and wit, that supplied new and engaging texts to pupils, and that trained those pupils to take their place in a milieu that valued learned amusement. As a man practised in both affection toward, and flattery of, royal personages, it was percipient of Alcuin to choose Pippin, the son of Charlemagne, as his dialogue partner.

To say that he chose Pippin, however, is to be less precise that one might think: in fact, Charlemagne's court was oversupplied with sons of Charlemagne named Pippin, there being two. The first was Pippin the Hunchback, Charlemagne's eldest son, born around 769 from a connection with a Frankish noblewoman, Himiltrude (it is unclear whether marriage was involved). In 777 Charlemagne's new wife, Hildegard, bore a son named Karlmann, who was destined early for great things. The boy was designated king of Italy at four, the same age in which he was baptised by the pope; at his baptism his name was changed to Pippin, for reasons that are not clear. It is almost certainly this younger Pippin who figures in the *Disputatio*.

To arrive at this conclusion requires some analysis of the likely date of the *Disputatio* and the circumstances of its composition. In so doing, it is necessary to pose a number of questions. First, does the *Disputatio* reflect a genuine conversation between Alcuin and Pippin? The answer here is certainly no: although the text is unique among literary dialogues for its moments of seemingly genuine and spontaneous exchange, as a whole it is much cleverer and more contrived – more literary – than real conversation. Secondly, was the dialogue intended to be presented to Pippin, or does it merely feature him as a character? It is unlikely that the text was intended exclusively for Pippin, as it is clearly a literary production; even

---

[32] The poems are edited by Karl Neff, *Die Gedichte des Paulus Diaconus* (Munich, 1908), nos. 16–22, pp. 82–105. See also Garrison, 'Emergence of Carolingian Latin literature', pp. 121–2. A library catalogue also gives evidence of riddles, now lost, composed by Joseph Scottus, a student of Alcuin from York also at the Carolingian court; see M. Garrison, 'The English and the Irish at the court of Charlemagne', in *Karl der Grosse und sein Nachwirken: Charlemagne and his Heritage*, ed. P. L. Butzer, M. Kerner and W. Oberschelp (Turnhout, 1997), pp. 97–123, at p. 105.

Alcuin's letters, like the letters of many other medieval authors, although ostensibly addressed to a sole recipient, were accomplished showpieces of literary endeavour, which were certainly meant to circulate among a wider audience, as indeed they did. In similar fashion, it is likely that Pippin was addressed in the first instance, but that Alcuin also envisioned a secondary audience of schoolboys. Indeed, schoolboys are mentioned twice in the dialogue, once in reference to a number riddle, hereafter simply cited as the number in parentheses (*'Pueri in scola sciunt'*, 'The boys in the school know that one' (100)), and again when the two interlocutors conspire to keep the answers a secret from them: ('. . . *sed pone digitum super os, ne pueri audiant quid sit'*, 'but put your finger on your lips, so the boys don't hear the answer' (95)). In this latter case, the solution is never revealed overtly, so the schoolboys do indeed never 'hear' the answer. The dialogue implies that the conversation is taking place between Alcuin and Pippin in the foreground, with the schoolboys in the background listening, but this apparent spatial distinction may in fact be a temporal one: Pippin is the privileged first reader of the dialogue, but it will be passed on to the schoolboys in turn.

As head of the school, Alcuin would have been in charge of Pippin's education, and so it is a very reasonable assumption that he did indeed address the *Disputatio* directly to Pippin. This would be not merely a pedagogical move but also a flattering one, since Alcuin's model text, as Pippin must have known, was a version of the *Altercatio Hadriani Augusti et Epicteti philosophi*. The strategy of casting Pippin in the role of Hadrian and himself in the role of Epictetus is of a piece with Alcuin's hallmark practice of assigning elevated classical identities to himself and the members of the court.

The question then remains: how old was Pippin when the dialogue was addressed to him? Certainly he is distinguished from the *pueri*, the boys in the schoolroom, not only by rank but also by age. Although the enjoyment of such dialogues was not confined to youngsters, dialogues and riddles have strong ties to early medieval school curricula, and the *Disputatio* in particular seems designed to appeal to youthful tastes.

Alcuin did not arrive to take charge of the court school until 781 or 782; he stayed at court continuously until 796 except for two sojourns in England, once in 786 and again from 790 to 793. Thus, when he arrived at court the elder Pippin, Pippin the Hunchback, would have been twelve or thirteen; at Alcuin's first return to England, seventeen; and at Alcuin's second journey, twenty-one to twenty-three. The younger

Pippin would have been around four when Alcuin arrived, nine at his first journey, between thirteen and sixteen at his second, and nineteen when Alcuin left the court in 796 to become abbot of Tours. The most important question remaining, then, is whether the *Disputatio* was written while Alcuin was in residence at the court or while he was abroad. There are a number of reasons to believe that the latter is the case, and that the text actually formed a letter sent to Pippin by Alcuin. As I shall show, the theme at the close of the dialogue is *epistola*, and Alcuin depicts the text itself as a letter Pippin is holding in his hand. At another point Pippin is depicted as saying '*Si scirem quid esset navis, prepararem tibi, ut venires ad me*' – 'If I knew what a boat was, I would make one ready for you, so you could come to me' (76). (This does not imply that Pippin was too young to be familiar with boats, but that he had not yet learnt the conventional wisdom-dialogue metaphor for boats, which Alcuin promptly supplies.) This suggests that Alcuin was overseas when he composed the text for Pippin, and thus the date can mostly likely be assigned to the period 790 to 793, when Alcuin's stay abroad was long enough to allow him the leisure to write. If one accepts the supposition that the dialogue is most likely to have been aimed at youthful tastes, then this would suggest the younger Pippin, who would be between thirteen and sixteen during these years, as its recipient.[33] This would be in keeping with Alcuin's attentiveness to the nuances of winning royal benefaction: although details of Pippin the Hunchback's early career are obscure, he seems to have been out of favour at court, and indeed was banished from the court to the monastery of Prüm in 792, on the grounds of conspiracy. To cast him as an analogue of the emperor Hadrian, when he was not destined for rulership of any sort, would have been a gaffe of the first order.

It seems likely, then, that the text addresses the younger Pippin, who was probably between thirteen and sixteen at the time, and that Alcuin sent the text from abroad. Pippin had presumably been his student for some years, as Alcuin had arrived at court when Pippin was four, and so there was already a bond of affection between them, as well as a grounding in basic texts and the dialogue form, so that Pippin would have been alive to the changes rung by the *Disputatio* on the conventions of the genre.

[33] There were also periods in which Alcuin remained at court and the younger Pippin was away – in 787, when he was ten, for example, Pippin was involved in leading troops from Italy into battle – but the reference to Alcuin coming to Pippin via boat suggests that this is not the separation referred to in the text.

The *Disputatio* begins in the form of a wisdom dialogue. Dialogues of this type go back to the late classical period, and a wilderness of related texts proliferated in the early medieval period. Unusually, Alcuin puts his *Disputatio* in the mouths of real interlocutors, but otherwise this section of the dialogue follows standard practice, with material borrowed, as usual, from the common store of proverbs and metaphors. The text consists of short and often poetic definitions of common concepts: Pippin asks, '*Quid est homo?*', 'What is man?' and Alcuin answers, '*Mancipium mortis, transiens viator, loci hospes*', 'The slave of death, a traveller passing by, the guest of a place' (8). '*Quomodo positus est homo?*', 'How is he situated?' '*Ut lucerna in vento*', 'Like a lantern in the wind' (10). '*Quid est terra?*', 'What is earth?'; '*Mater crescentium, nutrix viventium, cellarium vitae, devoratrix omnium*', 'The mother of growing things, the nurse of the living, the storehouse of life, the devourer of everything' (56). Not all the questions have this sombre tone: the text also asks '*Quid est venter? Custos fragilium*': 'What is the belly? The guardian of crumbs' (40); '*Quid sunt pedes? Mobile fundamentum*': 'What are the feet? Moveable pedestals' (44). The subjects of enquiry are cosmic as well as pedestrian: '*Quid est annus? Quadriga mundi. Quis ducit eam? Nox et dies, frigus et calor. Quid est aurgia eius? Sol et luna*': 'What is a year? A four-horse chariot of the world. Who pulls it? Night and day, heat and cold.' 'Who is its charioteer? The sun and the moon' (68–70). These are finely balanced between riddles and poetry, but their quality cannot be ascribed to Alcuin: the vast majority of the items he uses are paralleled in other wisdom dialogues.

Even at the beginning of the text, however, Alcuin displays a sharpness unusual to such dialogues. Other examples of the form shuffle the questions so that they appear in random order, but Alcuin begins with the building blocks of the enterprise. Pippin enquires, '*Quid est littera?*', 'What is a letter [of the alphabet]?' Alcuin replies, '*Custos historiae*', 'The guardian of history' (1). Pippin then expands his enquiry from the letter to the word: '*Quid est verbum? Proditor animi*', 'What is a word? The betrayer of the soul' (2). The dialogue then moves into conventional formulae, but the theme returns in the final subject of enquiry, a letter (*epistola*) – what has finally been built up when the letters and words with which the dialogue began have been assembled.

After this beginning, the text continues in conventional form to the tune of seventy-three questions. Uniquely among wisdom dialogues, however, this rather poetic and hence contrived interchange is transformed into something like real conversation. Pippin has been enquiring about the heavens, but at a certain point, he balks: '*Magister, timeo altum ire*',

'Master, I'm afraid to go up high.' Alcuin replies, '*Si times, descendamus; sequar quocumque ieris*', 'If you're afraid, let's go down; I'll follow wherever you go' (74–5). This diversion into subjective commentary is unprecedented in the genre. This is not merely personal commentary, but an exploration of the possibilities of words. When Pippin protests that he is afraid to go 'high', he opens the door to multiple meanings. The Latin word *altum* refers both to heights and to depths, so Pippin has also been expressing his fear of going out upon the deep. In saying 'let's go down', Alcuin is alluding back to the last topic of enquiry, the heavens, but Pippin now turns the double meaning upon its hinges and begins to talk about the depths of the ocean. Afraid to venture out to the depths, Pippin says, '*Si scirem quid esset navis, prepararem tibi, ut venires ad me,*' 'If I knew what a boat was, I would make one ready for you, so you could come to me' (76). This interchange involves an extraordinary convergence of images: the heights in the previous passages are transformed into the depths, and Pippin is afraid to set out upon these depths. The line also invokes the topos of beginning a literary enterprise as setting out across the sea, an image common to the period, employed both by Alcuin elsewhere and in a poem about Charlemagne ascribed to Einhard.[34] As I have suggested above, the passage also alludes to the fact that Alcuin genuinely was residing across the sea from Pippin. The sea voyage Pippin wishes Alcuin would make for him, then, may not be merely a literary expedition but also a literal one, back to court to answer Pippin's questions.

Once Pippin, in the text, has mentioned a boat, Alcuin, back safely in the conventions of the wisdom dialogue, responds with a conventional string of metaphors for boat: '*Navis est domus erratica, ubilibet hospitium, viator sine vestigiis, vicinus harenae,*' 'A boat is a wandering home, a shelter anywhere, a traveller without footprints, a neighbour of beaches' (76). Pippin makes a few more typical enquiries along these lines, on hope, friendship, faith and suchlike, when suddenly the dialogue again takes a turn away from formulaic phrases to original and self-reflexive answers. '*Quid est mirum?*', 'What is a wonder?' asks Pippin (86). Alcuin responds not with a formulaic definition but with an example. More than that, his unconventional response, absolutely unparalleled in other dialogue

---

[34] Alcuin's example is in the 'Versus de sanctis Euboricensis ecclesiae': *MGH PLAC* 1, ed. Dümmler, p. 198, lines 1321–3; the image also opens the poem from Einhard (ibid., p. 366; repr. and trans. Godman, *Poetry*, no. 25, p. 196). On the topos of beginning a literary work as equivalent to setting out to sea, see E. R. Curtius, *European Literature and the Latin Middle Ages*, trans. W. Trask (London, 1953), pp. 128–30.

literature, is a wonder itself; it constitutes its own definition. The exchange reads:

P. Quid est mirum? – A. Nuper vidi hominem stantem, molientem, ambulantem, qui numquam fuit. (86)

P. What is a wonder? – A. Recently I saw a person standing, moving, walking, who never was.

So Alcuin responds to the question 'What is a wonder?' with something that does not define a wonder but that embodies it. A further source of dislocation is the fact that, at the word 'wonder', the tables have been turned: now Pippin is answering rather than asking, an about-turn also unknown in the dialogue tradition. Alcuin proposes that he ask Pippin *'alia mira'* – 'other wonders' – and Pippin agrees.

At this point the text has let loose of its moorings in the wisdom tradition. A cascade of riddles follows. These riddles, moreover, are not just *enigmata*, but are genuinely enigmatic: in all but the first few, the answer is never supplied. Pippin appears to guess every one correctly, but he only supplies veiled hints to the reader: it is as if Alcuin is teasing Pippin, and then Pippin is teasing us. Riddle 92 may serve as an example. The riddle performs the typical riddle trick of characterising an inanimate object as 'dead', and then constructing a paradox between 'dead' things and 'live' ones. In this case the objects in question are bells, although the text never reveals the solution. The riddle reads: *'Audivi mortuos multa loquentes. – P. Numquam bene, nisi suspendantur in aëre'*, 'I heard the dead speaking copiously. – P. Not very well, unless they're hanging in the air' – a response which at once hints at the answer and magnifies the complexity of the original riddle.

Through the course of this riddle dialogue, Pippin's understanding increases: where initially he needs to be told the answer, he is soon alluding to – but not revealing – the answer himself. In this first instance, where Alcuin provides a 'wonder' – 'Recently I saw a person standing, moving, walking, who never was' – Pippin has to ask for the solution, and Alcuin reveals it: the person standing, moving and walking who never was is *'imago . . . in aqua'*, 'a reflection in water'. Pippin laments, *'Cur hoc non intellexi per me, dum toties vidi hunc ipsum hominem?'*, 'Why didn't I know that, when I've seen that person every day?' (88). This is typical of the conversational and self-mocking tone of this section of the dialogue, quite at odds with the formulaic interchange of earlier sections. In another example, Alcuin propounds a riddle about a pot boiling over:

'*Vidi mortuum sedentem super vivum, et in risu mortui moritur vivus*', 'I saw a dead one sitting on a live one, and in the laughter of the dead one the live one dies' (94). The dead one is a pot of water, the live one the fire on which it sits, and when the dead one laughs – boils over – the fire dies. None of this is explained, however. Pippin merely hints at the answer, '*Hoc coqui nostri norunt*', 'Our cooks know that one', and Alcuin increases the sense of collusion: '*Norunt, sed pone digitum super os, ne pueri audiant quid sit*', 'They do know it, but put your finger on your lips, so the boys don't hear what it is' (94–5).

The rapport between the two even gets to the point where Pippin dares to tease Alcuin. Alcuin asks a chick-in-egg riddle: '*Vidi quendam natum, antequam esset conceptus*', 'I saw someone born before he was formed.' '*Vidisti et forte manducasti*', 'You saw him', says Pippin, 'and perhaps you ate him' (96). '*Manducavi*' – 'That I did' – says Alcuin (97). Here the conventions of the riddle form, propounded in the first person with the formulaic 'I saw' introduction, are transmuted into the concrete world of the personal: 'You saw and perhaps you ate', 'So I did.' Typically when the riddle is elevated into literature, it is cast in verse and made elegant. Alcuin's interest is not stylistic display but communication in the service of affection.

The *Disputatio* contains seventeen riddles in all: four of these have close parallels in Symphosius, from whom they were probably borrowed, and seven have analogues in other early medieval riddle collections: Aldhelm, the *Ioca monachorum*, St-Gall 196, pseudo-Symphosius, and the pseudo-Bede *Collectanea*.[35] This leaves six that have no surviving analogues, but as the other questions in the *Disputatio* are derivative, it is probable that these riddles were part of the common stock of the time.

One surviving parallel provides an interesting contrast to the combination of succinctness, clarity and evasiveness that is the hallmark of this collection, as well as supplying an answer that has vexed a number of scholars. Alcuin's no. 101 is an animated paradox riddle: '*Quid est cui si caput abstuleris, et resurgit altior?*', 'What is it that when you take away the head, it springs back higher?' As with the other riddles, Pippin only hints at the answer: '*Vade ad lectulum et ibi invenies*', 'Go to your bed and you'll find it there' (101). The answer, as is clear from an analogue in Aldhelm, is a pillow: the trick of the riddle lies in the fact that it is the sleeper's head, rather than that of the object, that is taken away – an elegant example

---

[35] On these parallels, see 'Commentary', below.

of the misdirection common to medieval riddles.[36] In contrast to this simple formulation, Aldhelm's version is mired in the complexities of the rhetorical exercise:

Pulvillus
Nolo fidem frangas, licet irrita dicta putentur,
Credula sed nostris pande praecordia verbis!
Celsior ad superas possum turgescere nubes,
Si caput aufertur mihi toto corpore dempto;
At vero capitis si pressus mole gravabor,
Ima petens iugiter minorari parte videbor.[37]

Pillow
I do not want to strain belief, although these things may seem preposterous,
But open a trusting heart to my words!
I am able to swell toward the loftiest clouds on high
If the head is taken from me as the whole body is removed;
But if I am pressed down, burdened by the weight of a head,
Seeking the depths, straight away I will seem smaller in part.

Although Aldhelm's animated subject speaks in the first person, the poem itself is studiously impersonal; by contrast, Alcuin invites the listener not merely to guess from his own experience, but to bring his own world into the guessing-game of the riddle.

This use of familiar surroundings and practices is exemplified by one of the most problematic of the riddles, an example that has preserved its abstruseness to the present day. The riddle reads: '*Vidi hominem octo in manu tenentem, et de octonis subito rapuit septem, et remanserunt sex*', 'I saw a man holding eight in his hand, and from the eight he suddenly took away seven, and six remained.' Pippin replies, '*Pueri in scola sciunt*', 'The boys in the school know that one' (100). In fact the riddle is apparently a paraphrase of a verse riddle of pseudo-Symphosius:

De VIII tollas VII et remanet VI.
Nunc mihi iam credas, fieri quod posse negatur.

[36] The riddle has remained obscure in recent times, and modern scholars have tried to understand it as a logogriphic riddle. Friedrich Schwarz suggested that the answer might be 'castrum – astrum', in line with the two logogriphic riddles of Symphosius ('Das dritte der reichenauer *Aenigmata Risibilia*', *Zeitschrift für deutsches Altertum* 63 (Neue Folge 51) (1926), pp. 268–69, at p. 269, n. 1). Bengt Löfstedt has also suggested 'pediculus – ediculus' as the solution ('Zu den sog. *Ioca Monachorum*', *Eranos* 94 (1996), pp. 34–6, at p. 35).

[37] Aldhelm no. 41: *MGH Auctores Antiquissimi* 15, ed. Ehwald, p. 115; *Variae*, ed. Glorie, p. 425. The poem is also reprinted and translated by Hall Pitman, *Riddles of Aldhelm*; the pillow riddle is on pp. 22–3. The translation above is my own.

Octo tenes manibus, sed me monstrante magistro
Sublatis septem reliqui tibi sex remanebunt.³⁸

From 8 you take away 7, and 6 remain.
Now you should believe me, it is possible to do what you might discount.
You hold eight in your hands, but, as the schoolmaster showed me,
Lift seven away, and six will remain.

The pseudo-Symphosius is not supplied with an answer either, but
the references to school in both versions confirm Karl Menninger's suggestion that the riddle refers to finger-counting.³⁹ The system of representing the numbers by the position of the hands and fingers goes back
to the classical period, and descriptions of the technique occur in more
than fifty manuscripts of the early Middle Ages, as well as in those of
Bede's *De temporum ratione*, of which a treatise on finger-counting forms
the preface.⁴⁰ Bede's version 2 is typical:

Cum ergo dicis unum, minimum in laeua digitum inflectens, in medium palmae
artum infiges. Cum dicis duo, secundum a minimo flexum, ibidem impones.
Cum dicis tria, tertium similiter adflectes. Cum dicis quattuor, itidem minimum
leuabis. Cum dicis quinque, secundum a minimo similiter eriges. Cum dicis
sex, tertium nihilominus eleuabis, medio dumtaxat solo, qui medicus appellatur,
in medium palmae fixo. Cum dicis septem, minimum solum, caeteris interim
leuatis, super palmae radicem pones. Iuxta quem cum dicis octo, medicum.⁴¹

When, therefore, you say 'one', bend the little finger of your left hand and put
the tip in the middle of your palm. When you say 'two', bend the second finger,
next to the little one, and put it there likewise. When you say 'three', bend the
third finger likewise. When you say 'four', raise the little finger again. When you
say 'five', raise the second finger, next to the little finger, in the same way. When
you say 'six', you should lift the third finger, with the middle one [between the
third finger and the little finger – i.e. the ring finger], which is called the *medicus*,
alone placed in the middle of the palm. When you say 'seven', put the little
finger alone on the bottom of the palm, raising the rest. When you say 'eight',
lay the ring finger next to it.

---

³⁸ *Variae*, ed. Glorie, p. 723, no. 4.
³⁹ K. Menninger, *Number Words and Number Symbols: A Cultural History of Numbers*, trans. P. Broneer
   (Cambridge, MA and London, 1969), pp. 201–4. (The German original was *Zahlwort und Ziffer*,
   rev. edn 1958.) Menninger cites the pseudo-Symphosius version of the riddle, but was apparently
   unaware of Alcuin's version.
⁴⁰ See C. Cordoliani, 'A propos du chapitre premier du *De temporum ratione*, de Bède', *Le Moyen Âge*
   54 (1948), pp. 209–23; *Bedae Opera de Temporibus*, ed. Charles W. Jones (Cambridge, MA, 1943),
   pp. 329–30; *Bedae Venerabilis Opera, pars VI: Opera Didascalica 2*, *CCSL* 123B (Turnhout, 1977);
   and, for a wider survey of finger-counting, A. Rieche, 'Computatio Romana: Fingerzählen auf
   provinzialrömischen Reliefs', *Bonner Jährbücher* 186 (1986), pp. 165–92.
⁴¹ *Bedae Venerabilis Opera*, ed. Jones, p. 269.

The sign for eight, then, is to bend the little finger and the ring finger down; the sign for seven is to hold only the little finger down; and the sign for six is to hold only the ring finger down. Thus to make the sign for eight – or, as Alcuin says, 'hold eight in your hand' – and then suddenly to take away the sign for seven does indeed produce the sign for six.

There is also an identifiable source for the end of the *Disputatio*, and an examination of that source may reveal the skill with which Alcuin transformed standard texts into his own material. In a letter written sometime between 793 and 796, Alcuin quotes the wisdom dialogue that formed the inspiration for the *Disputatio*, the *Altercatio Hadriani*. Alcuin says:

De epistola interrogasti, quid esset? Nam 'epi' super, 'stola' habitus Grece dicitur. Unde Hadrianus imperator Epitetum philosophum inter alias inquisitiones interrogavit, quid esset cinctum? At ille videns eum epistolam manu tenentem respondit: 'Quod manu tenes.' Volens intellegere, quasi supercinctorium esset epistolae sigillum, quo a foris vestiatur cartula.[42]

You asked, what is a letter [*epistola*]? *Epi* means 'upon' in Greek, and *stola* means 'garb'. For this reason the emperor Hadrian asked Epitetus the philosopher, among other things, what is 'bound'? And he [Epitetus], seeing him holding a letter in his hand, answered, 'What you hold in your hand.' By this he meant that the seal of the letter was bound up, by which the document was garbed against the outside.

Alcuin was very fond of this image, of a letter being bound, and in a short poem he combines it with the image of opening, or solving; the image turns on the verb *solvere*, which has what in English is a double meaning, to open or solve, so that one opens or solves a letter as one might open or solve a riddle. His poem, enclosed with a letter, reads:

Nulla manus cartam discingat, ni tua, praesul;
Solve, pater sancte, et lege tu feliciter illam.
Succinctum solvat, cupiat qui abscondita scire . . .[43]

Let no hand unbind the letter, praesul, but yours;
Open [solve] it, holy father, and read it happily.
Let him solve [untie] the bound thing, who wishes to know hidden things . . .

Alcuin was so fond of the image of unbinding a missive that he used it in a different verse accompanying another letter.[44] In all these instances, a letter carries with it, in the name *epistola*, its own definition ('bound up')

---

[42] *MGH Epistolae* 4, ed. Dümmler, no. 88, pp. 132–3.
[43] *MGH PLAC* 1, ed. E. Dümmler, no. 29.2, p. 248.   [44] Ibid., no. 56.1, p. 268.

in riddle form, so that every letter is an invitation to unbinding on several levels.

In the *Altercatio Hadriani*, Alcuin's model text, this initial riddle about a letter serves as a preface to the conventional metaphor for letter: '*Quid est epistola? Tacitus nuncius*', 'What is a letter? A silent messenger.'[45] In Alcuin's version all these elements are transformed:

A. Quid est tacitus nuntius? – P. Quem manu teneo.
A. Quid tenes manu? – P. Epistulam tuam, magister.
A. Lege feliciter, fili! (108–10)

A. What is a silent messenger? – P. What I hold in my hand.
A. What do you hold in your hand? – P. Your letter, master.
A. Read happily, my son!

The *Disputatio* is framed as a dialogue, but of course it is not a conversation; it is a text. One can imagine Pippin reading this text as Alcuin sent it to him, as part of a letter. From the text, Alcuin asks, 'What do you hold in your hand?' and the real Pippin can answer, 'Your letter, master.' The *Disputatio*, a letter, an *epistola*, is, as its name suggests, something that has to be unbound, a document of 'hidden things', and this particular document above all is created to embody its name, a closed thing, full of hidden things to be opened and solved.[46]

THE RIDDLES OF THE *DISPUTATIO*: TEXT, TRANSLATION
AND COMMENTARY

Text

The text is reprinted from L. W. Daly and W. Suchier, *Altercatio Hadriani*; the punctuation of no. 88 has been altered.

86. P. Quid est mirum? – A. Nuper vidi hominem stantem, molientem, ambulantem, qui numquam fuit.
87. P. Quomodo potest esse? pande mihi. – A. Imago est in aqua.
88. P. Cur hoc non intellexi per me, dum toties vidi hunc ipsum hominem? – A. Quia bone indolis es iuvenis et naturalis ingenii, proponam tibi quaedam alia mira; tempta si per te ipsum possis conicere illa.

---

[45] *Altercatio Hadriani*, no. 2, in Daly and Suchier, *Altercatio Hadriani*, p. 104.
[46] For help and suggestions on this article I would like to thank Mary Garrison and Carol Lofmark. Any mistakes that remain are entirely my own.

89. P. Faciemus ita tamen, ut si secus quam est dicam, corriges me. –
    A. Faciam ut vis.
90. A. Quidam ignotus mecum sine lingua et voce locutus est, qui
    numquam ante fuit nec postea erit, et quem non audiebam nec
    novi. – P. Somnium te forte fatigavit, magister.
91. A. Etiam, fili; audi et aliud: Vidi mortuos generare vivum, et in ira
    vivi consumpti sunt mortui. – P. De fricatione arborum ignis natus
    est consumens arbores.
92. A. Verum est. Audivi mortuos multa loquentes. – P. Numquam
    bene, nisi suspendantur in aëre.
93. A. Vere. Vidi ignem inextinctum pausare in aqua. – P. Silicem in
    aqua significare vis reor.
94. A. Vidi mortuum sedentem super vivum, et in risu mortui moritur
    vivus. – P. Hoc coqui nostri norunt.
95. A. Norunt, sed pone digitum super os, ne pueri audiant quid sit.
    Fui in venatione cum aliis, in qua si quid cepimus, nihil nobiscum
    portavimus, et quod capere non potuimus, domum portavimus no-
    biscum. – P. Rusticorum est hec venatio.
96. A. Est. Vidi quendam natum, antequam esset conceptus. – P. Vidisti
    et forte manducasti.
97. A. Manducavi. Quis est qui non est et nomen habet et responsum
    dat sonanti? – P. Biblos in silvis interroga.
98. A. Vidi hospitem currentem cum domu sua, et ille tacebat et domus
    sonabat. – P. Para mihi rete, et pandam tibi.
99. A. Quis est qui videre non potest nisi clausis oculis? – P. Qui stertit
    tibi ostendit illum.
100. A. Vidi hominem octo in manu tenentem, et de octonis subito rapuit
    septem, et remanserunt sex. – P. Pueri in scola sciunt.
101. A. Quid est cui si caput abstuleris, et resurgit altior? – P. Vade ad
    lectulum et ibi invenies.
102. A. Tres fuere: unus numquam natus et semel mortuus, alter semel
    natus et numquam mortuus, tertius semel natus et bis mortuus. –
    P. Primus equivocus terre, secundus Domino meo, tertius homini
    pauperi.
103. A. Dic tamen primas litteras nominum. – P. .i., .v., .xxx.
104. A. Vidi feminam volantem, rostrum habentum ferreum et corpus
    ligneum et caudam pennatam, mortem portantem. – P. Socia est
    militum.

Translation

86. P. What is a wonder? – A. Recently I saw a person standing, moving, walking, who never was.

87. P. How can that be? Tell me. – A. It's a reflection in water.

88. P. Why didn't I know that, when I've seen that man every day? – A. Because you are a boy of good character and natural understanding, I will ask you some other wonders. Try and see if you can guess them yourself.

89. P. Let's do it so that if I guess wrong, you correct me. – A. I'll do as you wish.

90. A. A person I didn't know spoke to me without tongue or voice, who never was before nor ever will be, and whom I didn't hear or know. – P. Perhaps sleep had tired you out, master.

91. A. That's it, my son. And I heard another one: I saw the dead give rise to the living, and in the wrath of the living the dead were consumed. – P. From rubbing wood together fire is born as it consumes the wood.

92. A. It's true. I heard the dead speaking copiously. – P. Not very well, unless they're hanging in the air.

93. A. True. I saw fire unextinguished in the water. – P. You mean flint in water, I'm thinking.

94. A. I saw a dead one sitting on a live one, and in the laughter of the dead one the live one dies. – P. Our cooks know that one.

95. A. They do know it, but put your finger on your lips, so the boys don't hear what it is. I was on a hunt with some other people in which if we caught something, we took nothing back with us, and what we could not catch, that we carried home with us. – P. That's a hunt familiar to countryfolk.

96. A. It is. I saw someone born before he was formed. – P. You saw him and perhaps you ate him.

97. A. That I did. Who is it that is not, and has a name, and gives an answer to a sound? – P. Ask the rushes in the woods.

98. A. I saw a guest running along with his home, and he was silent and the home made noise. – P. Get me a net ready, and I'll show him to you.

99. A. Who is it that can only see with his eyes closed? – P. He who snores shows him to you.

100. A. I saw a man holding eight in his hand, and from the eight he suddenly took away seven, and six remained. – P. The boys in the school know that one.

101. A. What is it that when you take away the head, it springs back higher? – P. Go to your bed and you'll find it there.

102. A. There were three: one never born and died once, the second born once and never died, the third born once and died twice. – P. The first is equivalent to the earth, the second to my Lord, the third to a poor man.

103. A. Tell me the first letters of their names. – P. 1, 5, 30.

104. A. I saw a woman flying, with an iron beak and a wooden body and a feathered tail, carrying death. – P. That's a woman beloved of the soldiers.

Commentary

I have not cited riddles on the same subject with no discernible relation to the phrasing or content of those found in the *Disputatio*. These are my own notes and do not draw on the work by Daly and Suchier except where noted.

86–7. A reflection in water. No known early medieval parallels extant.

90. A man in a dream. No known early medieval parallels extant.

91. Fire kindled from sticks. No known early medieval parallels extant.

92. Bells. No known early medieval parallels extant.

93. Flint. No known early medieval parallels are extant, although the final line of Symphosius no. 76 [47] is possibly related in sense: '*Nec lignis ut uiuat eget, nec ut occidat undis.*'

94. A pot on the fire. There are parallels in St-Gall, Stiftsbibliothek 196,[48] pseudo-Bede *Collectanea* 197, and two late medieval German-language collections.[49]

95. Lice or fleas. Paralleled by Symphosius no. 30.[50]

96. Chick in egg. Paralleled by Symphosius no. 14.[51] Tullius no. 8.[52]

97. Echo. No known early medieval parallels extant.

98. Fish in river. This is derived from Symphosius no. 12.[53]

99. A dreamer. This may be related to Symphosius no. 99, on sleep, of which the last line is '*Sed me nemo uidet, nisi qui sua lumina claudet*'.[54]

100. Scholastic finger-counting. This is paralleled by pseudo-Symphosius no. 4.[55] On the solution, see explanation above.

---

[47] *Variae*, ed. Glorie, p. 697.   [48] Printed by Daly and Suchier, *Altercatio Hadriani*, p. 144, n. 91.

[49] See Bayless and Lapidge, *Collectanea*, pp. 144 and 245.

[50] *Variae*, ed. Glorie, p. 651.   [51] *Variae*, ed. Glorie, p. 635.   [52] Ibid., p. 554.

[53] *Variae*, ed. Glorie, p. 633.   [54] *Variae*, ed. Glorie, p. 720.   [55] *Variae*, ed. Glorie, p. 723.

101. Pillow. There is a distant parallel in Aldhelm no. 41.[56]
102–3. Adam; Enoch or Elijah; Lazarus. The first two are paralleled in numerous versions of the *Ioca monachorum* and *Adrianus et Epictetus*.[57] Early medieval dialogues containing versions of all three riddles (none with the answers encoded) include the B-version of the *Ioca monachorum*, contained in the Bobbio Missal[58] and the pseudo-Bede *Collectanea*.[59] The numerals '.i.' and '.v.' beginning the answers clearly refer to the place of the letter in the alphabet: 'i' is the A of Adam and 'v' the E of Enoch and Elijah. As Daly suggests,[60] the number 'xxx' was represented by the Greek lambda in certain medieval documents, and the lambda then represents the L of Lazarus. Adam, being made from the earth, is equivalent to it; Enoch and Elijah serve as antetypes of Christ; and Lazarus was a poor man.[61]
104. Arrow. No known early medieval parallels extant.

---

[56] *MGH Auctores Antiquissimi* 15, ed. Ehwald, p. 115, and *Variae*, ed. Glorie, p. 425.

[57] *Gespräch*, ed. Suchier.

[58] *The Bobbio Missal: A Gallican Mass-Book (MS Paris Lat. 13246)*, ed. E. A. Lowe (3 vols., London, 1917–24), vol. II, p. 6.

[59] Ed. Bayless and Lapidge, nos. 5 (p. 122) and 123–4 (p. 136), with commentary on pp. 202 and 228.

[60] Daly and Suchier, *Altercatio Hadriani*, p. 145, no. 103.

[61] On these clues see further Daly and Suchier, *Altercatio Hadriani*, p. 145.

CHAPTER 8

Laughter after Babel's fall: misunderstanding and miscommunication in the ninth-century west

Paul Kershaw

'How many languages are there? Seventy-two.' Thus ran the pithy treatment of the diversity of human tongues present in several eighth- and ninth-century collections of *Ioca monachorum*, 'Monkish jokes'.[1] Like early medieval wisdom dialogues, the *Ioca* were written to entertain and to educate, playfully testing biblical knowledge through riddling questions. On one level they serve as a reminder that a close relationship between levity and the classroom continued to exist long after schoolboys were amused, to Jerome's annoyance, by the testament of the piglet 'Grunnius Corocotta', and long before Peter Abelard's joking syllogisms elicited the laughter of his Paris students and the comparably cool comment of Otto of Freising.[2] More specifically, this particular question, 'how many languages are there?', encapsulates the themes I wish to discuss here, for the answer, 'seventy-two', originates in patristic exegesis on Genesis 10–11. This is, of course, the well-known account of the building and subsequent destruction of the Tower of Babel, the 'scattering of peoples' that followed in its wake and, with this, the creation of the 'confusion of tongues' that offered early medieval intellectuals an explanation for the multiplicity of earthly languages.[3]

---

[1] W. Suchier, *Das mittellateinische Gespräch Adrian und Epictetus nebstverwandten Texte (Joca monachorum)* (Tübingen, 1955) remains the standard edition. On the dialogue form, see Bayless, above, pp. 157–60; see also L. W. Daly and W. Suchier, *Altercatio Hadriani Augusti et Epicteti Philosophi* (Illinois Studies in Language and Literature 24) (Urbana, IL, 1939). M. Bayless, 'The *Collectanea* and medieval dialogues and riddles', in *Collectanea Pseudo-Bedae* (Scriptores Latini Hiberniae 14), ed. M. Bayless and M. Lapidge (Dublin, 1998), pp. 13–24, provides a discussion of the manuscript contexts of these collections, adding to the number of manuscripts known to Suchier and listing occurrences of this particular question at p. 232. See also Shanzer, above, pp. 26–7.

[2] For 'The testament of the piglet', and Jerome's comments on it, see J. Ziolkowski, *Talking Animals: Medieval Latin Beast Poetry, 750–1150* (Philadelphia, PA, 1993), pp. 38–9, citing Jerome, *Adversus Rufinum* (*PL* 23, col. 412), with a translation of the 'Testament' at cols. 299–300. On Abelard's use of humour in the classroom, and Otto's response, see M. T. Clanchy, *Abelard: A Medieval Life* (Oxford, 1997), pp. 132–3. See also Shanzer, above, p. 45.

[3] Genesis 10–11. On the image of the Tower of Babel in patristic thought and early medieval culture, A. Borst, *Das Turmbau von Babel. Geschichte der Meinungen über Ursprung und Vielfalt der Sprachen und*

As Arno Borst has shown in exhaustive detail, Babel stood at the centre of scripturally based explanations of the diversity of human culture and language. Differences in speech, and the incomprehensibility of the language of one people to another, occupied the very core of the antique notions of 'the barbarian', which continued into the early Middle Ages.[4] Writing in the 880s, for example, Notker the Stammerer, to whose sensitivity to language I shall return, told of the veteran Frankish warrior, Eishere, and his war stories of skewering Bohemians, Wilzi and Avars on his spear 'like little birds' whilst they 'squealed their incomprehensible lingo'.[5] For Carolingian intellectuals living in a world of Latin culture shared by Romance- and Germanic-language speakers, such ideas of barbarous speech shaped attitudes not only to the peoples beyond the Frankish frontiers, but to those around them, and to themselves.[6] A nagging sense that the *lingua theotisca* spoken by many Franks carried with it powerful connotations of barbarity prompted German-speaking Carolingian intellectuals such as Walahfrid Strabo and Ottfried of Weissenburg to mount defensive arguments for its right to a place alongside the three sacred languages of Hebrew, Greek and Latin as a valid vessel of Christian truth.[7]

Völker (Stuttgart, 1957–63), vol. II(1), pp. 366–581 remains the definitive study, with his treatment of the Carolingians at pp. 483–541; also H. Sauer, 'Die 72 Völker und Sprachen der Welt: ein Mittelalterliche Topos in der englischen Literatur', *Anglia* 101 (1982), pp. 29–48.

4 On this, see now G. Clark, 'Translate into Greek: Porphyry of Tyre on the new barbarians', in *Constructing Identities in Late Antiquity*, ed. R. Miles (London, 1999), pp. 112–32. For attitudes to barbarians, see Halsall, above, pp. 91–3, and Haldon, above, pp. 58–60. Pertinent in the present ninth-century context is Pope Nicholas I's letter of 865 to Emperor Michael III in which he refutes the Byzantine charge that the Latin west was barbarian: 'if you call the Latin language barbaric, because you do not yourself understand Latin, you should be careful: is it not ridiculous to call yourself emperor of the Romans when you do not know the language of the Romans?': translated and discussed by M. T. Fögen, 'Reanimation of Roman law in the ninth century: remarks on reasons and results', in *Byzantium in the Ninth Century: Dead or Alive?* ed. L. Brubaker (London, 1988), pp. 11–23, at pp. 17–22.

5 Notker Balbulus, *Gesta Karoli Magna Imperatoris* 2.12, in *MGH SRG* n.s. 13, ed. H. F. Haefele (Berlin, 1962). J. L. Nelson, 'Violence in the Carolingian world and the ritualization of ninth-century warfare', in *Violence and Society in the Early Medieval West*, ed. G. Halsall (Woodbridge, 1998), pp. 90–107, at p. 90.

6 See, for example, Einhard's account of one speaker of *barbara lingua*, a young girl from Lorsch, who was only able to speak Latin when possessed by the demon Wiggo: *Translatio et miracula sanctorum Marcellini et Petri* 3.14, in *MGH Scriptores* 15, ed. G. Waitz (Hanover, 1888), pp. 253–4. Borst, *Turmbau*, p. 501; P. Dutton, *The Politics of Dreaming in the Carolingian Empire* (London, 1994), pp. 94–6; P. J. E. Kershaw, 'Satanic conversations: talking to demons in the ninth century' (forthcoming).

7 Walahfrid Strabo, *De exordiniis et incrementis* 7, in *Walahfrid Strabo's Libellus de Exordiis et Incrementis Quarundam in Observationibus Ecclesiasticis Rerum: A Translation and Liturgical Commentary*, ed. and trans. A. Harting-Correa (Leiden, 1996), with Walahfrid's own observation on his tongue, *nostram barbariem, quae est Theotisca* at p. 70, and commentary at pp. 224–5. Ottfried of Weissenburg, *Evangelienbuch*, ed. D. Erdmann (Tübingen, 1957), pp. 4–7 and 11–14; J. Knight Bostock (rev. K. C. King and D. R. McLintock), *A Handbook of Old German High Literature* (Oxford, 1976), pp. 191–4;

In practice, this scriptural model for explaining linguistic diversity meant that when early medieval authors described comedy arising from miscommunication – and particularly from misunderstanding between the speakers of different languages – they also said something about humour's place in the broader scheme of man's fallen state. Moreover, laughter was in its own right symptomatic of the Fall, arising as it did from the absurdity, incongruity, obscenity and flawed nature of man's earthly condition.[8] In his treatise *On Free Will*, for example, Augustine conceded that the ability to laugh was part of being human, but cautioned that it belonged to man's lower nature.[9] Similar suspicions motivated Saint Benedict's wariness of laughter within the cloister, suspicions shared by his ninth-century commentators.[10] To laugh at misunderstanding, or to relate accounts of others doing so, was to participate in a double remembrance of man's fallen condition.[11] The essentially optimistic attitude to laughter that enabled an Islamic writer such as Notker's immediate contemporary, the Abbasid *litterateur* al-Jahiz, to ask, 'since laughter lies

F. P. Magoun, 'Otfrid's "Ad Liutbertum"', *Publications of the Modern Language Association of America* 58 (1943), pp. 869–90. On Carolingian attitudes to the three sacred languages see I. Resnick, '*Lingua Dei, lingua hominis*: sacred languages and medieval texts', *Viator* 21 (1990), pp. 51–74, esp. pp. 61–72.

[8] Jerome, *Commentarius in Ecclesiasten: Hebraicae Quaestiones in Libro Geneseos, Liber Interpretationis Hebraicorum Nominum, Commentarioli in Psalmos, Commentarius in Ecclesiasten, CCSL* 72, ed. P. Antin (Turnhout, 1959), on Eccles. 2.2.

[9] Augustine, *De libero Arbitrio* 1.8, in *Aurelii Augustini Opera* 2.2, *CCSL* 29, ed. W. M. Green (Turnhout, 1979). The notion that the capability to laugh was unique to man went back to Aristotle. On expressions of the idea in the ninth and tenth centuries, see H. Adolf, 'On medieval laughter', *Speculum* 22 (1947), pp. 251–3, replying to J. Tatlock, 'Medieval laughter', *Speculum* 21 (1946), pp. 289–94. For comparable ninth-century Jewish exegetical comment, see Saadia Gaon's *Kitab al'-Amanat wal-I'tikadat* [The Book of Beliefs and Opinions]: 'Thus he [Solomon] says: "I said in my heart: 'Come now. I will try thee with mirth, and enjoy pleasure'; and, behold, this was also vanity"' (Eccles. 2.1): *Saadia Gaon: The Book of Beliefs and Opinion* (Yale Judaica Series I), trans. S. Rosenblatt (New Haven, 1948), p. 363. As his reason for this conclusion he gives the fact that a person experiences, when he laughs and jests, a sense of degradation and debasement putting him on a level with the behaviour of beasts. That is the importance of his declaration: 'I said of laughter: "it is mad"; and of mirth: "What doth it accomplish?"' (Eccles. 2.2).

[10] Rule of Benedict 4, in *Benedicti Regula, Editio Altera Emendata, CSEL* 75, ed. R. Hanslik (Vienna, 1977). Hildemar of Corbie/Civitate, *Expositio Regulae S. Benedicti: Expositio Regulae ab Hildemaro Tradita et Nunc Primum Typis Mandata*, ed. R. Mittermüller (Regensberg, 1880), p. 172. Smaragdus of St-Mihiel, for example, felt a little like Brecht, that the man who laughed had not yet been told the terrible news: *Commentarium in Regulam S. Benedicti* 4.55, *PL* 102, cols. 783–4. J. Wilcox, 'Introduction', in *Humour in Old English Literature*, ed. J. Wilcox (Cambridge, 2000), pp. 1–10, at pp. 2–3, notes the same implicit relationship in the Old English translation of the Benedictine Rule and the significant wordplay therein between *hleahtor* (laughter) and *leahter* (sin). On the place of laughter in one ninth-century Carolingian monastery, see J. Ziolkowski, 'The spirit of play in the poetry of St Gall', in *Sangallensia in Washington: The Arts and Letters in Medieval and Baroque St Gall, Viewed from the Late Twentieth Century*, ed. J. C. King, (New York, 1993), pp. 143–69, esp. pp. 144–5. See Innes, above, pp. 142–3.

[11] H. Jacobson, *Seriously Funny: From the Ridiculous to the Sublime* (London, 1997), pp. 6–7.

at the root of human nature must it not have a considerable bearing on spiritual well-being and bodily health?' was almost entirely absent from the early medieval Christian west.[12]

With these issues in mind I analyse here several depictions of the failure of communication and comprehension in several texts from the Carolingian world and its penumbra, and the humour that arose from such episodes, paying particular attention to the polemical or, as in the *Ioca*, the didactic purpose underlying these comic misunderstandings. A substantial proportion of early medieval humour, at least in so far as it is recoverable from surviving texts, was predicated upon a comedy of miscommunication or misunderstanding.[13] In certain instances this was intentional, for example, in the *Scottus/sottus* wordplay of Theodulf of Orléans' description of a fellow scholar at Charlemagne's court,[14] or the 'angels not Angles' pun ascribed in variant forms to Gregory the Great in both Bede's *Historia Ecclesiastica* and the anonymous Whitby *Life*.[15] Confronted by English slave-boys in the market place of Rome, humour here arose from the quick-thinking Gregory's recasting of like-sounding words (*Angli/Angeli, Aelli/Alleluia, Deire/de ira Dei*), the similarity of which enabled him to 'translate' the youths' words into words that revealed

---

[12] *The Life and Work of Jahiz*, trans. C. Pellat (London, 1969), pp. 238–9. Al-Jahiz's position had a scriptural basis: Qu'ran 53.44–5, 'God said: "That it is He who makes men laugh and weep, that it is He who makes men live or die."' On one comic point, at least, ninth-century Muslim and Christian writers were of one mind: people wearing shoes on their heads were funny. On comedy and joking in early medieval Islamic culture, see S. Moreh, *Live Theatre and Dramatic Literature in the Medieval Arabic World* (Edinburgh, 1992), pp. 64–70. Compare the antics of the Abbasid *mudhikūn* (jester) Abū'l 'Ibar al-Hāshimī (d. 250 AH/864 AD) who appeared before the Caliph al-Mutawakkil with a slipper on his head and hats on his feet (Moreh, *Live Theatre*, p. 66, citing al-Husrī al-Qayrawānī, *Dhayl Zahr al-Ādāb* (Cairo, 1934), p. 66) with Notker's story of the man mocked for disguising his red hair with a boot when in church (*Gesta Karoli* 1.18).

[13] For one view of the nature of early medieval performative comedy, see M. Richter, *The Formation of the Early Medieval West: Studies in the Oral Culture of the Barbarians* (Dublin, 1989). This point is also made, in the context of Anglo-Saxon humour, by T. A. Shippey, 'Grim word-play: folly and wisdom in Anglo-Saxon humor', in *Humour in Old English Literature*, ed. J. Wilcox (Cambridge, 2000), pp. 33–48, at p. 48: 'characteristic of Anglo-Saxon humor is grim amusement . . . at the expense of those who cannot understand words and do not share their version of reality'.

[14] *MGH Poetae* i, ed. E. Dümmler (Berlin, 1881), no. 27, pp. 490–3, lines 63–4: '*Hic Scottus sottus cottus trinomen habebit/Guttare gentilupum clamat et ipse cavo.*' The joke was still funny in the twelfth century, when William of Malmesbury set down his well-known account of Eriugena's reply to Charles the Bald's question 'What separates a Scot from a Sot?' 'Only this table!': *De Gestis Regum Anglorum* 2.122, in *De Gestis Regum Anglorum*, ed. W. Stubbs (London, 1870). See J. J. O'Meara, *Eriugena* (Oxford, 1988), p. 214.

[15] Bede, *Historia Ecclesiastica* 2.1, in *Bede's Ecclesiastical History of the English People*, ed. and trans. B. Colgrave and R. A. B. Mynors (Oxford, 1969, rev. edn 1991); *Anonymous Life of Gregory the Great* 9, in *The Earliest Life of Gregory the Great*, ed. and trans. B. Colgrave (Cambridge, 1985). A. T. Thacker, 'Memorializing Gregory the Great: the origin and transmission of a papal cult in the seventh and eighth centuries', *EME* 7(1) (1998), pp. 59–84, discusses this anecdote at pp. 69–70.

a higher truth: that of the language of Scripture that lay beneath their speech. The closeness of their words to the language of the church intimated their ripeness for conversion.[16] In this series of associations the earthly gave clear intimations of the heavenly, as the Angles' names for themselves, their king and their homeland carried within them references to the angelic subjects and Divine Ruler of the Eternal Kingdom: the Christian's true *patria*.[17] For the Gregory of this tale earthly language, correctly interpreted, spoke of heavenly verities. Such wordplay was vindicated by patristic precedent. Occasionally, Jerome himself indulged in it, as his early medieval readers, including Bede, knew.[18] For Gregory the Great's own use of this technique there might be no better gloss than his own words from the *Moralia in Job*: 'When we surmise one thing from another, we easily recognise in the words that what they voice is one thing, what they intimate is another.'[19] Indeed, this episode is neatly emblematic of what Robert Markus has seen as Gregory's essentially optimistic notion of language as transparent to higher meaning, and his willingness to 'make the leap from sign to signified with less effort and less misgiving' than the more circumspect Augustine, for whom earthly systems of signs evoked an acute sense of the human word's inherent limitations.[20] Something of both Augustine's and Gregory's approaches

---

[16] The truth of the tale may be questionable, but the occurrence of a second pun on *gens Anglorum* in Gregory's letter to Bishop Eulogius of Alexandria gives it credibility: *Registrum Epistularum* 8.29, in *Registrum Epistularum, Libri viii–xiv*, CCSL 140A, ed. D. Norberg (Turnhout, 1982). See M. Richter, 'Bede's *Angli*: Angles or English?' *Peritia* 3 (1984), pp. 100–5; Thacker, 'Memorializing', p. 69; A. Scharer, *Herrschaft und Repräsentation. Studien zur Hofkultur König Alfreds des Großen* (Vienna, 2000), pp. 130–1. For Gregory's own view of the conversion of the English, and the barbarity of their language, see his *Moralia in Job* xxvii.21, in *Moralia in Job Libri xxii–xxxv*, CCSL 143B, ed. M. Adriaen (Turnhout, 1985).

[17] Gregorian notions of Heaven discussed by J. Burton Russell, *A History of Heaven: The Singing Silence* (Princeton, 1997), p. 96.

[18] Thacker, 'Memorializing', p. 69, citing, for example, the wordplay in Jeremiah 1.11, between the Hebrew words 'saced' (*nux*, 'nut-tree') and 'soced' (*vigilia*, 'watch'), discussed by Jerome, *In Hieremiam prophetam*, in *In Hieremiam Libri vi*, CCSL 74, ed. S. Reiter (Turnhout 1960), pp. 7–8. For Jerome's attitude to language, see D. Brown, *Vir Trilingualis: A Study in the Biblical Exegesis of St Jerome* (Kampen, 1992), with a discussion of this passage at pp. 81–2.

[19] R. Markus, *Signs and Meanings: World and Text in Ancient Christianity* (Liverpool, 1996), p. 65, citing and translating *Moralia in Job* v, pref., lines 24–6, in *Moralia in Job Libri i–x*, CCSL 143, ed. M. Adriaen (Turnhout, 1979). My understanding of Gregorian and Augustinian semiotics is heavily indebted to Markus' exposition.

[20] R. Markus, *Gregory the Great and his World* (Cambridge, 1997), pp. 48–50, noting at p. 50 Augustine's belief that, 'in our fallen state, we are constantly liable to fail to communicate: to find or to make the signs that we use opaque'. These ideas are explored more fully in his *Signs and Meanings*, pp. 1–70, and his 'Signs, communication and communities in Augustine's *De Doctrina Christiana*', in *De Doctrina Christiana: A Classic of Western Culture*, ed. D. W. H. Arnold and P. Bright (Notre Dame, IN, 1995), pp. 97–108. C. Straw, *Gregory the Great: Perfection in Imperfection* (London, 1988), with a discussion at pp. 49–50 of the distinction between Augustine's and Gregory's views of symbols.

to language will be found in the texts discussed in the remainder of this chapter.

BISHOP GRATIOSUS OF RAVENNA, A 'TRUE ISRAELITE'

During the 830s and 840s, Andreas Agnellus, a Ravennese priest, presented a series of *lectiones* to the episcopal *familia* and wider clerical community of Ravenna which collectively formed the history of the city and its see, and which were subsequently collated as a book, the *Liber pontificalis ecclesiae Ravennatis*.[21] In one *lectio*, probably written in the late 840s, Agnellus recounted the story of Charlemagne's visit to Ravenna in 787, and his encounter with its bishop, Gratiosus.[22] According to Agnellus, Gratiosus was a bishop whose lack of sophistication embarrassed not only his immediate entourage but the whole of Ravenna's clergy. It was a failing that manifest itself most immediately in the bishop's low mode of speech, presumably a form of local Romance.[23] The prospect of Gratiosus engaging the Frankish king in conversation horrified his entourage, and led to a deal being struck between bishop and *familia*. Gratiosus agreed to remain silent throughout the meal: 'No, my sons, no, I'll keep my mouth shut.'[24] Charlemagne duly arrived and the Frankish and Italian parties sat down to eat. In the course of the meal, however, Gratiosus forgot his promise, hospitality overriding discretion as he prompted his guest to eat. To understand the implications of this some elements of the text must remain in the original:

For the phrase 'the human word', see W. Benjamin, 'On language as such and on the language of man', in his *One Way Street and Other Writings*, trans. E. Jephcott and K. Shorter (London, 1985), pp. 107–23; B. Britt, *Walter Benjamin and the Bible* (New York, 1996), pp. 94–7.

[21] Agnellus of Ravenna, *Liber pontificalis ecclesiae Ravennatis* [*LPER*], *MGH Scriptores Rerum Langobardicarum et Italicarum*, ed. O. Holder-Egger (Hanover, 1878), pp. 265–391. On the stages of the work's composition, see A. Testi Rasponi, 'Note marginali al Libri pontificalis di Agnelo Ravennate', *Atti e memorie della R. Deputazione di Storia per la provincie di Romagna* (3rd ser.) 27 (1908–9), pp. 86–104 and 225–346. J. Martinez Pizarro, *Writing Ravenna: The Liber Pontificalis of Andreas Agnellus* (Ann Arbor, MI, 1995), provides the best English-language introduction to Agnellus' work, with extensive bibliography and much that is new and important. See also T. S. Brown, '*Romanitas* and *Campanilismo*: Agnellus of Ravenna's view of the past', in *The Inheritance of Historiography 350–900*, ed. C. Holdsworth and T. P. Wiseman (Exeter, 1986), pp. 107–14; G. V. B. West, 'Studies in representations and perceptions of the Carolingians in Italy, 774–875' (unpublished Ph.D. thesis, University of London, 1998), pp. 36–55.

[22] *LPER* 165. The treatment of Charlemagne by Agnellus is briefly discussed by G. Fasoli, 'Carlo Magno nelle Traduzioni Storico-Leggendarie Italianae', in *Karl der Grosse*, ed. W. Braunfels (Düsseldorf, 1966), vol. III, pp. 348–63.

[23] Pizarro, *Writing Ravenna*, p. 81, n. 21. In the present context it is worth noting Sylviane Lazard's analysis of Agnellus' Latin, and her conclusions that it contains a high occurrence of Hellenisms, Byzantinisms and non-classical forms: S. Lazard, 'De l'origine des hellénismes d'Agnello', *Revue de Linguistique Romane* 40 (1976), pp. 255–98.

[24] *Non, filii, non, sed oppilo os.*

'*Pappa, domine mi rex, pappa.*' Charlemagne was shocked, asking the clergy around the table, 'What is this talk, which is spoken by the priest, *pappa*, pappa?'[25]

The Ravennese clerics glossed Gratiosus' words for their Frankish guest:

Let our lord the king not fear that these are words of injury or deceit, but rather they are words of persuasion. This man, your servant and interlocutor, is of great simplicity, in the manner of a mother who coaxes her children, and from great love tries to persuade them to eat something, in the same way this man, with great affection, has invited your clemency to eat and be merry.[26]

Charlemagne's response to this explanation was to command silence, and to cite Christ's observation on Nathanael, from John 1.47: 'Behold, a true Israelite, in whom there is no guile.'[27] Gratiosus, as Pizarro has observed, spoke a form of Ravennese vernacular, in which 'pappa, pappa' was baby talk: 'Eat! Eat!'[28] But some commentators, understandably, have also seen it as a pun on '*papa*': 'pope', 'bishop', or simply 'father'. In Agnellus' narrative Gratiosus was calling the Frankish king 'pope', to his evident consternation. Charlemagne's incomprehension was understandable. Was the bishop so stupid, and so unaware of the hierarchies of eighth-century authority that he could confuse a king with a pope, or was Agnellus, as some have suggested, using Gratiosus as a mouthpiece for a dig at Charlemagne's so-called 'caesaro-papist' pretensions?[29]

This is a deceptively complex passage, for in it Agnellus played a number of games, not least with the ambiguity of the word *simplex*, meaning 'simple', 'simple-minded' and 'straightforward', that is to say 'plain-speaking'.[30] Charlemagne's initial confusion gave way to a realisation of Gratiosus' essential good-heartedness, manifest through his kindness. Whilst the Ravenna clergy were preoccupied by Gratiosus' speech, Charlemagne, displaying a sense of *discretio* comparable to Gregory's in the *Angli/angeli* episode, saw beyond the surface to the archbishop's inner nature. It was on his Christian qualities, rather than his low-born speech, that the Frankish visitor judged Gratiosus. But there are also absurdist

---

[25] *LPER* 165.   [26] Ibid.   [27] *Ecce vere Israhelita, in quo dolus non est.*

[28] Pizarro, *Writing Ravenna*, p. 81.

[29] As noted in ibid., p. 81. W. Ohnsorge, 'L'idea d'imperio nel secolo nono e l'Italia meridionale', *Atti del 3 Congresso Internazionale di Studi sull'Alto Medioevo, Benevento, Montevergine, Salerno, Amalfi, 14–18 Ottobre 1956* (Spoleto, 1959), pp. 255–72, at pp. 262–3; Brown, 'Romanitas', p. 109.

[30] Although dealing primarily with a later period, C. Waddell, 'Simplicity and ordinariness: the climate of early Cistercian hagiography', in *Simplicity and Ordinariness*, ed. J. R. Sommerfeldt (Kalamazoo, MI, 1980), pp. 1–48 usefully discusses the wide semantic range of *simplex*. P. Antin, 'Simple et simplicité chez saint Jérome', *Revue Bénédictine* 71 (1961), pp. 371–81, explores the Scriptural and patristic frameworks of the term.

currents in this narrative.[31] In 787 the historical Charlemagne was fresh from a series of bloody Saxon campaigns and the final stages of the destruction of Tassilo of Bavaria. Agnellus' Charlemagne, however, found himself treated like a child by the bishop in what comes close to being a parody of the concerned and solicitous pastor, as the stock parental metaphor of pastoral responsibility was acted out quite literally by the kindly bishop.[32] Here, however, the standard motif of bishop and flock as father and children ('no, no, my sons . . .'), often deployed in Agnellus' writing, underwent a subversive shift.[33] Gratiosus' *familia* chose to describe him not in established paternal but rather in maternal terms. He acted 'in the manner of a mother'. At a more basic level, there is the sheer incongruity of a bishop of Ravenna whose lack of urbanity reduced his clergy to embarrassment every time he opened his mouth. Viewed in the light of what some have seen as Agnellus' evident dislike of the Franks at other points in the *Liber* his account of Charlemagne in this anecdote is surprisingly favourable, not least in its willingness to place the words of Christ himself in the Frankish king's mouth.[34] Significantly, the chapter closed with Agnellus' observations that, following Charlemagne's seizure of the Lombard kingdom, ominous portents were seen in the sky. The following chapter continues this theme, presenting a long and detailed account of an apocalyptic vision (ascribed to Gratiosus in the margins of one of the *Liber pontificalis*' two extant manuscripts), which predicted natural and man-made disasters, floods, famines, families turning on themselves, wars and the despoliation of the church of Ravenna itself.[35] It was preceded by a speech in which Gratiosus defended his right to speak prophetically before the Ravenna clergy on the grounds that he was inspired by the Holy Spirit:

Therefore, most dear, do not linger, but take your places and listen to what the Lord will say through me, that you might know what will come to pass. I am not a prophet, but the Spirit itself, which speaks through prophets, is able similarly

---

[31] For incongruity in early medieval humour, see H. Magennis, 'A funny thing happened on the way to heaven: humorous incongruity in Old English saints' lives', in *Humour in Old English Literature*, ed. Wilcox, pp. 137–40.

[32] Pizarro, *Writing Ravenna*, pp. 45–6, drawing attention to Gratiosus' use of familial terminology; M. Sot, 'Historiographie épiscopale et modèle familial en Occident au XIe siècle', *Annales ESC* 33 (1978), pp. 433–49.

[33] Pizarro, *Writing Ravenna*, pp. 43–52.

[34] Brown, '*Romanitas*', pp. 107–8. On Agnellus' attitudes to the Franks, see also T. S. Brown, 'Louis the Pious and the papacy', in *Charlemagne's Heir: New Perspectives on the Reign of Louis the Pious*, ed. R. Collins and P. Godman (Oxford, 1990), pp. 297–307, at pp. 299–301, discussing Gratiosus' meeting with Charlemagne at p. 301.

[35] *LPER* 166.

to fill our hearts. As the Holy Spirit itself cried through Joel: 'I will pour out my spirit on all flesh' (Joel 2.28), and it was said to Jeremiah: 'Behold, I will place my words in your mouth' (Jeremiah 5.14), and Jacob the Patriarch said, 'Gather yourselves together, sons of Jacob, and listen to Israel your Father, that I may tell you what will befall' (Genesis 49.1–2), and the Son and Holy Father Himself said, 'For I will give you a mouth and wisdom' (Luke 21.5).[36]

Gratiosus went on to point out the prophets who, inspired by the Holy Spirit, had prophesied the coming of Christ, and how the Holy Spirit had spoken through the mouths of infidels such as 'the cruel tyrant' Nebuchadnezzar and Virgil, as well members of the weaker sex, Anna and the Sibyl. If God could speak through them, why not Gratiosus himself, with his simple speech but deep piety?

Paul Dutton has noted, surely correctly, that the prophecy ascribed to Gratiosus ought to be understood in terms of the political scene of the 840s rather than the late 780s, a time when the bishop of Ravenna, George, had seized many of the city's treasures, the Carolingian Empire had suffered the damage and divisions of Fontenoy, and other parts of coastal Italy had become the target for a renewed wave of Arab attacks.[37] What Gratiosus 'prophesied' were Agnellus' own comments on the woes of his own day, couched in apocalyptic terms and placed into the mouth of a former bishop.[38] In the light of this political prophecy, Charlemagne's earlier identification of Gratiosus with Nathanael takes on a deeper resonance, for it was Nathanael who recognised the true nature of Christ,[39] and who, consequently, was vouchsafed the gift of vision.[40] Within Agnellus' narrative, Gratiosus' prophecy had the effect of retrospectively demonstrating the validity of Charlemagne's observation. Gratiosus possessed the gift of vision: he *really was* like Nathanael.

Here, then, an initially comic encounter and the vision that succeeded it served to set the limits of human language's potential. The same mouth that the Ravenna clergy begged Gratiosus to keep closed, and that when

---

[36] Ibid., which might be compared with the *catena* of scriptural tags adduced by Agnellus at the work's opening to justify his use of ostensibly 'oral' sources: *LPER*, prologue.

[37] Dutton, *Politics of Dreaming*, pp. 125–6, and discussed by Pizarro, *Writing Ravenna*, pp. 60–5; see also T. S. Brown, *Gentlemen and Officers: Imperial Administration and Aristocratic Power in Byzantine Italy, AD 554–800* (Rome, 1984), p. 126. On the Arab attacks, see B. M. Kreuz, *Before the Normans: Southern Italy in the Ninth and Tenth Centuries* (Philadelphia, PA, 1991), pp. 24–7.

[38] Pizarro, *Writing Ravenna*, pp. 62–5, reads the prophecy as Agnellus' own, rather than his views mediated through the mouth of Gratiosus. On the political uses of apocalyptic prophecy, see P. Alexander, 'Medieval apocalypses as historical sources', *American Historical Review* 73 (1968), pp. 997–1018.

[39] John 1.48–50.

[40] John 1.51: 'Verily, verily, I say unto you, hereafter ye shall see Heaven open, and the angels of God ascending and descending upon the Son of Man.'

opened could only produce words incomprehensible to Charlemagne, served later as an instrument of the Holy Spirit and the revelation of future events, events which had, by Agnellus' day, actually happened.[41] Without divine inspiration Gratiosus' speech was flawed and ineffective. With it, Gratiosus spoke fluently, not only prophesying but also prefacing his vision of the future with a chain of quotations that validated his inspired speech with Scriptural precedent.

Agnellus' willingness to put himself in his work has long been noted by scholars, and there may even be a personal note encoded in this story.[42] The association of Nathanael, the guileless Israelite, with Saint Bartholomew was an exegetical commonplace,[43] and I showed above why there are compelling reasons for seeing the vision that Gratiosus 'described' as a coded criticism directed by Agnellus at the episcopate of George, his former friend. Agnellus had probably suffered most at George's hands, by his seizure and redistribution of one of Agnellus' two monastic holdings, Saint Bartholomew's.[44] Appropriate indeed that in this account it is Ravenna's own Bartholomew/Nathanael, the guileless Gratiosus, who foretold the depredations of the church of Ravenna during George's pontificate. For an audience able to make the link between John 1.47 ('Behold, a true Israelite, in whom there is no guile') and Nathanael/Bartholomew, and aware also of Agnellus' position in the 840s, there was, perhaps, a private joke for them to enjoy if they, like Gregory, could recognise that Agnellus' words voiced one thing but intimated another.

At various stages the *Liber pontificalis* betrays Agnellus' interest in repetitive patterns and typological structuring.[45] Long criticised for the incomprehensible nature of his 'historical logic', Agnellus combined a lack of engagement with correct chronology and clear analysis with a sustained concern with deeper narrative structures and cyclical historical patterning.[46] These interests are evident in his treatment of comic

---

[41] On the mouth as a symbol, see D. Williams, *Deformed Discourse: The Function of the Monster in Mediaeval Thought and Literature* (Exeter, 1996), pp. 141–9; Y. Carré, *Le Baiser sur la bouche au Moyen Age. Rites, symboles, mentalités, XIᵉ–XVᵉ siècle* (Paris, 1992), pp. 19–25, addresses the biblical context.

[42] Pizarro, *Writing Ravenna*, p. 5.

[43] U. Holzmeister, 'Nathanael fuitne idem ac S. Bartholomaeus Apostolus?', *Biblica* 21 (1940), pp. 28–39, with references to the patristic and early medieval identification of Bartholomew and Nathanael.

[44] *LPER* 64.

[45] Pizarro, *Writing Ravenna*, pp. 41–2, draws attention to Agnellus' repetitive patterning in his treatment of bishops' encounters with visiting leaders, and notes his repeated use of the same phrases in his description of their exchanges.

[46] Ibid., p. 4, citing the assessment of T. F. X. Noble, *The Republic of St Peter: The Birth of the Papal State, 680–825* (Philadelphia, PA, 1984), pp. 20, 22 and 104. On the tendency to criticise works

misunderstanding between the bishop of Ravenna and visiting secular figures: the Gratiosus–Charlemagne episode was not the only instance where such an encounter began with a comic misunderstanding but ended with the recognition of the power of Christian truth. Earlier, Agnellus recounted the story of the Huns' siege of Ravenna and the despatch of an embassy led by the then archbishop, John, to the Huns' leader, Attila. John asked Attila to spare the city, 'for the sake of his children'.[47] In Agnellus' account, this request was met with angry incomprehension. 'How was one man able to father so many children?' asked Attila. John explained that the bonds he spoke of were not the results of carnality, but rather the result of his episcopal position: the citizens were his spiritual children.[48] Chastened by the words, like Charlemagne after his encounter with Gratiosus, Attila went away deeply impressed by the archbishop's piety, agreeing not to destroy the city and even, Agnellus suggests, tempering the excesses of his subsequent behaviour.[49]

In both these accounts of meetings between an outside, secular leader and a bishop of Ravenna the language of Christian conduct – whether in the form of Gratiosus' hospitality and kindness or in John's deep concern for his flock – was that which communicated effectively. This contrasts with the words initially spoken by the two bishops, which served only to confuse.[50] Significantly, both anecdotes began with comic misunderstandings based around the mistaken identification of two paternal relationships. In the first instance, Gratiosus was mistakenly thought to have claimed Charlemagne as his 'father', whilst in the second, Archbishop John was though to be the father of Ravenna's entire population. As much as anything, Agnellus' work was an exercise in establishing typological patterns within which Ravenna, and its bishop, interacted with external secular power.

In its underlying assurance of earthly language's ability to communicate divine truth and effect profound change, Agnellus' approach to language closely resembles that of Gregory the Great. Like him, Agnellus believed that earthly language could encode higher truths, and that these truths had the power to effect change in those who heard and understood

---

organised by principles other than a strong narrative drive, see C. Cubitt, 'Memory and narrative in the cult of early Anglo-Saxon saints', in *The Uses of the Past in the Early Middle Ages*, ed. Y. Hen and M. Innes (Cambridge, 2000), pp. 29–66, at p. 63.

[47] *LPER* 37. For an extended and illuminating analysis of this passage, see Pizarro, *Writing Ravenna*, pp. 100–19.

[48] *LPER* 37: *Non ex conceptu carnis aut ex pollutione libidinis, sed spiritualis filii sunt.*

[49] Ibid.

[50] R. McKitterick, 'Latin and Romance: a historian's perspective', in *Latin and the Romance Languages in the Early Middle Ages*, ed. R. Wright (Pennsylvania, PA, 1996), pp. 130–45.

them, even if the hearer was a byword for barbarian brutality, such as Attila.[51] It was an optimistic, if understandable, notion, voiced by one whose written legacy, the *Liber* itself, directly witnesses his own engagement in the public promulgation of Christian values. Agnellus' views on the sign system of spoken language and individual conduct closely parallels his attitudes to the semiotics of visual imagery. Here, too, he presented accounts that spoke of a belief in the real presence of the holy in imagery. He recounts, for example, the intervention of Christ when a loan between two merchants that had been solemnly agreed in the Ravennese church of *Bracchium Fortis* was not repaid.[52] In the course of the agreement, the two men had used an icon of Christ as witness to, and guarantor for, their deal. When the borrower failed to meet on the agreed date in order to repay the loan, Christ repeatedly appeared to the defaulting debtor, fulfilling his role as guarantor, and forcing the man to make good the borrowed money.[53] Whether an icon of Christ, the articulation of spiritual truth or a Christian act of charity, all were earthly systems of signs that demonstrated the Gregorian notion that earthly language, no matter how clumsy or vulgar, could be transparent to higher truths. In the case of Agnellus' accounts of the bishops Gratiosus and John, their meetings with visiting leaders, and the misunderstandings that opened both, it might be said that he had grasped Gregory's notion of comic misinterpretation paving the way for the revelation of important truths. In one sense, these two anecdotes in which words were made the vehicles first of comic misunderstanding then of Christian truth could be seen as enacted versions of Gregorian punning.[54] In the works of my next author I discuss comic misunderstanding that followed a less optimistic route, one more akin to the attitude of Augustine than to that of Gregory.

---

[51] On the received image of Attila in late antique and early medieval historical writing, see P. Godman, *Poetry of the Carolingian Renaissance* (London, 1985), pp. 72–8; *The Poetic Edda*, vol. I, *Heroic Poems*, ed. and trans. U. Dronke (Oxford, 1969), pp. 32–45; H. De Boor, *Das AttilaBild in Geschichte, Legende und heroischer Dichtung* (Bern, 1932).

[52] *LPER* 30.

[53] The story is Byzantine, and has eastern parallels: see Pizarro, *Writing Ravenna*, p. 74, with references to earlier occurrences of the story. On Agnellus' attitude to icons, and its implications, see D. Mauskopf Deliyannis, 'Agnellus of Ravenna and iconoclasm: theology and politics in a ninth-century text', *Speculum* 71 (1996), pp. 559–76.

[54] Pizarro observes importantly that Gregory's injection of personal comments in a number of his *Homiliae in Evangelia*, particularly relating physical infirmity to oral delivery, influenced Agnellus' own style: Pizarro, *Writing Ravenna*, pp. 79–80. On the notion that certain early medieval narratives 'enacted' principles of belief, see P. Cramer, *Baptism and Change in the Early Middle Ages, c.200–1150* (Cambridge, 1995), pp. 201–2; M. M. Walsh, 'The baptismal flood in the Old English *Andreas*: liturgical and typological depths', *Traditio* 33 (1977), pp. 137–58; C. B. Hieatt, 'The harrowing of Mermedonia: typological patterns in the Old English *Andreas*', *Neuphilologische Mitteilungen* 77 (1976), pp. 49–62.

SIGNS THAT FAIL: NOTKER THE STAMMERER

Attitudes to humour, misunderstanding and the nature of language, which may at first seem comparable to Agnellus', can be found in the work of an author writing nearly half a century later in East Francia: Notker the Stammerer, who composed his *Gesta Karoli* between December 883 and May 887. Addressed to Charles the Fat, it has come to be seen, by some, as Notker's *speculum principis* for the young king, focussing upon the example of his great-grandfather and namesake. As David Ganz has observed, it might also be considered a kind of school text.[55]

In Notker's hands misunderstanding and miscommunication became key instruments of satire. Not only is he one of the few ninth-century authors to have articulated the central relationship of humour to humanity, the *Gesta* is one of the very few ninth-century texts to have been analysed explicitly for its comic content and its implications for his view of history.[56] Notker's *Gesta* is anecdotal, many of his anecdotes having Charlemagne at their centre, although often not, as I shall show, as their main protagonist.[57] I begin with one such story.

One feast day, Notker recounted, the royal household attended Mass at which an unnamed young *cognatus* of Charlemagne sang the 'Alleluia' with great beauty. Charlemagne turned to the bishop at his shoulder. 'How well that *clericus* sang', he said. The nameless bishop, thinking that Charlemagne was joking, and ignorant that young singer in question was a Carolingian, replied scathingly: 'Yes, that's how country-folk sing when they are following their oxen at the plough.'[58] At this, what Notker, with cutting irony, called 'a very imprudent response', the incensed Charlemagne knocked the bishop to the ground. Misunderstandings are legion in this passage: the bishop was unable to assess correctly the quality of the singing, to realise the singer's status and thus to read the crucial signs of *Königsnähe*. Nor was he even able to understand the spirit

[55] D. Ganz, 'Humour as history in Notker's *Gesta Karoli Magni*', in *Monks, Nuns and Friars in Medieval Society* (Sewanee Medieval Studies 4), ed. E. B. King, J. T. Schaefer and W. B. Wadley (Sewanee, TN, 1989), pp. 171–83, at p. 173. For humour in school texts, see Bayless, above, pp. 159–62; for other thoughts on Notker, see Innes, above, pp. 148–53.

[56] Ganz, 'Humour as history', pp. 171–83. H.-W. Goetz, *Strukturen der spätkarolingischen Epoche im Spiegel der Vorstellungen eines zeitgenössischen Mönchs. Eine Interpretation der 'Gesta Karoli' Notkers von Sankt Gallen* (Bonn, 1981); T. Siegrist, *Herrscher und Weltsicht bei Notker Balbulus: Untersuchungen zu den Gesta Karoli* (Geist und Werk der Zeiten; Arbeiten aus dem Historischen Seminar der Universität Zürich 8) (Zurich, 1963). On humour in the wider culture of early medieval St-Gall, see Ziolkowski, 'Spirit of play'.

[57] Ganz, 'Humour as history', pp. 177–8, on Notker's episodic style and its possible models.

[58] *Gesta Karoli* 1.19.

in which Charlemagne's comment was meant, mistaking as a joke an observation made in earnest. Seeking to laugh *with* Charlemagne, matching his jibe with one of his own, and thus sending back the signals of inclusion and sympathetic thought implicit in 'getting the joke' that would strengthen his own relationship with the king, the bishop achieved the exact reverse.[59] In Notker's mockery he became the target of the laughter he wished to direct towards the young Carolingian. Furthermore, Charlemagne's violent response to his words carries a powerful charge through its sheer incongruity. It is as comically literal an interpretation of Carolingian political theorists' notion of a good ruler 'casting down the proud' as Gratiosus' behaviour had been an overly rigorous fulfilment of the requirements of the notion of bishop as parent. Carolingian *Fürstenspiegeln* were, after all, silent on the correct circumstances under which a king could physically assault a churchman. The one environment where physical chastisement did have an accepted place in the correction of errors was the schoolroom, and in his mixture of violent rebuke and teaching by example there is more than a little of the schoolteacher in Notker's portrait of Charlemagne.[60]

In the *Gesta* the overwhelming subject of Charlemagne's correction was the figure of the proud but stupid bishop. One misunderstands Charlemagne's decision to eat at the seventh hour after Lent, castigating him for eating too early, without realising that Charlemagne did so out of consideration for the other members of his household who, in descending order, ate in sequential sittings after the emperor had finished. Had Charlemagne waited until the proper hour, the lowest members of his household would not have eaten until after midnight. Charlemagne's chastening parting comment was 'It seems to me, my dear bishop, that you must have realised by now that it is not greed which makes me eat before nightfall in Lent, but consideration for others.'[61] Another bishop, anonymous in the text but identifiable as Riculf of Mainz, was obsessed

---

59 Ganz suggests another level of irony at work in this passage – the 'Alleluia' was the churchman's worksong: 'Humour as history', p. 181. For a possibly more successful attempt to use humour to unify, see Halsall, above, pp. 93–6.

60 On the balance of corporal punishment and play in the classrooms of Notker's own St-Gall, Ziolkowski, 'Spirit of play', p. 145. Notoriously, it was fear of the rod that drove one pupil of St-Gall to start the fire of April 937, see Ekkehard IV, *Casus sancti Galli* 67, in *St. Galler Klostergeschichten*, ed. H. Haefele (Darmstadt, 1980).

61 *Gesta Karoli* 1.11. I have learnt much about the immediate political context of Notker's writing from the doctoral dissertation of S. MacLean, 'The reign of Charles III the Fat (876–888)' (unpublished Ph.D. thesis, University of London, 2000), who identifies the bishop as Riculf, and contextualises his portrayal by Notker, at pp. 237–47. For Einhard's comments on Charlemagne's attitude to fasting, see Innes, above, p. 138.

with exotica, and was tricked into parting with a large amount of silver in exchange for a spice-filled domestic mouse, in the mistaken belief that this was a rare creature from the east and a worthy addition to his collection.[62] The gullible bishop paid a substantial sum of silver in order to possess a worthless object. Even more damningly, this was silver intended for distribution to the poor and the needy. In a subsequent anecdote Riculf was again made to look foolish, as his vanity led him to go so far as to ask Charlemagne's wife Hildegard for the use of the king's sceptre as a replacement for his episcopal staff.[63] He was duly humbled for his pretensions. Yet another bishop behaved equally inappropriately, vaulting onto his horse in a way deemed more suited to a warrior than a man of God.[64]

In all these anecdotes Notker's bishops wander around in a semiological fog. They are incapable of placing themselves or the world around them in their proper place and unable to read the world's signs. They fail to assign the correct value to material objects, personal obligations or symbols of office.[65] Charlemagne occupies the still centre of many of these tales, passing effortlessly accurate judgements on those around him and intuitively aware of right order and correct value, a virtual embodiment of the qualities of both *discretio* and that Carolingian favourite, *correctio*.[66] In this sense Notker's Charlemagne is not so very far away from Thegan's portrait of the serene, unsmiling Louis. Both articulated – Notker by example, Thegan by description – the notion of the ruler as a fixed point of order.[67] The disorder apparent in the attitudes of the hapless bishops of Notker's tales serves to reinforce royal authority, the established social hierarchy and its modes of symbolic expression. There is a parallel here with the way in which strategies of inversion and formalised disordering famously discussed by Mikhail Bakhtin have been seen as superficially subversive, but ultimately supportive, of the prevailing order of society.[68] These accounts of confusion taught an unambiguous lesson to Charles the Fat about his own behaviour as a ruler.

[62] *Gesta Karoli* 1.16. [63] *Gesta Karoli* 1.17.
[64] *Gesta Karoli* 1.6. See Innes, above, pp. 144–7, for other examples of the problems of delineating secular from ecclesiastical appropriate behaviour.
[65] H. W. Goetz, *Strukturen der spätkarolingischen Epoche in Spiegel der Vorstellungen eines zeitgenössischen Mönchs: eine Interpretation der 'Gesta Karoli' Notkers von Sankt Gallen* (Bonn, 1981), pp. 86–98, provides a discussion of Notker's use of symbols and notions of hierarchy but offers a too one-dimensional view of early medieval semiology.
[66] On the rhetoric of *correctio* in Carolingian culture, see P. J. Fouracre, 'Carolingian justice: the rhetoric of improvement and contexts of abuse', *Settimane di Spoleto* 42(2) (1995), pp. 771–803.
[67] On Thegan's portrayal of Louis, see Innes, above, pp. 131–56.
[68] On Bakhtin see the excellent discussion of Bayless, *Parody*, pp. 178–84.

Like Agnellus, Notker was attuned to the comic possibilities of communication breakdown. Appointed to a newly vacant see, a churchman threw a party for palace officials and members of his diocese. As a consequence, he missed the night office, at which he had been given the task of singing the response. When the time came for the response to be given, the designated singer was absent, and it fell to a 'mean and humble' cleric, disliked by everyone but pitied by Charlemagne, to sing the missing man's part. Unable to perform it correctly, he had to be helped by the other members of the choir but, failing to stop when he should, he went into the Pater Noster: 'All the others wanted to stop him making such a mess of things but in his great wisdom Charlemagne forbade anyone to interfere with him.' Taking the place of the newly appointed bishop in the service, the humble cleric found himself given the absentee's see as well.[69] Just as in Agnellus' account of his encounter with Gratiosus, Charlemagne was able to see beyond the limits of the performed word, spoken or sung, to the inner man, choosing a flawed but humble bishop over one preoccupied with revelry and self-indulgence. Elsewhere in the *Gesta*, Notker recounted the story of a wandering monk who entered the choir at the beginning of a service. Ignorant of chant, he stayed silent when the singing began. Threatened with the choirmaster's stick, the monk, unable to sing but unwilling to be beaten, mimed, fooling no one but causing much amusement to those around him.[70] There can scarcely be a more powerful image of Notker's sensitivity to the comic capacity of non-communication.

Court ritual was also a form of language, and again Notker extracted comedy from its limitations. A Frankish envoy despatched to the Byzantine court was invited to dine with the emperor. In this anecdote, as in Agnellus' account of Charlemagne and Gratiosus, hospitality offered by one ethnic group and accepted by another drives the narrative, and the dining table is the focus of humour.[71] In Byzantium, Notker recounted, there was a law that nobody at the king's table could turn over any of the flesh served. Only meat from the exposed, upper side of the carcass could be touched. Unschooled in such Byzantine niceties a Frankish envoy turned over the fish before him. His fellow diners were horrified, and claimed that the emperor was dishonoured by this act. Reluctantly,

---

[69] *Gesta Karoli* 1.5.   [70] *Gesta Karoli* 1.8.

[71] The centrality of the dining table and the correct giving and taking of hospitality in early medieval culture scarcely needs stressing, but key analyses include: D. A. Bullough, *Friends, Neighbours and Fellow-drinkers: Aspects of Community and Conflict in the Early Medieval West* (Cambridge, 1991); M. J. Enright, *Ritual, Prophecy and Lordship in the European Warband from La Tène to the Viking Age* (Dublin, 1996); H. Magennis, *Scenes of Community in Old English Poetry* (Cambridge, 1995).

the emperor conceded that the Frank had to be put to death. The Frank, however, asked for, and was granted, one last wish: that anyone who saw him turn the fish over was to have his eyes put out. The previously voluble witnesses fell silent. They had seen nothing. The canny Frank, armed with characteristic Frankish *ingenium*, went free.[72]

In Notker's account of the reception of a Byzantine embassy at Charlemagne's court the Greeks were repeatedly given audiences with palace officials. At each stage they believed that they had finally met Charlemagne himself, only to be rebuked and moved on. Eventually, they arrived, awestruck, before the emperor himself.[73] This treatment was a response to the Byzantines' own treatment of Frankish envoys, themselves led 'through very many different places' before finally being allowed to leave.[74] As Karl Leyser pointed out, Liutprand of Cremona received similar treatment at Nicephoras Phocas' court. However, within the framework of Notker's pervasive concern with misunderstanding, this story can be read as yet another tale of the treachery of appearances and the potential for misreading earthly signs.[75]

Ganz has made the important suggestion that Notker's account of Charlemagne and his court was written in dialogue with Einhard's earlier biography: 'if Einhard was a school text and Notker a schoolmaster, it seems reasonable that Notker's *Gesta* represents his exposition of Einhard, even if Charles the Fat were his only pupil'.[76] A similar sense of Notker's *Gesta* as both counterpoint and variation on the more solemn themes of an earlier generation of Carolingian authors can be seen in his well-known account of Louis the Pious' reception of a party of Vikings for baptism. Unable to provide the requisite number of white robes, the Franks had made tunics and 'overalls' from old clothes. These found little favour with one seasoned Viking visitor to the Carolingian court:

Now, I've been washed about twenty times before, but then I was clothed in the finest white vestments, but look, this sacking is more appropriate for a swineherd than a soldier. If it wasn't for fear of being embarrassed by my nakedness,

---

[72] *Gesta Karoli* 2.5. For the place of Notker's attitudes to the Greeks, see C. Wickham, 'Ninth-century Byzantium through western eyes', in *Byzantium in the Ninth Century*, ed. Brubaker, pp. 245–56, with references.

[73] *Gesta Karoli* 2.6.   [74] Ibid.

[75] It may also further support Innes' contention that Notker was drawing from a fund of already-extant tales about Charlemagne in the creation of the *Gesta*: M. Innes, 'Memory, orality and literacy in an early medieval society', *Past and Present* 158 (1998), pp. 1–36. On Frankish–Byzantine relations and the misunderstanding implicit in them, see Haldon, above, pp. 58–9, and Balzaretti, above, p. 123.

[76] Ganz, 'Humour as history', p. 173.

as you've taken my clothes away, I'd leave these old clothes to you and your Christ![77]

For the Franks the clothing was purely symbolic, representative of the spiritual rebirth of the new Christian.[78] The Vikings, however, were resolutely literal. The clothes had no such symbolic value, nor had the baptismal rite itself, beyond providing the Vikings with an easy means of acquiring a new wardrobe. As in his earlier anecdote about the bishop's unfortunate comparison of the Carolingian cleric with a common ploughman, Notker had a keen sense of the centrality of status at the Carolingian court. The visiting Dane felt the tunic he had received was more suggestive of a worker than the warrior he was. The story is amusing in its own right, but is made all the more so if placed alongside the highly solemn set-piece accounts of the baptism of Vikings found in earlier Carolingian texts, notably the one that occupies a large part of Book 4 of Ermold the Black's 'In Honour of Louis the Pious'.[79] Ermold used the description of such a scene as the medium for a high-minded linkage of Carolingian authority and Christianity. The speech he placed in the mouth of the Viking convert Harald was one of awe and respect for both Christianity and Louis the Pious, its disseminator and leading exponent. It was a speech that also revealed Harald's understanding of the central symbols of the baptismal rite.[80] Notker's Viking, with his wilful lack of any insight into the meaning of the rite, and material preoccupations, can be read as a parodic subversion of Ermold's, and a parody also of the catechumenal exchange that began the baptismal rite itself, for here the Viking *senior* ends by repudiating, rather than accepting, Christ.[81] This willingness to subvert earlier Carolingian generations' set-piece accounts of royal authority is a powerful indicator of his awareness of the literary conceits of Carolingian image-building.

---

[77] *Gesta Karoli* 2.19: *Iam vities hic lotus sum et optimis candissimisque vestibus indutus; et ecce talis saccus non milites sed subulcos addecet. Et nisi nuditatem erubescerem, meis privatus nec a te datis contectus, amictum tuum cum Christo tuo tibi relinquerem.*

[78] Ermoldus Nigellus, *Carmen in honorem Hludovici Christianissimi Caesaris Augusti* 4, line 2209, in *Ermold le Noir, poème sur Louis le Pieux et Epitres au Roi Pépin* (Les Classiques de l'histoire de France au moyen âge 14), ed. E. Faral (2nd edn, Paris, 1964).

[79] *In honorem* 4, lines 2167–247. Ermold was not, however, beyond extracting mileage from episodes of misunderstanding similar to those found in Notker; see, for example, his tale of Datus, the Frank who prized his horse higher than his own mother, and refused to swap the former for the latter with the Muslims of Barcelona: *In honorem*, lines 242–301.

[80] *In honorem* 4, lines 2205–28.

[81] On contemporary rites and attitudes to baptism, see P. Cramer, *Baptism and Change in the Early Middle Ages, c.200–c.1150* (Cambridge, 1993), pp. 130–78; J. D. C. Fisher, *Christian Initiation: Baptism in the Medieval West. A Study of the Disintegration of the Primitive Rite of Initiation* (Alcuin Club Collections 47) (London, 1965), pp. 47–77.

On a different, but no less profound, level, Notker was making a point about the non-translatability of Christian symbols. The Vikings had little awareness, and less interest in finding out, that there was a leap to be taken from sign to signified. In sharp contrast to Agnellus' account of Attila, for whom even a brief brush with the Christian concepts of spiritual kinship was enough for an apparently fundamental shift of attitudes, Notker's Vikings are left comically unchanged by their encounter with Frankish Christianity and its paradigmatic ritual of transformation.

This contrast tells more than a little about the essentially different attitudes of Agnellus and Notker to earthly language, a contrast that in some senses echoes those between Augustine and Gregory. I have shown Agnellus' essentially optimistic view of the ability of earthly language to disclose higher truth whilst Notker, like Augustine, grasped its inadequacies, its inherent slipperiness and tendency to opacity. The flawed nature of earthly discourse was made all the more explicit by Notker's inclination to show its limits operating in episodes that took explicitly flawed figures as their protagonists. As much as it embodied Notker's anxiety about the future of the Carolingian polity under Charles the Fat, the *Gesta* exemplified his resignation about earthly kingdoms of any kind.

Notker's sense of the limits of earthly language is made most explicit in his account of the infant Louis the German's encounter with Charlemagne. Impressed by the boy's conduct, and his spirited assertion of his warrior status, Charlemagne commented: 'If that little boy lives, he will be someone great.'[82] In the *Gesta*, however, the words Charlemagne 'spoke' were not his own. Rather, they were those spoken by Ambrose's father in the fifth-century *Vita Ambrosii* by Paulinus of Milan upon observing a swarm of bees expelled heavenwards from his son's mouth, a prefiguration of the words he would produce in adulthood, 'which would tell of heavenly gifts and raise the minds of human beings from earthly to heavenly things'.[83] 'I have adapted these words from the *Vita Ambrosii*', Notker explained, 'because the words which Charlemagne actually said cannot be translated into Latin.'[84] Notker's ready admission of non-translatability has evoked a range of responses. 'Can we do anything to this passage other than reject it as a literary invention?' a recent student of the *Gesta* has asked, finding the answer to his question in Notker's

---

[82] *Gesta Karoli* 2.10.

[83] Paulinus, *Vita Ambrosii* 3, citing Prov. 16.24, 'Good words are a honeycomb' , in *Paolino di Milano: Vita di S. Ambrogio 1*, ed. M. Pellegrino (Rome, 1961); see also *Ambrose*, trans. B. Ramsey (London, 1997), pp. 195–218, at p. 197.

[84] *Gesta Karoli* 2.10: *Que verba ideo de Ambrosio mutuati sumus, quia Karolus que dixit, non possunt examussim in Latinum converti.*

overriding belief in the importance of textual models, and the centrality to his world view of the repetitive patterns of human history.[85] Viewed from this perspective the phrase functions like a hagiographic topos, reflecting the deeper, universal truth implicit in the specific. Such an approach, however, sidesteps the quotation's most immediate context, namely Notker's acute sense of the limits of human language. Just as the symbols of baptism could not carry across to the Viking visitors, neither could Charlemagne's vernacular find the same meaning in Latin. Despite the positive view of language implicit in the account of the infant Ambrose upon which he drew – that there could be a genuine relationship between earthly language and the disclosure of higher truths – Notker used the quotation to assert the very opposite. The comment is all the more telling coming from a figure who, as one of St-Gall's *ellinici fratres*, and working in a different mode, played a key part in the translation of Greek Scripture.[86]

There is a further level to Notker's choice of the *Vita Ambrosii* as a source for Charlemagne's words, for it also points out the distinctive character of his conception of royal authority. As seen above, many of the *Gesta*'s humorous tales revolved around Charlemagne instilling humility into overbearing churchmen.[87] Ambrose, of course, was the archetypal agent of *humilitas*, presiding over Theodosius' penance in Milan in 390, and in the process providing a template for subsequent demonstrations of royal humility.[88] As Robert Deshman and Mayke De Jong have both shown, over the course of the ninth century humility moved to the centre of the battery of royal virtues.[89] Notker stood resolutely, and almost certainly

---

[85] Innes, 'Memory, orality', p. 15.

[86] The phrase is Notker's, on which see W. Berschin, *Greek Letters and the Latin Middle Ages: From Jerome to Nicholas of Cusa* (trans. J. C. Frakes, rev. edn, Washington, DC, 1988), pp. 145–9, with substantial references to Notker's role in the translation enterprise at St-Gall in the later ninth century.

[87] A theme of the work that Notker refers to explicitly, *Gesta Karoli* 1.16, echoing Matthew 23.12.

[88] R. Schieffer, 'Von Mailand nach Canossa. Ein Beitrag zur geschichte der christliche Herrscherbuße von Theodosius d. Gr. bis zu Heinrich IV', *Deutsches Archiv* 28 (1972), pp. 333–70; see also S. Hamilton, 'A new model for royal penance? Helgaud of Fleury's *Life* of Robert the Pious', *EME* 6(2) (1997), pp. 189–200.

[89] M. De Jong, 'Power and humility in Carolingian society: the public penance of Louis the Pious', *EME* 1(1) (1992), pp. 29–51; R. Deshman, 'The Galba Psalter: pictures, texts and context in an early medieval prayerbook', *Anglo-Saxon England* 26 (1997), pp. 109–38, at pp. 128–38; also his 'The exalted servant: the ruler theology of the prayerbook of Charles the Bald', *Viator* 2 (1980), pp. 385–417; P. E. Dutton and H. L. Kessler, *The Poetry and Paintings of the First Bible of Charles the Bald* (Ann Arbor, MI, 1995), pp. 81–4, reiterating H. L. Kessler, 'A lay abbot as patron: Count Vivian and the first Bible of Charles the Bald', *Settimane di studio del Centro Italiano di Studi sul'alto medioevo* 39 (1992), pp. 647–79, esp. pp. 662–5. P. J. E. Kershaw, 'Illness, power and prayer in Asser's *Life of King Alfred*', *EME* 10(2) (2001), pp. 201–24.

consciously, outside this development, for, although he could refer in passing to Charlemagne undertaking penance when he felt he had acted wrongly,[90] Notker was overwhelmingly concerned with Charlemagne as the agent, rather than the subject, of acts of humility.[91] Rather than the ruler submitting to episcopal authority, as Theodosius did at Milan, or Louis the Pious in 822 or 833, in the *Gesta* it was bishops who were invariably cast down.[92]

Was this a sense of language that carried a personal perspective? Notker's *Gesta* includes one story that has puzzled scholars. Ganz, for example, the most perceptive reader of Notker's humour, has called it his 'most surprising'.[93] This is the story of a 'perfect' cleric in Charlemagne's retinue:

It was said of him what has never been said of any other man, that he excelled all others in his knowledge of secular and divine literature, in the singing of both church and popular music, in the composition of poems and their recitation, and above all in the sweet fullness of his voice and the inestimable pleasure which he gave when he spoke.[94]

These abilities made this great communicator vain. He forgot that his gifts came from God and was neither grateful for them, nor humble. 'He who does not know whence his talents come or, if he does know, has failed to be duly grateful to the Giver of these gifts, has lost all', commented Notker, and proceeded to show how this particular figure lost all.[95] One day, when standing besides Charlemagne he suddenly vanished. On the spot where he had stood was a smouldering piece of coal. Notker's tale of this hubristic churchman, punished for the pride he took in his speech, might be read as an allegory of Babel. Both stories confirmed the teachings of the Evangelist John: control of the Word was the province of God, not man.[96] Might there even be an intentional echo of Babel, built by Noah's children from 'burnt bricks', in the curious smoking coal that was all that was left of the churchman?[97] What is more certain is that the notion that fluency was no substitute for pious humility is particularly noteworthy when expressed by an author known to himself, his peers and posterity as Balbulus, 'the Stammerer', for whom the limits of earthly language were no mere abstraction but an everyday reality.[98]

[90] *Gesta Karoli* 1.32.   [91] *Gesta Karoli* 1.32.

[92] See also Notker's explicit parallel of Louis the German with Ambrose: *Gesta Karoli* 2.10.

[93] Ganz, 'Humour as history', p. 178.   [94] *Gesta Karoli* 1.33.

[95] Ibid. On this story, see also Innes, above, p. 151.   [96] John 1.1.   [97] Genesis 11.3.

[98] As Ganz points out, the description is Notker's own: 'Humour as history', p. 173, n. 14 with references.

'I WANT TO DRINK': THE 'PARIS CONVERSATIONS'

Notker saw the linguistic diversity of Babel's legacy as an unbridge-able gulf. Other Carolingian authors, however, sought practical means to cross the barrier.[99] It was an awareness of the gap in under-standing between Romance- and Germanic-language speakers in the Carolingian territories that lay behind the composition of the so-called 'Paris Conversations' in the late ninth century, preserved uniquely in a tenth-century Paris manuscript.[100] In this short text useful terms and questions were translated for a visitor to Germany from a Romance-speaking area.[101] In contrast to the narrative treatments of communica-tion failure seen in Agnellus and Notker, in the 'Paris Conversations' the comedy lay not in the failure of communication to cross the language barrier, but rather the way in which that barrier was breached. The list of terms began with the names for body-parts, working from the head down, and including various significant refinements – 'stomach' (*guanbe, venter*), 'full stomach' (*follo guanbe, plenus venter*)[102] – before moving on to questions such as 'where do you come from?',[103] 'what country are you from?',[104] 'give me my sword',[105] before returning to alimentary issues: 'I want a drink' (*erro, e guille trenchen, ego volo bibere*).[106] Many of the phrases are suggestive of exchanges between a Romance-speaking master and a German servant.[107] The general tenor is humorous, with occasional flashes of the dissolute and the obscene, such as this exchange between *senior* and *vasallus*:

'Why weren't you at Matins?'
'I didn't want to go.'
'You were in bed with your wife.'[108]

Here, then, the actual process of communicating in another language was parodied. Useful phrases were provided, but the value of communication was subverted, and its limits in any case made explicit in one phrase:

---

[99] On the linguistic complexity of the Frankish kingdoms, see A. Joris, 'On the edge of two worlds in the heart of the new empire: the Romance regions of northern Gaul during the medieval period', *Studies in Medieval and Renaissance History* 33 (1966), pp. 1–52.

[100] 'Paris Conversations' (*PC*): text: W. Braune, *Althochdeutsche Lesebuch* (Tübingen, 1965), pp. 9–11; discussion: C. Edwards, 'German vernacular literature: a survey', in *Carolingian Culture: Emulation and Innovation*, ed. R. McKitterick (Cambridge, 1994), pp. 141–70, at p. 143; Knight Bostock, *Handbook*, pp. 101–3; J. A. Huisman, 'Die Pariser Gespräche', *Rheinischer Vierteljahrsblätter* 33 (1969), pp. 272–96. The tenth-century dating of the manuscript is given by Knight Bostock, *Handbook*, pp. 102 and 160, whilst the ninth-century context for the composition of the 'Conversations' themselves is argued by Edwards, 'Vernacular', p. 143, which I follow here.

[101] Edwards, 'Vernacular', pp. 143–4; Knight Bostock, *Handbook*, p. 102.

[102] *PC*, paras. 1–12.   [103] *PC*, para. 17.   [104] *PC*, para. 20.   [105] *PC*, para. 53.

[106] *PC*, para. 71.   [107] See, for example, *PC*, paras. 31, 34, 36 and 79.   [108] *PC*, paras. 60–2.

'I don't know this word.'[109] The result was a knowingly comic sketch that trivialised the attempt to bridge the German–Romance linguistic divide, revealing a resolutely earthly range of needs and appetites and, simultaneously, producing a biting parody of lay culture.[110] In spirit, if not in fact, the nobleman of the 'Paris Conversations', with his preoccupation with weaponry and his stomach, is a close relation of Theodulf of Orléans' Wibod, the *membrosus heros* of Charlemagne's court and the possessor, according to Theodulf, of no mean stomach himself.[111] Opinion is divided as to whether the 'Paris Conversations' were based upon actual interchanges recorded on an actual journey or were intended as pure parody.[112] That the 'Conversations', like the *Vocabularius St Galli*, owed a clear debt to the third-century Greek–Latin school manual the *Hermeneumata pseudodositheana* and its derivatives, points surely to a scholastic, and almost certainly monastic, place of composition and suggests a third possible explanation: the 'Conversations' were a form of applied parody, a means of teaching the essentials of conversational *lingua theotisca*.[113] As several of Lupus of Ferrières' letters make clear, instruction in German was undertaken at least at certain Frankish monasteries, notably Fulda, in the ninth century.[114]

LAUGHTER AFTER BABEL'S FALL

In the narratives of Agnellus and Notker, symbols were misinterpreted, words lost their meaning: confusion reigned. For Agnellus the higher

---

[109] PC, para. 90: '*begott eh ne uitst nen hurt – nullum uerbum scio de hoc*'.

[110] Compare with the similarly drink-preoccupied parody of *Lex Salica* from the late eighth century, discussed by M. Banniard, *Viva Voce: Communication écrite et communcation orale du IVᵉ au IXᵉ siècle en Occident latin* (Paris, 1992), pp. 299–300, with the text at p. 551; M. Garrison, 'The Franks as the New Israel?', in *Uses of the Past*, ed. Hen and Innes, pp. 114–61, at pp. 133–4; G. Beckmann, 'Aus den letzten Jahrzehnten des Vulgärlateins im Frankenreich', *Zeitschrift für Romanische Philologie* 79 (1963), pp. 305–34, at p. 307.

[111] *MGH PLAC* 1, ed. Dümmler, pp. 483–9.

[112] Edwards, 'Vernacular', p. 143, 'a guide book'; Knight Bostock, *Handbook*, p. 103: 'the *Gespräche* have a character of their own, based on the interesting adventures or lively imagination, or both, of the writer'.

[113] Knight Bostock, *Handbook*, p. 100. On the *Hermeneumata Pseudodositheana*, see R. Copeland, *Rhetoric, Hermeneutics, and Translation in the Middle Ages: Academic Traditions and Vernacular Texts* (Cambridge, 1991), pp. 21–2 and 38. On the use of *Hermeneumata* by insular Latin grammarians see V. Law, 'Notes on the dating and attribution of anonymous Latin grammars of the early Middle Ages', in her *Grammar and Grammarians in the Early Middle Ages* (Harlow, 1997), p. 42. Compare the 'Conversations' structure and content with the Latin conversation lesson, glossed in Old Welsh, found in the tenth-century 'codex Oxoniensis posterior', Oxford Bodleian MS 572, fols. 41–50, discussed by W. M. Lindsay, *Early Welsh Script* (Oxford, 1912), pp. 26–8.

[114] Lupus of Ferrières, *Loup de Ferrières*, ed. L. Levillain (Paris, 1964), *Epp.* 35, 58, 65 and 70. See also W. Haubrichs, 'Althochdeutsche in Fulda und Weissenburg – Hrabanus Maurus und Otfried von Weissenberg', in *Hrabanus Maurus: Lehrer, Abt und Bischof*, ed. R. Kottje and H. Zimmerman, (Wiesbaden, 1981), pp. 182–93.

truths of Christian belief could cut through this fog of meaning. Notker was less sure of its powers of penetration. When, as in the 'Paris Conversations', there is an attempt to overcome the language barrier the results were both studiedly comic and pointedly earthy. The flawed layman of the 'Conversations', concerned with his stomach and fond of his bed, was as much an inhabitant of the *civitas terrena* as Notker's foolish bishops. In their own ways, both betray something of a monastic disapproval of aspects of secular life.[115] Certainly the image of lay life in the 'Conversations', very much outside the codes of reformed monastic life rather than informed by them, stands in sharp contrast to some other images found elsewhere in Carolingian literature, which betrayed an attempted fusion of the monastic and the lay.[116] For both Notker and the anonymous author of the 'Conversations' it was man's comic potential that signposted his limits, his moral weaknesses and, ultimately, his fallen nature. Yet humour was, as I showed at the outset, a tool for teaching and all three of the texts I have discussed here made use of it as a means of effectively communicating the points their authors wished to make. In this sense, these anecdotes of non-communication were paradoxical, for even as they recounted failure to communicate they taught acute lessons about language and man's condition. Moreover, even as humour brought this reality into sharper relief, whether for Agnellus, Notker or the anonymous author of the 'Conversations', it perhaps made their sojourn in the earthly kingdom more bearable. Laughter was, after all, an aspect of humanity, and humanity, as Augustine and Gregory agreed, carried within itself the hope of salvation.[117]

---

[115] On Notker's attitude to Riculf, bishop of Mainz, see MacLean, 'Charles the Fat', pp. 237–65.

[116] Innes, above, pp. 142–5; S. Airlie, 'The anxiety of sanctity: Gerard of Aurillac and his Maker', *Journal of Ecclesiastical History* 42 (1992), pp. 372–95; also his 'Private bodies and the body politic', *Past and Present* 161 (1999), pp. 1–38, J. L. Nelson, 'Monks, secular men and masculinity, c.900', in *Masculinity in Medieval Europe*, ed. D. M. Hadley (London, 1999), pp. 121–42.

[117] I express my debt to G. Steiner, *After Babel: Aspects of Language and Translation* (2nd edn, Oxford, 1992), whose title my own echoes. Laughter, of course, speaks of community and here is the appropriate place to acknowledge the debt I owe to my fellow London early medievalists, Guy Halsall, Mark Handley, Matt Innes, Simon MacLean, Alan Thacker and Geoff West, and to Mary Garrison in York. I have learnt much from discussions about Notker and Agnellus with Simon MacLean and Geoff West respectively, and much about laughter from them all.

Index